AF806308

Synthese Library

Studies in Epistemology, Logic, Methodology, and Philosophy of Science

Volume 456

Editor-in-Chief

Otávio Bueno, Department of Philosophy, University of Miami, Coral Gables, USA

Editorial Board Members

Berit Brogaard, University of Miami, Coral Gables, USA

Anjan Chakravartty, Department of Philosophy, University of Miami, Coral Gables, USA

Steven French, University of Leeds, Leeds, UK

Catarina Dutilh Novaes, VU Amsterdam, Amsterdam, The Netherlands

Darrell P. Rowbottom, Department of Philosophy, Lingnan University, Tuen Mun, Hong Kong

Emma Ruttkamp, Department of Philosophy, University of South Africa, Pretoria, South Africa

Kristie Miller, Department of Philosophy, Centre for Time, University of Sydney, Sydney, Australia

The aim of *Synthese Library* is to provide a forum for the best current work in the methodology and philosophy of science and in epistemology, all broadly understood. A wide variety of different approaches have traditionally been represented in the Library, and every effort is made to maintain this variety, not for its own sake, but because we believe that there are many fruitful and illuminating approaches to the philosophy of science and related disciplines.

Special attention is paid to methodological studies which illustrate the interplay of empirical and philosophical viewpoints and to contributions to the formal (logical, set-theoretical, mathematical, information-theoretical, decision-theoretical, etc.) methodology of empirical sciences. Likewise, the applications of logical methods to epistemology as well as philosophically and methodologically relevant studies in logic are strongly encouraged. The emphasis on logic will be tempered by interest in the psychological, historical, and sociological aspects of science.

In addition to monographs *Synthese Library* publishes thematically unified anthologies and edited volumes with a well-defined topical focus inside the aim and scope of the book series. The contributions in the volumes are expected to be focused and structurally organized in accordance with the central theme(s), and should be tied together by an extensive editorial introduction or set of introductions if the volume is divided into parts. An extensive bibliography and index are mandatory.

More information about this series at https://link.springer.com/bookseries/6607

Hein Duijf

The Logic of Responsibility Voids

Springer

Hein Duijf
Ludwig-Maximilians-Universität
München, Germany

ISSN 0166-6991 ISSN 2542-8292 (electronic)
Synthese Library
ISBN 978-3-030-92654-0 ISBN 978-3-030-92655-7 (eBook)
https://doi.org/10.1007/978-3-030-92655-7

© The Editor(s) (if applicable) and The Author(s), under exclusive license to Springer Nature Switzerland AG 2022
This work is subject to copyright. All rights are solely and exclusively licensed by the Publisher, whether the whole or part of the material is concerned, specifically the rights of translation, reprinting, reuse of illustrations, recitation, broadcasting, reproduction on microfilms or in any other physical way, and transmission or information storage and retrieval, electronic adaptation, computer software, or by similar or dissimilar methodology now known or hereafter developed.
The use of general descriptive names, registered names, trademarks, service marks, etc. in this publication does not imply, even in the absence of a specific statement, that such names are exempt from the relevant protective laws and regulations and therefore free for general use.
The publisher, the authors, and the editors are safe to assume that the advice and information in this book are believed to be true and accurate at the date of publication. Neither the publisher nor the authors or the editors give a warranty, expressed or implied, with respect to the material contained herein or for any errors or omissions that may have been made. The publisher remains neutral with regard to jurisdictional claims in published maps and institutional affiliations.

This Springer imprint is published by the registered company Springer Nature Switzerland AG.
The registered company address is: Gewerbestrasse 11, 6330 Cham, Switzerland

Preface

Responsibility, liability, and accountability play a vital role in human societies. Sometimes, however, there might be a threat of a shortfall of responsibility. Prototypical examples include attributions or exemptions of responsibility for climate change, failures to attribute accountability for machine actions, and corporate wrongdoings without member liability. In these cases, responsibility voids may arise: there may be situations where some morally undesirable outcome results from the interaction of several individuals even though none of them can be held responsible for their involvement. This book collects my thinking on the subject of moral responsibility, collective responsibility, and responsibility voids since the start of my academic career as a PhD candidate in 2014. The purpose of this book is to study the *possibility* and *scope* of the problem of responsibility *voids*.

This research would not have been possible without the generous financial support of the European Research Council (ERC) via the projects "Responsible Intelligent Systems" (REINS, No. 616512) and "Social Epistemology of Argumentation" (SEA, No. 771074).

There are many people who have contributed to making this book possible. Let me spend a few words to express my gratitude. First and foremost, I would like to thank Jan Broersen for the freedom and support in the early stages of my academic career and for various fascinating and stimulating conversations. I would also like to thank Allard Tamminga, to whom I owe a lot of academic maturity and whom I thank for many gratifying collaborations. Special thanks go to John-Jules Meyer for his enthusiasm and unconditional trust. I want to thank Catarina Dutilh Novaes and Martin van Hees for encouraging and supporting me to write this book, and I would like to thank Otávio Bueno for his incredibly swift and professional editorial guidance and support. I also want to thank Sander Beckers, Daniel Cohnitz, Sjur Dyrkolbotn, Natalie Gold, Martin van Hees, Jeff Horty, Jurgis Karpus, Michael Klenk, Alexandra Kuncová, Tsz Yuen Lau, Christian List, Niels van Miltenburg, Jesse Mulder, Aldo Iván Ramírez Abarca, Werner Raub, Olivier Roy, Robert Sugden, Frederik Van De Putte, and anonymous reviewers at several journals and Springer for insightful comments and discussions.

I want to apologize for the inevitable incompleteness of this list and thank my colleagues at Utrecht University and Vrije Universiteit Amsterdam and participants at various conferences for their constructive and open-minded discussions that helped shape my academic character, in general, and the ideas that make up this book, in particular.

Finally, thanks are due to my family and friends for providing an essential dose of healthy distractions that make life colorful. Above all, I want to thank Maxime for her loving support.

Maastricht, The Netherlands
25 October 2021

Hein Duijf

Contents

About the Author

Dr. Hein Duijf is currently an assistant professor at the Ludwig-Maximilians-Universität Munich and has a PhD in philosophy and artificial intelligence from Utrecht University. He was previously a postdoctoral researcher at Utrecht University and the Vrije Universiteit Amsterdam. His work can be roughly divided into two strands. In the first line of research, which started as part of the project the *Social Epistemology of Argumentation*, he investigates the epistemic risks and potential benefits of group deliberation by developing agent-based models and by taking inspiration from behavioral sciences (including social psychology, economics, and the social sciences). In the second line of work, which began as part of the project *Responsible Intelligent Systems*, he studies moral responsibility, collective agency, machine ethics, and deontic reasoning.

Chapter 1
Introduction: The Problem of Responsibility Voids

The detrimental effects of climate change are starting to materialize. The renowned research by the IPCC undoubtedly confirms that human emissions play a pivotal role. The mitigation of these climate risks requires a fundamental and radical transformation of society at large. Industrialized societies need to transition from coal and oil, and other fossil fuels, towards renewable energy, like wind and solar energy. Although this transition is well under way, it is indicative that the 'renewable energy directive' of the European Union set its target to achieving 20% in renewable energy by 2020, which means that 80% of the energy would *not* originate from renewable sources. At a more individual level, a change in individual's behaviour is required. For example, Project Drawdown estimated that two of the top five solutions are reducing food waste and switching to a plant-rich diet.[1] Coming up with solutions to climate change is a top priority, but this leaves open the question of who has to implement them. To address the latter question, we need a clear and compelling theory that tells us who can be held responsible for what.

On a global level, many countries signed the Paris Agreement in December 2015, which deals with the mitigation, adaptation and finance of emissions that causally influence our climate. However, one of the biggest drawbacks is that the agreement is ineffective, since the actual commitments of many countries worldwide are insufficient for meeting the agreed targets. We could ask whether any of the parties of the political community can be held responsible for these failures. Recently, in the so-called Urgenda court case, the State of the Netherlands has been held accountable for not doing enough to reduce greenhouse emissions. On a local level, we may ask whether an individual can be held morally co-responsible if she opts for a meat-heavy diet. Or, in virtue of the inefficiency of certain political actors, we could ask whether voters can be held co-responsible for the omissions of these political leaders. In any case, it is important to ask whether a given individual or political agent can be held morally co-responsible for these environmental outcomes.

[1] See https://www.drawdown.org/solutions-summary-by-rank.

© The Author(s), under exclusive license to Springer Nature Switzerland AG 2022
H. Duijf, *The Logic of Responsibility Voids*, Synthese Library 456,
https://doi.org/10.1007/978-3-030-92655-7_1

1.1 Responsibility Voids

It may be hard to determine who is to be held responsible in these complex cases. It is therefore vital to explore and systematize theories of moral responsibility so that we can enhance our capacity to determine the responsible individuals and agents. With regard to the allocation of responsibility, two perspectives need to be distinguished. On the one hand, the complexity of these situations requires a clear and compelling theory of moral responsibility. That is, we need to identify the general conditions for assigning responsibility. Let us call this the *responsibility system*: it determines who is to be held responsible and for what.

On the other hand, we need to determine whether a given responsibility system yields desirable distributions of responsibility. For the purposes of this book, I will focus on the worry that the responsibility system may allocate *too little* responsibility. In particular, we run the risk of *responsibility voids*: situations in which a combination of actions of several individuals leads to an outcome for which none of the involved agents can be held responsible. The general concern is that the responsibility system fails to track the responsibility of the involved agents; there may be cases where bad outcomes result although none can be held responsible. This is morally undesirable.

In the literature on the ethics of technology, there is a growing concern for responsibility voids:

> Presently there are machines in development or already in use which are able to decide on a course of action and to act without human intervention. Traditionally we hold either the operator/manufacturer of the machine responsible for the consequences of its operation or "nobody" (in cases, where no personal fault can be identified). Now, it can be shown that there is an increasing class of machine actions, where the traditional ways of responsibility ascription are not compatible with our sense of justice and the moral framework of society because *nobody* has enough control over the machine's actions to be able to assume the responsibility for them. (Matthias, 2004, p. 177 – emphasis added)

AI techniques that bring about a lack of control over the machine's actions are increasingly adopted: for example, some local governments in the Netherlands have adopted these technologies to estimate whether someone is likely to commit tax fraud, banks are experimenting with algorithms that determine people's eligibility for mortgages, and these technologies are a vital component in self-driving cars. Hence, examples of responsibility voids may include a traffic accident that is caused by a self-driving car, an unjust denial of a mortgage, and a false suspicion of tax fraud.

We can rephrase Andreas Matthias' observation in the terminology introduced above: there is an growing class of machine actions for which it holds that nobody can be held responsible for those actions. Consequently, if such a machine action brings about some harm, then nobody can be held responsible. To determine whether this class of machine actions allows for the possibility of such responsibility voids, a clear and compelling theory of moral responsibility is required. After all, the existence of responsibility voids depends on the adopted responsibility system.

From a more general perspective, the potential injustice of a responsibility void could be characterized by considering the following roles in a decision-making scenario: the harm-exposed and the decision-makers. If a given responsibility system allows for a responsibility void, then there are two possible responses. On the one hand, one could say that the responsibility system must be flawed. That is, the possibility of responsibility voids highlights that some of the blameworthy decision-makers may be off the hook for harms imposed on some individuals. In these cases, the responsibility system does not enable the harm-exposed agents to demand rectification from the responsible decision-makers. For example, if we were to agree with Matthias, this would mean that the *traditional* responsibility system is flawed and needs to be revised.[2]

On the other hand, one could say that the responsibility system is correct and that we cannot hold anyone accountable for certain harms. After all, if a manufacturing team responsibly designed a self-driving vehicle, then it would seem unjust to require compensation from this team whenever the vehicle causes a traffic accident. However, this would mean that either the harm-exposed agents cannot demand any rectification or it would require compensation from blameless individuals. The first horn of the dilemma emphasizes that the responsible actions of several individuals may be transformed by the structure of interaction into morally undesirable outcomes.[3] Moreover, "the fact that that no one can be meaningfully called to account after the event also means, however, that no one need feel responsible beforehand" (Bovens, 1998, p. 49). On the second horn of the dilemma, the decision-makers would be held accountable even if they had acted responsibly beforehand.

In any case, if responsibility voids turn out to be pervasive, then it makes sense to ask how we may *revise* a given responsibility system in order to cope with responsibility voids. For example, to address Matthias' concern regarding machine actions, there are two plausible ways to revise a given responsibility system. Both consist in broadening the notion of responsibility, that is, to hold an agent responsible who could not be held responsible under the traditional responsibility system: (1) We could expand the realm of agents that are fit to be held responsible so as to include machines;[4] and (2) In contrast, we may

[2] In accordance with this perspective and on a more statistical interpretation, this emphasizes that it is important to investigate the potential false negatives of a given responsibility system. After all, a responsibility void may demonstrate that the responsibility system does not identify some of the agents that should be held responsible.

[3] Bovens (1998, p. 49) concurs:"A meaningful calling to account is rendered extremely difficult and sometimes even impossible by the above variations on the problem of many hands. This frustrates the need for compensation and retribution on the part of the victims ('the guilty still run around freely'). More important still, such outcomes signify that what began as a conscious and rational human act can be transformed by the structure and the dynamics of complex organisations into a sort of 'act of God' with its own dynamic which seems to be independent of any specific individual human action ('there are no guilty ones')."

[4] There are various reasons for being sceptical of machine responsibility, these include—but are not limited to: (a) the machine is not an agent, (b) the machine cannot make moral decisions, (c)

revise the traditional responsibility system in such a way that these responsibility voids are avoided or reduced. These revisionary strategies emphasize a conflict between two responsibility systems. After all, these revisionary strategies may rule out responsibility voids only at the expense of disagreeing with the traditional responsibility system. Some prudence is thus recommended for those pursuing revisionary strategies.

However, the severity of the above-mentioned risks of responsibility voids could be exaggerated and it may be that they only arise in exotic circumstances.[5] We therefore need to determine the exact conditions under which responsibility voids may arise. If such voids are pervasive, then the threat of responsibility voids is of great interest. If such voids are rare, then it would seem appropriate to direct our attention at other threats.

One of the main goals of this book is to study the *possibility* and *scope* of the problem of responsibility *voids*. I'd like to emphasize that the problem of responsibility voids derives from a unique perspective on responsibility. To explain this perspective, it is helpful to briefly mention an analogy to a paradox in social dilemmas. A group finds itself in a social dilemma if it is in everybody's personal interest to act in a certain way, yet each of them would be better off if they together acted differently. One well-known example is the prisoner's dilemma, where it is in everyone's personal interest to defect, even though all would be better off if they had all cooperated as opposed to defected. These social dilemmas illustrate that acting in the pursuit of one's own self-interest may yield unexpected and undesirable outcomes. By analogy, a responsibility void demonstrates that acting *responsibly* may yield unexpected and sometimes even *morally undesirable* outcomes. A responsibility system explicates what it means to act responsibly, while a responsibility void highlights an anomaly in the relation between individual norms and collective outcomes.

This perspective on responsibility is the unique and defining characteristic of the analysis in this book. As indicated above, this perspective yields a novel analysis of responsibility systems and, in particular, of the existence of responsibility voids. But, it also opens up other lines of inquiry. One example that complements responsibility voids is the worry that the responsibility system may allocate *too much* responsibility. In particular, we run the risk of responsibility gluts: situations where too many agents are held responsible. The general concern would be that the responsibility system unjustly holds some agents responsible.[6] In this book,

---

the machine is not sentient, (d) the machine cannot repay the risk-exposed, and (e) by holding the machine responsible, people may dodge their responsibilities.

[5] Braham and van Hees (2011, p. 6) argue that "the conditions for these voids are so restrictive as to reduce the philosophical or institutional significance they might be thought to possess".

[6] Another example is the property of fragmentation introduced by Braham and van Hees (2018, F96): "Fragmented responsibility occurs when a combination of actions by different individuals leads to an outcome for which at least some of the responsible individuals are responsible for different features of the outcome."

however, the focus is restricted to the problem of responsibility voids and the study of other properties is left for future research endeavours.

Another example would be the general issue of allocating *too little* responsibility. Any analysis of this more general issue would require a quantitative measure of moral responsibility. Although it is surely interesting and important to investigate such quantitative measures, the philosophical literature on moral responsibility chiefly concerns qualitative considerations. Moreover, the philosophical literature on qualitative notions of moral responsibility is already vast and diverse enough that a single book cannot cover all of its complexities.

1.2 Collective Responsibility and Gaps

In this book, I will apply and extend the above considerations to the current debates on *collective moral responsibility*. In recent years, several authors have proposed the legitimacy and possibility of a notion of *irreducible* collective responsibility. The claim is not that all collections of individuals are fit to be held collectively responsibility. After all, the collection consisting of the king of the Netherlands and the author of this book can hardly be thought of as a group that is fit to be held collectively responsible. Rather, the claim is that, in suitable circumstances, a group can be fit to be held collectively responsible for an outcome even though none of the individual members can be held responsible for their involvement.

Although there may be various reasons for endorsing a notion of collective responsibility, one central reason involves the threat of responsibility voids. The idea is that there are some problematic instances of responsibility voids where there is reason to think that we can hold the group responsible. Philip Pettit endorses this line of argument when he writes:

> I hold that even when all the relevant enactors in a group action have been identified and held responsible, still it may be important to hold the group agent responsible as well. The reason for this, very simply, is that it is possible to have a situation in which there is ground for holding the group agent responsible [...], but not the same ground for holding individual enactors responsible. The responsibility of enactors may leave a deficit in the accounting books, and the only possible way to guard against this may be to allow for the corporate responsibility of the group in the name of which they act. (Pettit, 2007, p. 194)

So, from the perspective of this book, Pettit's argument says that a given responsibility system allows for an individual responsibility void and to guard against this, we need to update the responsibility system so that we can expand the realm of agents that are fit to be held responsible so as to include some collectives.

With respect to collective responsibility, I prefer to use the phrase *responsibility gaps*, rather than responsibility voids, to refer to situations where a morally bad outcome results from the interaction of several individuals, none of the individuals can be held responsible for their involvement, yet the group can be held collectively responsible. Simply stated, a responsibility gap is a responsibility void plus collective responsibility. Phrased differently, responsibility gaps indicate a space between the collective responsibility of a group and the individual responsibility of its members.

One of the main goals of this book is to study the *possibility* and *scope* of the problem of responsibility *gaps*. Such gaps arise only in circumstances where it makes sense to hold the group collectively responsible. When can we hold a group collectively responsible? I propose to specify the nature of collective responsibility on the basis of the philosophy of collective action.[7] My analysis will cover different ways of representing collective action and, consequently, collective responsibility.

Although the problem of responsibility voids could sometimes be solved by introducing collective responsibility, it is unclear whether collective responsibility genuinely solves the issue or merely introduces new pathologies. First, expanding the realm of agents that are fit to be held morally responsible requires a careful defence. We need a clear and compelling theory that provides the general conditions under which a collection of individuals can be held *collectively* morally responsible.[8] Second, in cases of responsibility gaps, it is unclear how the harm-exposed agents ought to be compensated. After all, it would seem that only the group, not its members, should offer rectification. But, how would the group act without placing any constraints or demands on its blameless members? Lastly, there may be cases where all members of a group are morally responsible and, in addition, the group is also collectively responsible. That is, we would hold an individual agent responsible and also hold the group collectively responsible. It would seem that we're double counting responsibilities and, as a result, we may introduce a responsibility glut, i.e. too many agents are held morally responsible.

Although these considerations are not definitive, they strongly suggest to err on the side of caution with regard to introducing an irreducible notion of collective responsibility. Rather than assessing the plausibility and nature of irreducible collective responsibility, this book treats the largely orthogonal issue of scrutinizing the *possibility* and *scope* of responsibility gaps. The analysis takes seriously the idea that the conditions for the existence of responsibility gaps depend on the specifics of the responsibility system and on the criteria for collective action and responsibility.

1.3 Methodology

One of the novel aspects of the present approach is the *pluralistic position* regarding responsibility systems. Let me illustrate and emphasize this position by contrast. In the analytical-philosophical tradition much attention has been given to the grounds of responsibility: who can be held accountable for what and why. In this body

[7] In comparison, Pettit (2007, p. 174–175) proposes three conditions that are necessary and sufficient for someone to be fit to be held responsible in a given choice: Value relevance, value judgement, and value sensitivity.

[8] List and Pettit (2011) provide a very thorough account of group agency.

of work, philosophers often search for and defend the one true notion of moral responsibility. In contrast, I do not defend a single notion of moral responsibility. Rather, I endorse a pluralistic position regarding the responsibility system and will study several responsibility systems. The issue of responsibility voids is, thus, carefully examined for a broad range of responsibility systems.[9]

The pluralistic position can also be viewed as a robustness test for the phenomenon of responsibility voids. This robustness has two dimensions. First, simply stated, one can examine whether responsibility voids are possible under a wide range of responsibility systems. If this is the case, then the phenomenon of responsibility voids is robust under *a variety of responsibility systems*. This is where the pluralistic position is helpful. Second, one can study whether responsibility voids can arise in a wide range of circumstances, given a particular responsibility system. If this is the case, then we could say that the phenomenon of responsibility voids is robust in *a variety of circumstances*, given a particular responsibility system.

From the perspective of robustness analysis, it is important to explore the *scope* or *extent* of the problem of responsibility voids for a given responsibility system. It is hence vital to study, for any given responsibility system, the range of circumstances where responsibility voids may arise. In particular, we need to identify the conditions under which responsibility voids may arise and, alternatively, to study the conditions under which responsibility voids may be ruled out. After all, if it turns out that responsibility voids can only arise in exotic circumstances, then we need not worry about them too much. Their practical relevance depends on the plausibility and abundance of these conditions.

In a nutshell, the purpose of this book is to study the possibility and scope of the problem of responsibility voids and gaps for a variety of responsibility systems. To make these responsibility systems precise, I propose to adopt and conceptually amend two prominent formalisms of action: the modal-logical treatment of agency, and rational choice theory. Although these formal frameworks are simple and well-known, the conceptual interpretation is adapted to the analysis of moral responsibility. One of the appealing features of the book is that a relatively small range of models is used to investigate a variety of responsibility systems.

The overall structure of the book is as follows. In Chap. 2, I will introduce these formalisms of action, show that they are intimately related, and study a basic notion of agentive responsibility (disregarding any subjective features). In Chap. 3, I will specify an objective responsibility system based on dominance theory and inspired by the theory of obligations by Horty (2001). Roughly stated, I assume that an agent

[9] I am partly inspired by criminal law, where it is common and vital to distinguish between different modes of acting, that is, mental states that accompany the act, which correspond to different levels of culpability. Although legal and moral responsibility need not align, I think that these modes of acting affect our attributions of moral responsibility and that studying them helps provide a systematic study of moral responsibility. The North American legal system uses the following distinctions regarding modes of acting, in decreasing order of culpability: purposefully, knowingly, recklessly, negligently, and strict liability (Dubber, 2002; Weigend, 2014).

can be held responsible if (and only if) she failed to fulfil some of her obligations.[10] I will demonstrate that responsibility voids and gaps can exist and, subsequently, study a sense of joint action in which the members of a group design and then publicly adopt a group plan. I will examine the conditions under which a group plan is a good plan, that is, one that guarantees that if each member fulfils her member obligation then the group fulfils its collective obligation. In Chap. 4, I will study informational responsibility system, that is, one that includes an epistemic condition for moral responsibility. An agent's moral responsibility thus depends on the practical knowledge of that agent. I will develop an account of individual and collective knowing-how and, then, apply them to the study of responsibility voids and gaps. In Chap. 5, I will investigate intentional responsibility systems, where attributions of moral responsibility are assumed to depend on the intentions of the agents. I will study the relation between collective and individual intentionality and explicate which facts must obtain if responsibility voids and gaps are to exist. In Chap. 6, I will present a reasoning-based framework for moral responsibility, which explicates the idea that an agent's moral responsibility is determined by the reasons bearing on the actions available to her. Inspired by the team-reasoning literature, I will use practical-reasoning schemas to distinguish between competitive and cooperative decision contexts. For each of these contexts, I will study which facts must obtain if responsibility voids or gaps are to exist. In the concluding chapter I will summarize the main findings of the book and provide an outlook for future work.

Let me elaborate on the style and method of this book. Although my analysis of responsibility voids is firmly rooted in mathematical frameworks, the emphasis is on conceptual analysis rather than technical results. To aid readability, the formal proofs are relegated to the appendix. Readability should not trump precision, however, so I have stated the definitions and results rigorously. The discussion should be intelligible to any reader with an understanding of modal logic, game theory, and/or elementary mathematics.

I am aware that a book like this one presents some focal risks. Ethicists who do not care about formal work may be unsatisfied by the whole formal approach and demand that I forcefully argue how the formal definitions and logical results could have any bearing on fundamental issues regarding moral responsibility. Mathematical philosophers and logicians who appreciate formal work will ask why there is so little of it: where is the exploration of the technical aspects of the logics presented here, and of their connections to other formal work on moral responsibility and deontic logic? Computer scientists will be perplexed to find out that I do not develop algorithms for reasoning about responsibility nor for verifying blame in multi-agent systems. Economists interested in studying and modelling human decision-making will be puzzled by a lack of empirical work, and wonder why I take virtually no effort to prove empirical validity. I have tried to manage these

[10] Notice that there is no reference to the mental state of the agent, which is why I call this a causal of objective responsibility system.

risks as well as possible, in full knowledge that no one will be satisfied entirely. I hope that my work is attractive to a broad readership from these various disciplines and that this book provides a stepping stone for those interested in the formal and conceptual study of moral responsibility and blame.

On a positive note, mathematical modelling offers distinct benefits: it stimulates interdisciplinary collaborations and in particular, it helps to bridge the playing field between philosophy, economics, and artificial intelligence. The models used in these disciplines share many characteristics and thereby enable fruitful synergies. This interdisciplinary potential highlights that these models can be used for multiple purposes: to help clarify and understand philosophical doctrines and arguments, to aid microeconomic theorizing, and to provide the tools for designing and verifying complex agent-based artificial intelligence. For the purposes of this book, formal modelling helps to explicate a variety of responsibility systems and to characterize the conditions under which responsibility voids and gaps are ruled out.

References

Bovens, M. (1998). *The quest for responsibility: Accountability and citizenship in complex organisations*. Cambridge: Cambridge University Press.

Braham, M., & van Hees, M. (2011). Responsibility voids. *The Philosophical Quarterly, 61*(242), 6–15.

Braham, M., & van Hees, M. (2018). Voids or fragmentation: Moral responsibility for collective outcomes. *The Economic Journal, 128*(612), F95–F113.

Dubber, M. D. (2002). *Criminal law: Model penal code*. New York: Foundation Press.

Horty, J. F. (2001). *Agency and deontic logic*. New York: Oxford University Press.

List, C., & Pettit, P. (2011). *Group agency: The possibility, design, and status of corporate agents*. Oxford: Oxford University Press.

Matthias, A. (2004). The responsibility gap: Ascribing responsibility for the actions of learning automata. *Ethics and Information Technology, 6*(3), 175–183.

Pettit, P. (2007). Responsibility incorporated. *Ethics, 117*(2), 171–201.

Weigend, T. (2014). Subjective elements of criminal liability. In M. D. Dubber, & T. Hörnle (Eds.), *The oxford handbook of criminal law* (pp. 490–511). Oxford: Oxford University Press.

Chapter 2
Games and Agency

> *The most helpful invention of game theory for the social sciences is the payoff matrix.*
>
> *Schelling (2010, p. 29)*

> *We followed and extended the idea of treating agency as a modality—a modality that represents through an intensional operator the agency, or action, of some individual in bringing about a particular state of affairs.*
>
> *Belnap, Perloff and Xu (2001, p. 28)*

2.1 Introduction

This book studies moral responsibility for outcomes. I endorse the commonly recognized intuition that agents can be held morally (co-)responsible for a given outcome if and only if they are somehow involved in the process that brought about the morally undesirable outcome and their involvement was avoidable. In other words, on my view, moral responsibility requires the positive condition of agency and the negative condition of the possibility of avoidance.[1]

The concept of *agency* thus plays a pivotal role in discussions about moral responsibility. It can be illustrated by considering statements of the form:

(i) 'agent i makes it the case that φ',
(ii) 'φ is guaranteed true by a prior choice of agent i',
(iii) 'agent i brought it about that φ obtains',
(iv) 'agent i sees to it that φ obtains'.

---

[1] The idea that the ability to do otherwise plays a key role in responsibility attributions goes back to Aristotle (see *Nichomachaen Ethics*, 2019, 1113b7-8) and it is closely related to the principle of alternative possibilities (Frankfurt, 1969; Van Inwagen, 1999). More precisely, my formalization is related to recent work on moral responsibility and the avoidance of blame (Hetherington, 2003; McKenna, 1997; Otsuka, 1998; Wyma, 1997). Formalisms that capture this idea in a somewhat different way than mine are presented by Vallentyne (2008) and Braham and van Hees (2012).

© The Author(s), under exclusive license to Springer Nature Switzerland AG 2022
H. Duijf, *The Logic of Responsibility Voids*, Synthese Library 456,
https://doi.org/10.1007/978-3-030-92655-7_2

To elaborate on the notion of agency and moral responsibility, I propose to build on the theory of games and the theory of 'seeing to it that' to get a formal framework within which one can specify different conceptions of moral responsibility. The theory of 'seeing to it that', which is often abbreviated to *stit theory*, provides a precise and compelling semantics of agency within an overall framework of indeterminism. The central idea of stit theory is to treat agency as a modality that represents the agency, or action, of some individual in bringing about a given state of affairs.

Moreover, the problem of responsibility voids requires us to focus on *interdependent* decision scenarios, that is, on scenarios where the resulting outcome depends on the actions and interactions of several individuals. *Game theory* offers a precise and fruitful framework for studying such interdependent decision scenarios.

In this chapter, I will introduce these two theoretical frameworks and show that they are intimately related by elaborating on a correspondence result. There are at least three benefits of elaborating on this correspondence between stit theory and the theory of games. First, such a correspondence supports and facilitates collaborations between game theorists and stit theorists because game models can be translated into stit models, and often *vice versa*. Second, the upshot is that certain advances in game theory can be carried over to stit theory, and *vice versa*. Two recent examples come to mind: game theory has benefitted from a synergy with modal logic in the field of epistemic game theory (see Aumann, 1999); and stit theory has benefited from a synergy with decision theory in the field of deontic logic (see Horty, 2001). Third, with regard to the general aim of investigating moral responsibility, this correspondence means that the analysis of moral responsibility using game models can be carried out using stit models, and (often times) *vice versa*.[2]

The chapter proceeds as follows. I will start by introducing the theory of games (Sect. 2.2), stit theory (Sect. 2.3) and my simplified atemporal version of stit theory (Sect. 2.3.2). Then, I will elaborate on the correspondence between these two frameworks (Sect. 2.4). In the conclusion, I will use these frameworks to demonstrate some preliminary insights on individual moral responsibility.

2.2 Deontic Games

Starting with the seminal work by von Neumann and Morgenstern (1944), the theory of games has been further developed and applied to study a wide range of phenomena and subjects. The theory provides a useful framework for thinking about interdependent decision problems (Schelling, 1960). Interdependent decision

[2] Strictly speaking, because I will prove that game models correspond to a *subclass* of stit models, it follows that there exist stit models for which there is no corresponding game model. Hence, there might be cases where the analysis of moral responsibility using stit models cannot be carried out using game models. At least, my correspondence results do not exclude this possibility.

Fig. 2.1 Driving game

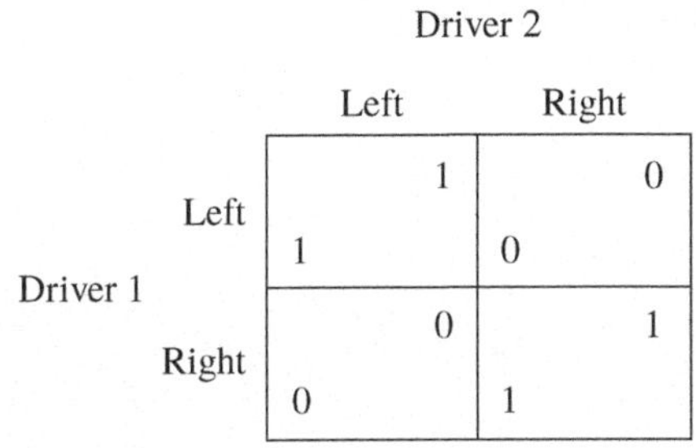

problems are paradigmatically used to study scenarios involving two or more agents where the outcomes depend on the actions of these agents. To illustrate how the application of the framework might work in practice, I will start by discussing some well-known examples. Then I will provide enough detail to set out a cogent introduction to the theory of games. It is therefore not my aim to provide an elaborate overview of all the theoretical and applied work done in the field of game theory. Rather, I will use and develop a framework to the degree necessary for my philosophical theorizing in later chapters. Consider the following trio of examples.

Driving Game Two drivers approach one another in a two-lane road. Each can either keep left or keep right. They are both better off if they both choose the same respective side, otherwise they will have to stop, wasting precious time, or crash. We can use a simple matrix to describe this scenario; see Fig. 2.1. (The number in the lower left corner represent Driver 1's utility and the number in the upper right corner represent Driver 2's utility.) Most importantly, this is a scenario in which the drivers must coordinate to solve the problem, there are many ways to solve the problem, and the drivers are indifferent about which way they do it.[3]

Many-Hands Problem Two tourists are enjoying the sunny weather on the beach when each of them independently spots a drowning child in the ocean. Each can perform either of two actions: swim or wait. Each tourist would save the drowning child by swimming; see Fig. 2.2. Again, there are multiple ways of solving this coordination problem, and each is indifferent about the way it is done.[4]

---

[3] I take this description from Guala (2016, p. 24), who uses game-theoretical models to study institutions. Guala is inspired by Lewis (1969), who uses game-theoretical models for his philosophical analysis of conventions.

[4] This game is meant to highlight some game-theoretical aspects of cases of overdetermination and the so-called bystander effect. The murder of Kitty Genovese has prompted research into the bystander effect (Darley & Latané, 1968; Gansberg, 1964). The game-theoretical structure of the case of the bystander effect is similar, although I will not investigate its psychological precursors. Braham and van Hees (2009) argue, on the basis of such problems of overdetermination, for a quantitative notion of causation. Later, they connect this work on causality to the distribution of responsibility in collective action problems (Braham & van Hees, 2012).

Fig. 2.2 Many-hands problem

		Tourist 2	
		Swim	Wait
Tourist 1	Swim	1 1	1 1
	Wait	1 1	0 0

Fig. 2.3 Hawk-dove game

		Player 2	
		Dove	Hawk
Player 1	Dove	2 2	3 0
	Hawk	0 3	-5 -5

Hawk-Dove Game Think of two individuals who come into conflict over some valuable resource. To play dove is to offer to share the resource but to back down if the other attempts to take it all; to play hawk is to demand the whole resource, backed by a readiness to fight for it. We assume that fighting is costly for both parties and that the utility value of a half share of the resource is greater than half of the utility value of the whole; see Fig. 2.3.[5]

These examples highlight the two fundamental components of a game model: the game form and the utilities. A *game form* involves a finite set N of individual agents. Each individual agent i in N has a non-empty and finite set A_i of available individual actions.[6] I use a_i and a_i' as variables for individual actions in the set A_i. The Cartesian product $\times_{i \in N} A_i$ of all the individual agents' sets of actions gives the full set A of action profiles.

Definition 2.1 (Game Form) A *game form* S is a tuple $\langle N, (A_i) \rangle$, where N is a finite set of individual agents and for each agent i in N it holds that A_i is a non-empty and finite set of actions available to agent i. The set of action profiles A is given by $\times_{i \in N} A_i$.

[5] I take this description from Gold and Sugden (2007, p. 111), who use game-theoretical insights to challenge prominent accounts of collective intentionality.

[6] In this book I will only use such finite game forms for my theorizing. There is, of course, a branch of game theory that deals with infinite games. The most famous example is the infinitely repeated prisoner's dilemma (see Axelrod, 1984).

Some notational conventions: I use a and a' as variables for action profiles in the set A.[7] For each group $\mathcal{G} \subseteq N$ the set $A_{\mathcal{G}}$ of group actions that are available to group $\mathcal{G}$ is defined as the Cartesian product $\times_{i \in \mathcal{G}} A_i$ of all the individual group members' sets of actions. I use $a_{\mathcal{G}}$ and $a'_{\mathcal{G}}$ as variables for group actions in the set $A_{\mathcal{G}}$ $(= \times_{i \in \mathcal{G}} A_i)$. Moreover, if $a_{\mathcal{G}}$ is a group action of group $\mathcal{G}$ and if $\mathcal{F} \subseteq \mathcal{G}$, then $a_{\mathcal{F}}$ denotes the subgroup action that is $\mathcal{F}$'s component subgroup action of the group action $a_{\mathcal{G}}$. I let $-\mathcal{G}$ denote the relative complement $N - \mathcal{G}$. Finally, if $\mathcal{F} \cap \mathcal{G} = \emptyset$, then any two group actions $a_{\mathcal{F}}$ and $a_{\mathcal{G}}$ can be combined into a group action $(a_{\mathcal{F}}, a_{\mathcal{G}}) \in A_{\mathcal{F} \cup \mathcal{G}}$.

A *utility function* u assigns to each action profile a a value $u(a)$, and can be used to represent many different things. It is typically used by game and decision theorists to represent the preferences of an agent, or to represent the revealed preferences of an agent (Okasha (2016) provides a useful discussion on decision-theoretical interpretations of utility). But this is not the only available interpretation. Deontic logicians, for instance, use a binary utility function to represent a single moral code (see Hilpinen, 1971).[8] Depending on the interpretation of the utility function, derived game-theoretical notions should be interpreted differently. The value that an agent i's utility function u_i assigns to an action profile is usually given by a real number, which straightforwardly induces a comparison between action profiles, viz. a is more valuable than b according to u_i if and only if $u_i(a) > u_i(b)$. Depending on the interpretation of the utility function this means that (i) agent i prefers a over b, (ii) agent i always chooses a over b, or (iii) a is deontically better than b.[9]

Definition 2.2 (Game) A *game* S is a triple $\langle N, (A_i), (u_i) \rangle$, where $\langle N, (A_i) \rangle$ is a game form, and for each agent i in N it holds that u_i is a utility function that assigns to each action profile a in A $(= \times_{i \in N} A_i)$ a value $u_i(a) \in \mathbb{R}$.

In this book, I consider *deontic games* (Tamminga & Duijf, 2017; Tamminga & Hindriks, 2020). These are games involving a single *binary* utility function which afford the *deontic* interpretation of utilities. These can be thought of as games where the agents have identical, binary utility functions.[10] The main reason for focusing on binary utility functions is that they naturally relate to standard possible-worlds models for deontic logic. The role of possible worlds is played by possible action profiles and the set of deontically ideal worlds is given by those action profiles that are assigned deontic utility 1 (those assigned deontic utility 0 are considered to

---

[7] I adopt the notational conventions of Osborne and Rubinstein (1994, Sect. 1.7) and omit braces if the omission does not give rise to ambiguities.

[8] Alternatively, in Chap. 5 I will use a binary utility function to represent the intention of an agent.

[9] One may ask whether it is always possible to represent an agent's preferences by a real-valued utility function. The most influential result is that of Savage (1954), who gives conditions under which it is possible to model an agent as if she were maximizing her expected utility, using a credence function and a real-valued utility function.

[10] Deontic games are similar to Schelling's (1960, p. 84) *pure-collaboration games* and Bacharach's (2006, p. 122) *coordination contexts*.

not be deontically ideal). It is common to take deontically ideal action profiles to represent a single moral code, similar to deontically ideal worlds in the possible-worlds semantics for standard deontic logic (Hilpinen, 1971, pp. 13–15).[11] This binary ordering of the action profiles in terms of deontic ideality can also be taken to reflect a simple preference ordering of agents who classify action profiles unanimously as 'good' or 'bad'.

Definition 2.3 (Deontic Game) A *deontic game* S is a triple $\langle N, (A_i), (d)\rangle$, where $\langle N, (A_i)\rangle$ is a game form, and d is a utility function that assigns to each action profile a in A a value $d(a) \in \{0, 1\}$.

For my current purposes, deontic games in which no action profile is deontically ideal are uninteresting. I therefore restrict the analysis to non-flat deontic games:

Definition 2.4 (Flat) Let S be a deontic game. Then S is *flat* if and only if for all action profiles $a \in A$ it holds that $d(a) = 0$.

For readability, I drop the adverb 'non-flat'.

It may be helpful to point out that these games are generally called *normal-form* games (also sometimes called strategic-form games). These normal-form games can be taken to represent a situation in which several agents act simultaneously. These are contrasted with extensive-form games, which drop this simultaneity assumption and can be taken to represent sequential moves. It is important to note that each extensive-form game can be transformed into a normal-form game, although this transformation will remove the temporal structure.[12] Nonetheless, my analysis in this book is restricted to normal-form games.

Game and decision theory deal with the following questions: 'What do people choose in certain decision problems?' and 'What should people choose in certain decision problems?'. The first question is descriptive and seeks to answer how people actually make decisions; the second is normative and studies how people should make decisions. In both enquiries game theorists have put forward many solution concepts. I will briefly discuss two of these that will be relevant throughout the book.[13]

The *Nash equilibrium*, named after John Nash (1950, 1951), is perhaps the most well-known solution concept. Stated simply, Ann and Bob are in a Nash equilibrium

[11] Deontic logicians study the logical aspects of normative expressions, like obligations, duties, permissions, right, and other related expressions. The seminal work by von Wright (1951) has sparked the field of deontic logic. Kanger (1971) and Anderson (1958) give semantical interpretations of deontic logic using deontically ideal worlds that represent what "morality prescribes" (Hilpinen, 1971, p. 21).

[12] It may be interesting to note that normal-form games are typically assumed to imply complete, imperfect information, that is, the 'rules' of the game and the utility functions are commonly known and the agents cannot observe each other's simultaneous choice. In Chap. 4, however, I relax both these requirements by adding an epistemic dimension to normal-form games.

[13] The maximization of expected utility will not be discussed because my study will largely do without probabilities. Although this means that my investigations may not be fully general, for my purposes this gap will be irrelevant.

if Ann is making the best decision she can, given Bob's actual decision, and Bob is making the best decision he can, given Ann's actual decision. Likewise, a group of agents are in a Nash equilibrium if each agent is making the best decision she can, given the actual decisions of the others. A Nash equilibrium is typically taken to represent a state in which no one has an incentive to deviate, given the choices of the others.[14]

Definition 2.5 (Nash Equilibrium) Let S be a game. Then an action profile a is a Nash equilibrium if and only if for each agent i in N and for every $b_i \in A_i$ it holds that $u_i(a) \geq u_i(b_i, a_{-i})$.

To illustrate, the Nash equilibria in the three discussed games are as follows: (left, left) and (right, right) in the driving game; (swim, wait), (swim, swim), and (wait, swim) in the many-hands problem; and (hawk, dove) and (dove, hawk) in the hawk-dove game.

Another intuitive principle is that of dominance, which comes in two guises: strict dominance and simple dominance.[15] An action a_i *strictly dominates* action b_i in S, notation: $a_i \gg_S b_i$, if and only if a_i always yields a strictly better outcome than b_i, regardless of what the others do. An action a_i *simply dominates* action b_i in S, notation: $a_i \succeq_S b_i$, if and only if a_i promotes the utility at least as well as b_i, regardless of what the other agents do. Simple dominance relates to Leonard Savage's "sure-thing principle"; he writes:[16]

> I know of no other extralogical principle governing decisions that finds such ready acceptance. (Savage, 1972, p. 21)[17]

Definition 2.6 (Dominance) Let S be a game. Let $a_i, b_i \in A_i$ be individual actions available to i. Then

$a_i \gg_S b_i$ iff for all $c_{-i} \in A_{-i}$ it holds that $u_i(a_i, c_{-i}) > u_i(b_i, c_{-i})$.
$a_i \succeq_S b_i$ iff for all $c_{-i} \in A_{-i}$ it holds that $u_i(a_i, c_{-i}) \geq u_i(b_i, c_{-i})$.

---

[14] Although the Nash equilibrium concept is widely accepted, it cannot be straightforwardly justified (Risse, 2000). Justifications based on epistemic conditions gave rise to the field of epistemic game theory (see Perea, 2012), originating from the work on rationalizability (Bernheim, 1984; Pearce, 1984).

[15] My notion of 'simple dominance' is the same as Horty's (2001) notion of 'weak dominance', and my notion of 'weak dominance' is the same as his 'strong dominance'. This choice of terminology for 'weak dominance' follows standard practice in game and decision theory and the term of 'simple dominance' is an invention.

[16] My personal inspiration is from Horty (1996, 2001), who provided a similar analysis in deontic logic, which is the formal study of obligations and permissions, by introducing "an ordering on actions available to the agent through a state-by-state comparison of their results", where "we will identify the states confronting the agent at any given moment with the possible patterns of actions that might be performed at that moment by all other agents" (Horty, 2001, p. 67 and p. 66).

[17] In their axiomatic approach to decision theory, Luce and Raiffa (1957, see Section 13.3, and p. 306) express the admissibility requirement in Axiom 5 and write: "Axioms 1 through 5 seem quite innocuous and, so far as we are aware, all serious proposals for criteria satisfy them."

Weak dominance is defined in terms of simple dominance: a_i weakly dominates b_i, notation: $a_i \succ_S b_i$, if and only if $a_i \succeq_S b_i$ and $b_i \not\succeq_S a_i$.

The set of *admissible individual actions* that are available to an individual agent i in a game S are defined in terms of the weak dominance ordering of A_i. An individual action a_i in A_i is admissible if and only if it is not weakly dominated by any individual action in A_i:

Definition 2.7 (Admissible Actions) Let S be a game. Let i be an individual agent. Then the set of i's *admissible actions in* S, denoted by $Admissible_S(i)$, is given by

$$Admissible_S(i) = \{a_i \in A_i : \text{ there is no } a_i' \in A_i \text{ such that } a_i' \succ_S a_i\}.$$

Admissibility captures the idea that an agent takes all actions of the other agents into consideration; none is entirely ruled out.[18] The admissibility concept has a long tradition in decision theory (see the discussion by Kohlberg and Mertens (1986, Sect. 2.7)).

Note that this definition implies that there is at least one admissible action for each individual agent (a special case of Lemma B.1 in Appendix 3.6). It may be useful to add that these three types of dominance are related in a straightforward way: strict dominance entails weak dominance, which entails simple dominance. To illustrate the admissibility requirement, let us reconsider the previously discussed games: in both the driving game and the hawk-dove game, any individual action is admissible, because neither simply dominates the other; in the many-hands problem, only choosing swimming is admissible.

This concludes the brief introduction to the theory of games, showing its application in practice; highlighting its relevance to a range of topics; developing the basic framework; and discussing some solution concepts.

2.3 An Introduction to Stit Theory

The theory of 'seeing to it that', or simply *stit*, has been developed in a series of papers by Belnap, Perloff, and Xu, culminating in their book (2001). It is a theory of agency that is cast against the background of branching time, which neatly models the indeterministic nature of time. Although I will eventually settle for a different modelling, it will be useful to present the ideas of stit theory within this branching-time semantics (Sect. 2.3.1) before giving my simplified version of it that abstracts away from the temporal dimension (Sect. 2.3.2).

[18] Selten (1975) argues that even rational players, having made their choice, may with non-zero probability do something else by accident. It can easily be shown that any action that maximizes expected utility with respect to a probability function that assigns positive probabilities to each move of the opponent is also admissible. This means that an expected utility maximizer should avoid inadmissible actions, but it is foreseeable that some admissible actions do not maximize expected utility with respect to some such probability functions.

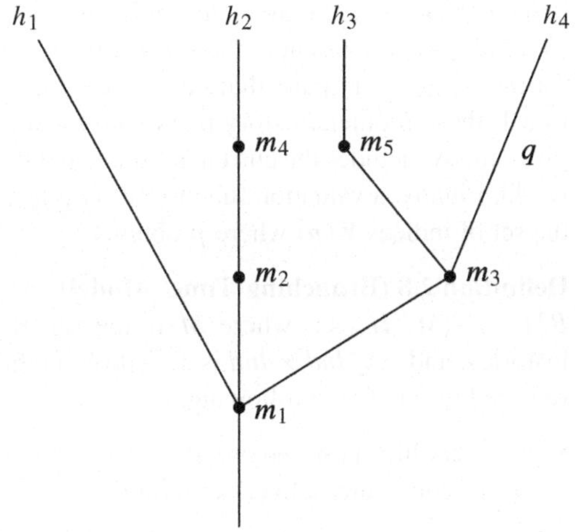

Fig. 2.4 A branching-time structure

2.3.1 Agency in Branching Time

The seminal contributions of Prior (1967) and Thomason (1970, 1984) gave rise to the theory of branching time that would later serve as the backbone for stit semantics (Belnap et al., 2001; Horty, 2001). The branching-time models originate from a philosophical enquiry into the truth-values of temporal sentences, for example, so-called future contingencies. Belnap et al. (2001) present a detailed account of how our indeterministic world can be modelled.[19] The fundamental idea is to represent the world as moments ordered in a tree of histories. (It is important to note a possible confusion: 'histories' are taken to include future moments.) Figure 2.4 presents such a structure.[20] The upward branching of histories represents the openness of the future. Although histories may branch at a particular moment, it is conceivable that there are moments at which no history branches. The absence of backward branching represents the determinateness of the past, that is, the fact that every moment has only a single past sequence of events. Each history in this tree-like structure represents a complete temporal evolution of the world.

A *branching-time model* involves a set of moments M, a set of histories $H \subseteq 2^M$, and a relation $<$ between moment/history pairs which represents the progression of events along a history. I use m, m' as variables for moments in M and h, h' as variables for histories in H. When a moment m and a history h satisfy $m \in h$, this can be taken to mean that m occurs on h, or that h passes through m. Because of

[19] Perloff and Belnap (2011, pp. 583–584) write: "Part of the idea of indeterminism as we conceive it is that at any given moment there are a variety of ways in which the world might proceed. Such possibilities are real, not merely epistemic; they are possibilities."

[20] It may be helpful to point out a convention for interpreting the figures: when a formula φ is written next to a history h emanating from a moment m, then this means that φ holds at that moment/history pair. For example, this means that q holds at m_3/h_4.

indeterminacy, there may be multiple histories that pass through m, so I let $H_m = \{h \in H \mid m \in h\}$ denote the set of histories through m. I use m/h as a variable for moment/history pairs that satisfy $m \in h$ or, equivalently, $h \in H_m$. It is common to call these moment/history pairs *indices*; we let *Ind* denote the set of indices. A given index includes the current moment and the complete temporal evolution of the world. Finally, a valuation function V assigns to each propositional variable $p \in \mathcal{P}$ the set of indices $V(p)$ where p obtains.

Definition 2.8 (Branching-Time Model) A *branching-time frame* is a tuple $BTF = \langle M, H, < \rangle$, where M is the set of moments, $H \subseteq 2^M$ is the set of histories, and $< \subseteq Ind \times Ind$ is a relation on the set of indices. Moreover, *BTF*s are required to satisfy the following:

- for every history h, the ordering $<_h$ on h induced by $<$, viz. $m <_h m'$ iff $m/h < m'/h$, constitutes a linear ordering.
(Linear Histories)
- for every moment m and all histories h, h' such that $m \in h \cap h'$, it holds that $\{m' \in h \mid m' <_h m\} = \{m' \in h' \mid m' <_{h'} m\}$. In other words, there is a single past sequence of events.
(Past Determinacy)

A *branching-time model* $BTM = \langle M, H, <, V \rangle$ is a branching-time frame supplemented with a valuation $V : \mathcal{P} \to 2^{Ind}$.

These branching-time models are typically used to provide semantics for a logical language that includes a past operator P, a future operator F, and a historical necessity operator $\Box$.[21] Intuitively, $\mathsf{P}\varphi$ is true at a moment/history pair m/h if and only if there is a moment m' before m on h where φ obtains; $\mathsf{F}\varphi$ holds at an index m/h if and only if there is a moment m' after m on h where φ obtains. The historical necessity operator $\Box\varphi$ expresses that φ holds at the current moment in the index m/h regardless of how the future unfolds. The dual $\Diamond\varphi$ expresses that there is a possible way for the future to unfold such that φ holds now.

Definition 2.9 (Evaluation Rules Temporal Formulas) Let *BTM* be a branching-time model and let φ be a formula constructed using propositional constants and temporal operators P, F, and $\Box$. Then the truth of φ, at a moment/history pair m/h in *BTM*, notation: $BTM, m/h \vDash \varphi$, is given by the following (suppressing the standard propositional clauses and the model *BTM*):

$m/h \vDash \mathsf{P}\varphi$ iff there is an $m' \in h$ satisfying $m' <_h m$ and $m'/h \vDash \varphi$;
$m/h \vDash \mathsf{F}\varphi$ iff there is an $m' \in h$ satisfying $m <_h m'$ and $m'/h \vDash \varphi$;
$m/h \vDash \Box\varphi$ iff every $h' \in H_m$ satisfies $m/h' \vDash \varphi$.

[21] The literature also discusses other temporal operators; the most common additional operators are the next operator and the until operator.

Definition 2.8 says that indices emanating from the same moment can have different valuations of atomic propositions. This captures the Ockhamistic view that the present moment does not determine the truth of every proposition. Although these branching-time models do not explicitly model agency, one intuitive reason for positing alternative histories through a particular moment is that they witness different actions that the agents can perform. On this view, two histories branch at the current moment if the agents currently perform different actions along these histories.[22] In particular, temporal conditions expressed by $\mathsf{F}\varphi$ may evaluate to different truth values at indices that emanate from the same moment.

Indeed, given these semantics, the idea that the future may still be open is represented by the invalidity of the formula $\mathsf{F}\varphi \rightarrow \Box\mathsf{F}\varphi$. In particular, notice that the branching time model depicted in Fig. 2.4 is such that $m_3/h_4 \vDash \mathsf{F}\varphi$ while $m_3/h_4 \nvDash \Box\mathsf{F}\varphi$. Or, equivalently, $m_3/h_4 \vDash \mathsf{F}\varphi \wedge \Diamond\neg\mathsf{F}\varphi$.

The fundamental idea of agency in stit theories builds on these branching-time models. At a particular moment m we may view H_m as representing the possibilities that are still open. Conversely, the histories outside H_m are no longer possible, or accessible, at moment m. Given that the histories in H_m are still open, an action, or choice, of an agent is viewed as restricting the possible histories to a subset K of H_m. Accordingly, 'the agent sees to it that φ' means that the truth of φ is guaranteed by an action or choice K of the agent. When Ann empties her glass of milk, the nature of her action on this view is to constrain the possible histories to those where the glass of milk is emptied. Hence, an action is identified with a subset of the possible histories. This induces the reading that an agent sees to it that φ only if she performs an action, thereby constraining the possible worlds to only φ-worlds.

A *branching-time agency model* supplements a branching-time model with a finite set of agents *Ags* and sets of available actions, one for each group of agents at each moment. Given a moment m and a group of agents $\mathcal{G}$ (possibly a singleton), the set of available actions is given by a collection of subsets of the possible histories $Act_{\mathcal{G}}^{m} \subset 2^{H_m}$.[23] Since a history can be viewed as the complete temporal evolution of the world, it includes the actions that the agents are performing. The particular action that the group $\mathcal{G}$ executes at a moment/history pair m/h is given by $Act_{\mathcal{G}}^{m}(h)$, which is the action $K \in Act_{\mathcal{G}}^{m}$ satisfying $h \in K$.[24]

[22] Note the absence of the 'only if' here, which only holds for deterministic models (see Definition 2.14).

[23] Stit theorists are ambiguous about the interpretation of *Act* as either choices or actions. According to Horty (1996, p. 274—emphasis added), "*Act* is a device for representing the constraints that an agent is able to exercise upon the course of history at a given moment, the *actions* or *choices* open to him at that moment". Belnap et al. (2001, pp. 33–34—notation adapted and emphasis added) writes: "The equivalence classes belonging to *Act* can be thought of as the possible *choices* or *actions* available." For my current purposes, the elements of *Act* are best thought of as actions.

[24] The fact that there is a unique action $K \in Act_{\mathcal{G}}^{m}$ satisfying $h \in K$ follows from the requirement that $Act_{\mathcal{G}}^{m}$ be a partition of H_m (see below).

Definition 2.10 (Branching-Time Agency Model) A *branching-time agency frame* is a tuple $BTAF = \langle M, H, <, Ags, (Act^m_{\mathcal{G}})\rangle$, involving a branching-time frame $\langle M, H, <\rangle$, a finite set of agents Ags, and for each moment m and each group of agents $\mathcal{G} \subseteq Ags$ it holds that $Act^m_{\mathcal{G}} \subset 2^{H_m}$ is a finite set of actions available to group $\mathcal{G}$ at moment m, satisfying the following:

- for every moment m and every group $\mathcal{G}$, $Act^m_{\mathcal{G}}$ is a partition of H_m.
(Partition)
- for every moment m, every group $\mathcal{G}$, and all histories $h, h' \in H_m$, if there is a moment m' such that $m' \in h \cap h'$ and $m <_h m'$, then $h \in Act^m_{\mathcal{G}}(h')$.
(No Choice between Undivided Histories)
- for every moment m and all groups $\mathcal{F}$ and $\mathcal{G}$, if $\mathcal{F} \subseteq \mathcal{G}$ then $Act^m_{\mathcal{F}} \supseteq Act^m_{\mathcal{G}}$.[25]
(Agent Monotonicity)
- for every moment m, all histories h, h', and all groups $\mathcal{F}$ and $\mathcal{G}$, if $\mathcal{F} \cap \mathcal{G} = \emptyset$ then $Act^m_{\mathcal{F}}(h) \cap Act^m_{\mathcal{G}}(h') \neq \emptyset$.[26]
(Independence of Agency)

A *branching-time agency model* is a branching-time agency frame supplemented with a valuation $V : \mathcal{P} \to 2^{Ind}$.[27]

Figure 2.5 depicts such a branching-time agency model. For example, at m_1, agents i and j both have two available actions, where each action is identified with a subset of the possible histories, in particular, $Act_i^{m_1} = \{\{h_1, h_6, h_7\}, \{h_2, h_3, h_4, h_5\}\}$. These branching-time agency models are used to interpret a logical language that includes agency operators $[\mathcal{G}\ \mathsf{stit}]$, one for each group $\mathcal{G}$. Intuitively, $[\mathcal{G}\ \mathsf{stit}]\varphi$ is true at a moment/history pair m/h if and only if the truth of φ is guaranteed by the action of the group $\mathcal{G}$. That is, the group $\mathcal{G}$ performs an action K thereby constraining the possible histories to only those where φ holds. It may be useful to add that $[\mathcal{G}\ \mathsf{stit}]\varphi$ may be interpreted, relative to a moment/history pair m/h, as 'group $\mathcal{G}$ guarantees that φ holds regardless of what the others do'.[28]

[25] One may wonder why these models are not required to satisfy the *intersection property*, which states that $Act^m_{\mathcal{G}} = \bigcap_{i \in \mathcal{G}} Act^m_i$ (see Definition 2.14). All of the models used in my conceptual analysis actually satisfy this stronger intersection property. My main reason is technical rather than conceptual: the agent monotonicity property enables and simplifies the proof of completeness (Theorem 4.1). For more discussion on the intersection property, see Sect. 2.4.

[26] See Horty (2001, Sect. 2.4) for a useful discussion of the independence of agency requirement.

[27] Branching-time models are often conceived as trees. However, for some purposes a branching-time model is better thought of as a forest consisting of several independent trees. This may, for instance, be important when adding an epistemic indistinguishability relation. For example, to allow for the possibility that an agent does not know the exact past, a branching-time model needs to be interpreted as a forest, rather than a tree.

[28] The stit operator is naturally connected to α-effectivity as used in game theory. I will discuss the relation between stit theory and game theory in Sect. 2.4.

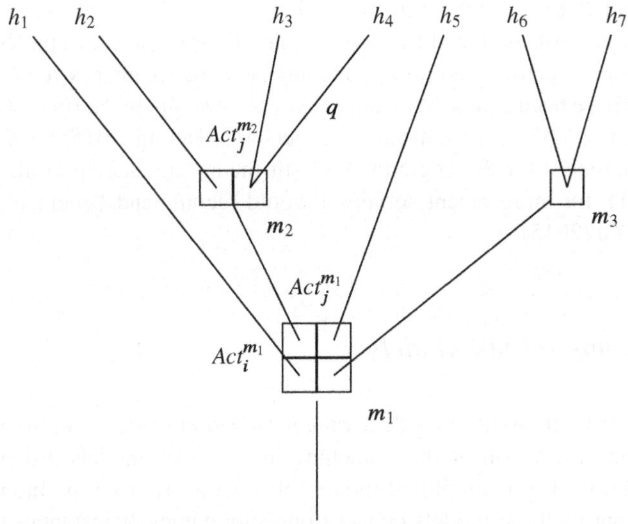

Fig. 2.5 A branching-time agency model

Definition 2.11 (Evaluation Rule Agency) Let *BTAM* be a branching-time agency model. Then the evaluation rule for the stit operator is given by the following (suppressing the model *BTAM*):

$m/h \vDash [\mathcal{G}\ \mathsf{stit}]\varphi$ iff for every $h' \in Act_{\mathcal{G}}^m(h)$ it holds that $m/h' \vDash \varphi$.

It might be helpful to briefly revisit the branching-time agency model depicted in Fig. 2.5. Let us focus on moment m_2. At m_2, agent j has two available actions, where each action is identified with a subset of the possible histories, in particular, $Act_j^{m_2} = \{\{h_2\}, \{h_3, h_4\}\}$. Note that at index m_2/h_4 it is the case that q holds even though it is not the case that agent j sees to it that q holds. That is, $m_2/h_4 \vDash q \wedge \neg[j\ \mathsf{stit}]q$. The second conjunct follows from the fact that q does not hold at m_2/h_3. This illustrates that it is foreseeable that not everything that happens is brought about by an agent.[29]

This concludes my discussion of the traditional stit framework. To those familiar with stit theory, note that the discussed operator is known as the Chellas stit operator (named after Chellas, 1992). Other operators have been introduced and discussed in the literature, most importantly, the deliberative and the achievement stit operator (originally proposed by Belnap and Perloff (1988), and later simplified

[29] Horty and Belnap (1995) propose that we characterize the ability of an individual by a combination of impersonal possibility and agency of the form $\Diamond[i\ \mathsf{stit}]\varphi$, which is to be read as saying that it is possible that agent i sees to it that φ obtains (it should be noted that they use a deliberative stit operator). A model similar to the one depicted in Fig. 2.5 reveals that this proposal escapes an objection raised by Kenny (1975, 1976) that is based on the example of a poor darts player who accidentally hits the bull's-eye (see Horty & Belnap, 1995, pp. 610–611).

by Horty and Belnap, 1995). Stit theory is related to logics of bringing it about (Elgesem, 1993, 1997); the difference is that stit frameworks typically build on branching-time structures and impose the independence of agency requirement. Stit frameworks have been extended to include *strategic action* by Horty (2001, Chap. 7) and Broersen (2009) (see, for instance, Broersen & Herzig, 2015, Sects. 3–6). The standard references for the beginnings of stit theory are Belnap et al. (2001) and Horty (2001); for more recent surveys I would recommend Broersen and Herzig (2015) and Xu (2015).

2.3.2 Atemporal Stit Models

In this section I will briefly introduce *atemporal stit models*, or simply *stit models*, which are an abstraction of the branching-time agency models discussed in the previous section. These simplified models abstract away from the branching-time structure. That is, these models concern one-shot games or instantaneous actions instead of extensive form games or temporally extended actions. Although this is a limitation, the additional complexity is unnecessary for the difficulties addressed in my study. I do believe that that my present study and ideas can be transferred to these extensive form games or temporally extended actions.

Stit models can be taken to represent alethic possibilities and group actions at a single moment in time. These models abstract away from the temporal progression of the worlds. A stit model involves a finite set of agents Ags and a set of moments M, a set of histories H, and a set of indices or moment/history pairs $Ind \subseteq M \times H$. Instead of taking histories to be linearly ordered sets of histories (as is standard in stit theory), we assume a primitive set of indices Ind. We say that history h passes through moment m if $m/h \in Ind$.[30] Furthermore, given a moment m, we let Ind_m denote the set of indices that are based on moment m. Given a group of agents $\mathcal{G}$ and a moment m, the set of available group actions is given by a collection of subsets of the possible indices $Act_{\mathcal{G}}^m \subset 2^{Ind_m}$. The particular action that the group $\mathcal{G}$ executes at an index m/h is given by $Act_{\mathcal{G}}(m/h)$, which is the action $K \in Act_{\mathcal{G}}$ satisfying $m/h \in K$.

Definition 2.12 (Stit Models) A *stit frame* is a tuple $\langle M, H, Ind, Ags, (Act_{\mathcal{G}})\rangle$, involving a set of moments M, a set of histories H, a set of indices $Ind \subseteq M \times H$, a finite set of agents Ags and for each moment $m \in M$ and each group of agents $\mathcal{G} \subseteq Ags$ it holds that $Act_{\mathcal{G}}^m \subset 2^{Ind}_m$ is a finite set of actions available to group $\mathcal{G}$, satisfying the following:

- for every moment m and every group $\mathcal{G}$, $Act_{\mathcal{G}}^m$ is a partition of Ind_m. (Partition)

[30] In comparison, in standard stit theory histories are thought of as linearly ordered sets of moments and we can *define* the set of indices Ind as the set of moment/history pairs m/h such that $m \in h$.

- for all moments m and for all groups $\mathcal{F}, \mathcal{G}$, if $\mathcal{F} \subseteq \mathcal{G}$ then $Act^m_{\mathcal{F}} \supseteq Act^m_{\mathcal{G}}$.
(Agent Monotonicity)
- for all indices $m/h, m/h'$ and all groups $\mathcal{F}, \mathcal{G}$, if $\mathcal{F} \cap \mathcal{G} = \emptyset$ then $Act_{\mathcal{F}}(m/h) \cap Act_{\mathcal{G}}(m/h') \neq \emptyset$.
(Independence of Agency)

A *stit model* is a stit frame supplemented with a valuation $V : \mathcal{P} \rightarrow 2^{Ind}$. A *rich stit model* is a stit model supplemented with utility functions $u_i : Ind \rightarrow \mathbb{R}$, one for each agent $i \in Ags$.[31] A *deontic* stit model is a stit model supplemented with binary utility functions $d_i : Ind \rightarrow \{0, 1\}$, one for each agent $i \in Ags$.

Notice that stit models can be viewed as standard Kripke structures, where the indices *Ind* play the role of the possible worlds. One important aspect of stit models is that such indices are two-dimensional in that they involve both a moment and a history. From the perspective of modal logic, this aspect is *non-standard*. This two-dimensional feature is helpful in that it forces the interpretation of possible worlds as including the temporal evolution of the world. This, for instance, makes it natural to speak of the action performed by an agent at an index, whereas this might be fallacious or elusive for standard possible worlds that do not include such a temporal evolution.

The (rich) stit models closely resemble *choice structures* and *consequentialist models* (Kooi & Tamminga, 2008, Sect. 2), *stit choice structures* (van Benthem & Pacuit, 2014, Sect. 2), and *choice Kripke models* and *consequentialist choice Kripke models* (Ciuni & Horty, 2014, Sects. 23.2–23.3). These models have been fruitfully applied to study meta-logical aspects of various stit logics, such as completeness and axiomatization (see, for instance, Herzig & Schwarzentruber, 2008, Sects. 5–6).

Stit models can be used to interpret a logical language that includes the historical necessity operator $\Box$ and agency operators $[\mathcal{G}\ \mathsf{stit}]$, one for each group $\mathcal{G}$. The evaluation rules for these operators in stit models mirror those for branching-time agency models (see Definitions 2.9 and 2.11). These models can therefore be used to provide semantics for the following logical language:

Definition 2.13 (Syntax) The formal language $\mathfrak{L}_{stit}$ is as follows:

$$\varphi := q \mid \neg\varphi \mid \varphi \wedge \varphi \mid \Box\varphi \mid [\mathcal{G}\ \mathsf{stit}]\varphi,$$

where q ranges over a given countable set of propositions $\mathcal{P}$, i ranges over a given finite set of agents *Ags*, and $\mathcal{G}$ ranges over subsets of *Ags*.

To illustrate these definitions, consider the stit model depicted in Fig. 2.6. This stit model involves two moments, m and m', and two agents, i and j. The indices that pass through m are represented by the matrix on the left and those that pass through m' are represented by the matrix on the right. At moment m, agent i has three actions available to her, K_i, K_i' and K_i'', while agent j only has two actions

[31] See the discussion of utility functions in game theory in Sect. 2.2.

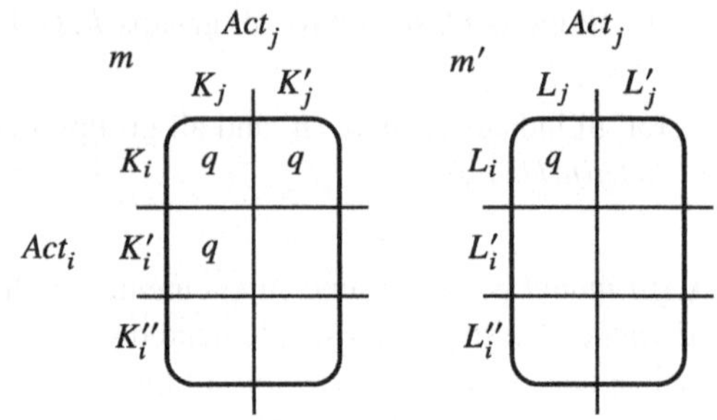

Fig. 2.6 A stit model

available to her, K_j and K'_j. It may be helpful to point out a few conventions for interpreting the figures. When a formula φ is written in a given cell of the matrix, then this means that φ holds at any moment/history pair emanating from that cell. For example, this means that q holds at any index m/h such that $Act_i(m/h) = K_i$ and $Act_j(m/h) = K_j$. Moreover, in the figures, we commonly assume that the group actions are given by the intersections of the actions of the group's members. For instance, $K_i \cap K_j$ is one of the group actions available to the group consisting of agents i and j (see also, the intersection property discussed in Sect. 2.4).

It may be helpful to briefly consider a few properties of the particular model depicted in Fig. 2.6. First, take any index m/h in the upper-left cell, that is, $m/h \in K_i \cap K_j$. Then, we see that, at m/h, agent i sees to it that q. After all, for any index $m/h_0 \in Act_i(m/h) = K_i$ it holds that $m/h_0 \models q$. Second, consider any index m/h' in the mid-left cell, that is $m/h' \in K'_i \cap K_j$. Notice that, at m/h', it is not the case that agent j sees to it that q, because q does not hold in the lower-left cell. Likewise, it is also not the case that agent i sees to it that q. Hence, $m/h' \models q \wedge \neg[i \text{ stit}]q \wedge \neg[j \text{ stit}]q$. This illustrates that it is foreseeable that not everything that happens is brought about by an individual agent.

2.4 Correspondence Between Stit Models and Games

In this section I will demonstrate that stit theory and the theory of games are very similar. More precisely, the stit models presented in Sect. 2.3.2 and the games presented in Sect. 2.2 are closely related: game-theoretical models correspond to a subclass of stit models. The goal of this section is to clarify the exact nature of this correspondence by postulating some mathematical correspondence results. (The proofs are relegated to Appendix A.)

Under this correspondence, an agent can see to it that some state of affairs is realized if and only if she is α-effective for that state of affairs. We need to do a bit of formal work in order to fully grasp this correspondence. This connection has already been noticed and exploited by Horty (2001) to provide semantics for group obligations.[32] Others have subsequently further developed and exploited this analogy (see Bartha, 2014; Ciuni & Horty, 2014; Goranko et al, 2013; Tamminga, 2013; Turrini, 2012).

To establish a straightforward connection with games, three conditions for stit models are crucial. First, the *intersection property* requires that any group action can be identified with a combination of individual actions. Second, *determinacy* requires that each group action of the grand coalition determines a unique moment/history pair. Third, the *solo* property requires that the stit model is based on a single moment.

Definition 2.14 (Intersection Property & Determinacy & Solo) Let $\mathcal{F}$ be a stit frame. We say that $\mathcal{F}$ satisfies the *intersection property* if and only if

(IP) for every index m/h and for every group $\mathcal{G}$ it holds that $Act_{\mathcal{G}}(m/h) = \bigcap_{i \in \mathcal{G}} Act_i(m/h)$.

We say that $\mathcal{F}$ is *deterministic* if and only if

(Det) for every index m/h it holds that $Act_{Ags}(m/h) = \{m/h\}$.

We say that $\mathcal{F}$ is *solo* if and only if

(Solo) for all indices $m/h, m'/h'$ it holds that $m = m'$.

We say that a stit model or rich stit model satisfies any of the above properties—(IP), (Det) or (Solo), respectively—if and only if the stit frame it is based on satisfies the corresponding property.

To state the correspondence theorem that connects stit models to games, we need to elaborate on the notion of *effectivity for outcomes*. An outcome can be thought of as a (non-empty) set of possible indices. Roughly speaking, an agent is effective for a given outcome in the model—stit or game—if and only if she can ensure that outcome by some action, regardless of what the other agents do.

Definition 2.15 (Effectivity) Let $\mathcal{F}$ be a solo rich stit frame and let $X \subseteq Ind$ represent an outcome. I submit that a group $\mathcal{G} \subseteq Ags$ *is effective for* X in $\mathcal{F}$ if and only if

there is a $K \in Act_{\mathcal{G}}$ such that $K \subseteq X$.[33]

A similar definition can be given for games (recall Definition 2.2). Let $S = \langle N, (A_i), (u'_i) \rangle$ be a game and let $Y \subseteq A$ represent an outcome. I submit that a group $\mathcal{G} \subseteq N$ *is effective for* Y in S if and only if

there is an $a_{\mathcal{G}} \in A_{\mathcal{G}}$ such that $\{a' \in A \mid a'_{\mathcal{G}} = a_{\mathcal{G}}\} \subseteq Y$.[34]

---

[32] My study in Chap. 3 relies on Horty's analysis of collective and individual obligations.

[33] Note that if X is represented by a proposition φ in a stit model $\mathcal{M}$, then a group $\mathcal{G}$ is effective for X in $\mathcal{M}$ if and only if $\mathcal{M} \models \Diamond[\mathcal{G}\ \mathsf{stit}]\varphi$.

[34] It may be useful to add that this is equivalent to saying that there is an $a_{\mathcal{G}} \in A_{\mathcal{G}}$ such that $\{(a_{\mathcal{G}}, a'_{-\mathcal{G}}) \mid a'_{-\mathcal{G}} \in A_{-\mathcal{G}}\} \subseteq Y$.

Stated simply, we say that two models $\mathcal{M}_1$ and $\mathcal{M}_2$—solo stit or games—are *equivalent* if and only if for any given outcome X and every group of agents $\mathcal{G}$ it holds that $\mathcal{G}$ is effective for X in $\mathcal{M}_1$ if and only if $\mathcal{G}$ is effective for X in $\mathcal{M}_2$. The correspondence theorem states that every solo, deterministic rich stit frame that satisfies the intersection property corresponds to an equivalent game, and *vice versa*.

Definition 2.16 Let $\mathcal{F} = \langle M, H, Ind, Ags, (Act_{\mathcal{G}}), (u_i)\rangle$ be a solo, deterministic rich stit frame that satisfies the intersection property. The corresponding game $S^{\mathcal{F}} = \langle N, (A_i), (u'_i)\rangle$ is defined as follows:

- $N := Ags$;
- for every $i \in Ags$, $A_i := Act_i$;
- $u'_i(a) := u_i(m/h)$, where $\{m/h\} = \bigcap_{i \in Ags} A_i$.

Because $\mathcal{F}$ is deterministic, a profile $a \in A$ can be identified with the index $m/h \in Ind$ that satisfies $\{m/h\} = \bigcap_{i \in Ags} A_i$. Likewise, an index $m/h \in Ind$ can be identified with the tuple $(Act_i(m/h))_i$. In the following we therefore loosely speak of members of *Ind* as profiles in $S^{\mathcal{F}}$.[35]

Definition 2.17 Let $S = \langle N, (A_i), (u'_i)\rangle$ be a game. The corresponding rich stit frame $\mathcal{F}^S = \langle M, H, Ind, Ags, (Act_{\mathcal{G}}), (u_i)\rangle$ is defined as follows:

- $M := \{m\}$, $H = A$, $Ind := \{m\} \times H$, $Ags := N$, and $u_i = u'_i$;
- for every $\mathcal{G} \subseteq Ags$ and for every $a \in A$, $Act_{\mathcal{G}}(m/a) := \{m/a' \in A \mid a'_{\mathcal{G}} = a_{\mathcal{G}}\}$.

Note that $\mathcal{F}^S$ is solo and deterministic, and it satisfies the intersection property.[36]

Theorem 2.1 (Correspondence Theorem)

1. *Let $\mathcal{F}$ be a solo, deterministic rich stit frame that satisfies the intersection property. Then for the corresponding game $S^{\mathcal{F}}$ we have the following:*
   - *for every group $\mathcal{G}$ and every $X \subseteq Ind$ it holds that $\mathcal{G}$ is effective for X in $\mathcal{F}$ if and only if $\mathcal{G}$ is effective for X in $S^{\mathcal{F}}$.*
2. *Let S be a game. Then for the corresponding rich stit frame $\mathcal{F}^S$, which is solo, deterministic and satisfies the intersection property, we have the following:*
   - *for every group $\mathcal{G}$ and for every $Y \subseteq A$ it holds that $\mathcal{G}$ is effective for Y in S if and only if $\mathcal{G}$ is effective for Y in $\mathcal{F}^S$.*

---

[35] It is important to note that this construction works because the rich stit frame is assumed to satisfy (Det) and (IP). An indeterministic rich stit frame would not allow for a straightforward identification of an index m/h with $\bigcap_{i \in Ags} A_i$. A violation of the intersection property undermines the condition in the corresponding game that $A_{\mathcal{G}} = \times_{i \in \mathcal{G}} A_i$.

As an aside, it can be proven that a solo, *indeterministic* rich stit frame $\mathcal{M}_1$ that satisfies the intersection property can be transformed into a solo, *deterministic* rich stit frame $\mathcal{M}_2$ that satisfies the intersection property while preserving the effectivity for all groups $\mathcal{G} \subset Ags$, i.e. excluding the grand coalition (see my joint work Van De Putte et al., 2017).

[36] The proofs are straightforward: determinism follows from the fact that $A = \times_{i \in Ags} A_i$ and $Act_{Ags}(m/a) = \{m/a' \in A \mid a'_{Ags} = a_{Ags}\}$; the intersection property follows from the fact that $A_{\mathcal{G}} = \times_{i \in \mathcal{G}} A_i$.

Since I will use logical machinery in my analysis it may be helpful to restate this correspondence theorem in terms of a *logical* correspondence. On the one hand, this logical correspondence may help the reader familiar with game theory to understand what the stit formalism is meant to capture. On the other hand, it helps, for instance, to connect my theories of individual and collective know-how to some discussions in game theory (in particular, see Sect. 4.3.2). To establish this logical correspondence, we need to be able to interpret the logical language on games (Kooi & Tamminga, 2008; Tamminga, 2013). A game model is a game supplemented with a valuation. The evaluation rules for the modal operators are straightforward:

Definition 2.18 (Game Models) A *game model* is a tuple $\langle N, (A_i), (u_i), V\rangle$ involving a game $\langle N, (A_i), (u_i)\rangle$ and a valuation $V : \mathcal{P} \to 2^A$. The truth of a formula $\varphi \in \mathfrak{L}_{stit}$ at a profile a in a game model S, notation: $S, a \vDash \varphi$, is given by the following (suppressing the standard propositional clauses):

$S, a \vDash [\mathcal{G}\ \mathsf{stit}]\varphi$ iff for every $a' \in A$ satisfying $a_\mathcal{G} = a'_\mathcal{G}$ it holds that $S, a' \vDash \varphi$;[37]
$S, a \vDash \Box\varphi$ iff for every $a' \in A$ it holds that $S, a' \vDash \varphi$.

The previous Theorem 2.1 entails that a game model and its corresponding rich stit model validate exactly the same formulas in $\mathfrak{L}_{stit}$. The same holds for any solo, deterministic rich stit model that satisfies the intersection property and its associated game model.

Corollary 2.1 (Logical Correspondence)

1. *Let $\mathcal{M}$ be a solo, deterministic rich stit model that satisfies the intersection property, and let $m/h \in Ind$. Then*
   - *for every formula $\varphi \in \mathfrak{L}_{stit}$ it holds that $\mathcal{M}, m/h \vDash \varphi$ if and only if $S^{\mathcal{M}}, m/h \vDash \varphi$.*
2. *Let S be a game model, and let $a \in A$. Then*
   - *for every formula $\varphi \in \mathfrak{L}_{stit}$ it holds that $S, a \vDash \varphi$ if and only if $\mathcal{M}^S, m/a \vDash \varphi$.*

So, if we use formulas in $\mathfrak{L}_{stit}$ to study moral responsibility, then the analysis of responsibility in game models can be carried out using stit models. Conversely, often times, the analysis of responsibility in stit models can be simulated using game models.

[37] In the terminology of Braham and van Hees (2012), $S, a \vDash [\mathcal{G}\ \mathsf{stit}]\varphi$ corresponds to saying that $a_\mathcal{G}$ is a sufficient condition for realizing that φ obtains.

2.5 Discussion: Agentive Responsibility Systems

Consider the idea that an agent is morally responsible for the realization of a given state of affairs if and only if her actions guarantee its realization. That is, moral responsibility for the realization of φ would then be characterized by $[i \text{ stit}]\varphi$. This would mean that moral responsibility requires that your actions were sufficient to bring about that state of affairs. There are some counterexamples to this intuition that are helpful to briefly discuss. First, there is a common intuition that in order to be an appropriate target of blame, the realization of that state of affairs would have to be open. That is, if the state of affairs were unavoidable, then an agent cannot be held responsible for it. After all, the agent's actions had no effect on whether or not that state of affairs is realized. If this is correct, then the responsibility system formalized by $[i \text{ stit}]\varphi$ may sometimes unjustly attribute responsibility to certain agents. We can accommodate the idea that the states of affairs need to be open by considering the *deliberative stit* operator of the form $[i \text{ dstit}]\varphi$, where $[i \text{ dstit}]\varphi := [i \text{ stit}]\varphi \wedge \Diamond\neg\varphi$ (Belnap et al., 2001; Horty & Belnap, 1995).

Notice that this intuition entails that the notion of moral responsibility should be *narrower*. After all, it is easy to see that $\models [i \text{ dstit}]\varphi \rightarrow [i \text{ stit}]\varphi$, which means that deliberately seeing to it that φ logically entails guaranteeing φ. In other words, if an agent is morally responsible under the deliberative stit, then that agent is morally responsibility under the regular stit.

To illustrate the second worry, consider an example where two firms bring about an environmental harm by simultaneously emitting amounts of some toxin into a river and in which no firm could have brought about the harm alone. We can simplify the scenario by assuming that each firm i has two options available: to emit the toxin into the river or to refrain from doing so, represented by a_i and b_i respectively. Then, this example can modelled in terms of the deontic game depicted in Fig. 2.7 and, in particular, by considering action profile $a = (a_1, a_2)$. Notice that neither firm guaranteed that the environmental harm obtains. After all, for instance, $[\text{Firm 2 dstit}]q$ is false at a. Hence, if we endorse the notion of moral responsibility that is characterized by $[i \text{ dstit}]\varphi$, then we would conclude that neither firm can be held morally responsible for the harm they together brought about. This example supports the claim that the responsibility system formalized by $[i \text{ dstit}]\varphi$ sometimes fails to attribute responsibility. As a result, we would conclude that this responsibility system readily produces responsibility voids: voids can arise whenever no member has full control over the realization of some morally undesirable state of affairs.

Fig. 2.7 A deontic game of the environmental harm

Firm 1 \ Firm 2	a_2	b_2
a_1	0 / q	1
b_1	1	1

One way to address this second worry is to broaden the conception of moral responsibility by relying on the idea that agents cannot be held responsible for φ only if they did their best to avoid the realization of φ. To account for this intuition, and similar to the analysis of Braham and van Hees (2012), I propose that an agent cannot be held responsible for a given outcome if she maximally avoided it. At the current stage, this can be made precise using the decision-theoretic notion of *admissibility*.[38] To understand this notion of maximal avoidance, it is important to consider the counterfactual scenarios where an individual unilaterally deviated from her actual course of action. That is, we may ask whether there is an alternative action by which that individual would have changed the state of affairs *while fixing the actions of the other agents*. In the example above, each firm would have avoided the environmental hazard if it had unilaterally refrained from emitting the toxin in the river. Accordingly, emitting toxin is weakly dominated by refraining from doing so, that is, $a_i \prec b_i$. Hence, neither firm maximally avoided the realization the environmental harm and, therefore, each can be held responsible.

Although inconclusive, the lesson to be drawn from this discussion is that agentive statements play an important role in our moral responsibility attributions. In this chapter, the goal has been to propose a framework for studying the agency of individuals and groups. In formulating my framework I draw from two formal traditions: game theory and stit theory. In addition, I briefly discussed some formal and conceptual links between these two traditions. I demonstrated that these formal frameworks can be used to specify several responsibility systems, and that these formalisms readily enable us to study the problem of responsibility voids. The next chapter follows up on the discussion above and studies the possibility and scope of responsibility voids and gaps under the responsibility system that is based on dominance theory.

Appendix A: Games and Agency

Theorem 2.1 (Correspondence Theorem)

1. *Let $\mathcal{F}$ be a solo, deterministic rich stit frame that satisfies the intersection property. Then for the corresponding game $S^{\mathcal{F}}$ we have the following:*
   - *for every group $\mathcal{G}$ and every $X \subseteq Ind$ it holds that $\mathcal{G}$ is effective for X in $\mathcal{F}$ if and only if $\mathcal{G}$ is effective for X in $S^{\mathcal{F}}$.*
2. *Let S be a game. Then for the corresponding rich stit frame $\mathcal{F}^S$, which is solo, deterministic and satisfies the intersection property, we have the following:*
   - *for every group $\mathcal{G}$ and for every $Y \subseteq A$ it holds that $\mathcal{G}$ is effective for Y in S if and only if $\mathcal{G}$ is effective for Y in $\mathcal{F}^S$.*

[38] The main distinction with the work of Braham and van Hees is that I spell out the notion of maximal avoidance in non-probabilistic terms.

Proof

1. Because $\mathcal{F}$ satisfies (Det), (Solo) and (IP), each index m/h corresponds to the group action $Act_{Ags}(m/h)$, which is given by $\bigcap_{i \in Ags} Act_i(m/h)$, and therefore corresponds to the action profile $(Act_i(m/h))_{i \in Ags}$ in $S^{\mathcal{F}}$. The converse also holds: to each action profile a in $S^{\mathcal{F}}$ corresponds exactly one index, viz. the element of $\bigcap_{i \in Ags} a_i$. Since $K \in Act_i$ in $\mathcal{F}$ can be represented by an index m/h such that $K = Act_i(m/h)$, it holds that $K = \{m/h' \in Ind \mid Act_i(m/h') = Act_i(m/h)\}$, which corresponds to $\{a' \in A \mid a'_i = a_i\}$ in $S^{\mathcal{F}}$, where $K = a_i \in A_i$.
   Let $X \subseteq W$, and let $\mathcal{G} \subseteq Ags$. Then the following are equivalent: (1) $\mathcal{G}$ is effective for X in $\mathcal{F}$, (2) there is a $K \in Act_{\mathcal{G}}$ such that $K \subseteq X$, (3) there are $K_i \in Act_i$, one for each $i \in \mathcal{G}$, such that $\bigcap_{i \in \mathcal{G}} K_i \subseteq X$, (4) there are $a_i \in A_i$, one for each $i \in \mathcal{G}$, such that $\{a' \in A \mid a'_i = a_i \text{ for each } i \in \mathcal{G}\} \subseteq X$, (5) there is an $a_{\mathcal{G}} \in A_{\mathcal{G}}$ such that $\{a' \in A \mid a'_{\mathcal{G}} = a_{\mathcal{G}}\} \subseteq X$, (6) $\mathcal{G}$ is effective for X in $S^{\mathcal{F}}$.
2. Follows immediately from unravelling the definitions and noting that a group action $a_{\mathcal{G}} \in A_{\mathcal{G}}$ in S corresponds to the group action $\{a' \in A \mid a'_{\mathcal{G}} = a_{\mathcal{G}}\} \in Act_{\mathcal{G}}$ in $\mathcal{F}^S$. □

Corollary 2.1 (Logical Correspondence)

1. *Let $\mathcal{M}$ be a solo, deterministic rich stit model that satisfies the intersection property, and let $m/h \in Ind$. Then*
   - *for every formula $\varphi \in \mathfrak{L}_{stit}$ it holds that $\mathcal{M}, m/h \models \varphi$ if and only if $S^{\mathcal{M}}, m/h \models \varphi$.*
2. *Let S be a game model, and let $a \in A$. Then*
   - *for every formula $\varphi \in \mathfrak{L}_{stit}$ it holds that $S, a \models \varphi$ if and only if $\mathcal{M}^S, m/a \models \varphi$.*

Proof This can be proven by standard induction on the complexity of the formula using the correspondences alluded to in the proof of Theorem 2.1. Let us consider the proof of 1. for the induction step involving formulas of the form $[\mathcal{G}\ \mathsf{stit}]\varphi$.

Let $\mathcal{M}$ be a stit model that satisfies the abovementioned constraints and let m/h be an index. By the induction hypothesis, for every index m^*/h^* it holds that $\mathcal{M}, m^*/h^* \models \varphi$ if and only if $S^{\mathcal{M}}, m^*/h^* \models \varphi$. Note that $\mathcal{M}, m/h \models [\mathcal{G}\ \mathsf{stit}]\varphi$ if and only if for every $h' \in Act^m_{\mathcal{G}}(h)$ it holds that $\mathcal{M}, m/h' \models \varphi$. By the intersection property, the latter is equivalent to: (a) for every h' such that for all $i \in \mathcal{G}$ we have $Act_i(m/h) = Act_i(m/h')$ it holds that $S^{\mathcal{M}}, m/h' \models \varphi$. By the correspondences alluded to in the proof of Theorem 2.1, we can view m/h as an action profile a in $S^{\mathcal{M}}$. Moreover, by the same token, every m/h' satisfying $h' \in Act^m_{\mathcal{G}}(h)$ can be viewed as an action profile a' such that for all $i \in \mathcal{G}$ it holds that $a'_i = a_i$, and vice versa. By the induction hypothesis, (a) is equivalent to (b) for every a' such that for all $i \in \mathcal{G}$ we have $a'_i = a_i$ it holds that $S^{\mathcal{M}}, a' \models \varphi$, which is in turn equivalent to (c) for every a' such that $a'_{\mathcal{G}} = a_{\mathcal{G}}$ it holds that $S^{\mathcal{M}}, a' \models \varphi$. In other words, (a) is equivalent to $S^{\mathcal{M}}, m/h \models [\mathcal{G}\ \mathsf{stit}]\varphi$, as desired. □

References

Anderson, A. R. (1958). A reduction of deontic logic to alethic modal logic. *Mind, 67*(265), 100–103.

Aristotle (2019). *Nicomachean ethics* (3rd ed.). T. Irwin (Trans.). Indianapolis: Hackett Publishing Company.

Aumann, R. J. (1999). Interactive epistemology I: Knowledge. *International Journal of Game Theory, 28*(3), 263–300.

Axelrod, R. M. (1984). *The evolution of cooperation*. New York: Basic Books.

Bacharach, M. (2006). *Beyond individual choice: Teams and frames in game theory*, N. Gold & R. Sugden (Eds.). Princeton: Princeton University Press.

Bartha, P. (2014). Decisions in branching time. In T. Müller (Ed.), *Nuel Belnap on indeterminism and free action* (pp. 29–56). Springer.

Belnap, N., & Perloff, M. (1988). Seeing to it that: A canonical form for agentives. *Theoria, 54*(3), 175–199.

Belnap, N., Perloff, M., & Xu, M. (2001). *Facing the future. Agents and choices in our indeterminist world*. Oxford: Oxford University Press.

van Benthem, J., & Pacuit, E. (2014). Connecting logics of choice and change. In T. Müller (Ed.), *Nuel Belnap on indeterminism and free action* (pp. 291–314). Springer.

Bernheim, B. D. (1984). Rationalizable strategic behavior. *Econometrica, 52*(4), 1007–1028.

Braham, M., & van Hees, M. (2009). Degrees of causation. *Erkenntnis, 71*(3), 323–344.

Braham, M., & van Hees, M. (2012). An anatomy of moral responsibility. *Mind, 121*(483), 601–634.

Broersen, J. (2009). A stit-logic for extensive form group strategies. In P. Boldi, G. Vizzari, G. Pasi, & R. Baeza-Yates (Eds.), *Proceedings of the International Joint Conference on Web Intelligence and Intelligent Agent Technology* (Vol. 3, pp. 484–487). Washington: IEEE Computer Society.

Broersen, J., & Herzig, A. (2015). Using STIT theory to talk about strategies. In J. van Benthem, S. Ghosh, & R. Verbrugge (Eds.), *Models of strategic reasoning* (pp. 137–173). Springer.

Chellas, B. F. (1992). Time and modality in the logic of agency. *Studia Logica, 51*(3/4), 485–517.

Ciuni, R., & Horty, J. (2014). Stit logics, games, knowledge, and freedom. In A. Baltag & S. Smets (Eds.), *Johan van Benthem on logic and information dynamics* (pp. 631–656). Springer.

Darley, J. M., & Latané, B. (1968). Bystander intervention in emergencies: Diffusion of responsibility. *Journal of Personality and Social Psychology, 8*(4), 377–383.

Elgesem, D. (1993). *Action theory and modal logic*. PhD Thesis, University of Oslo.

Elgesem, D. (1997). The modal logic of agency. *Nordic Journal of Philosophical Logic, 2*(2), 1–46.

Frankfurt, H. G. (1969). Alternate possibilities and moral responsibility. *The Journal of Philosophy, 66*(23), 829–839.

Gansberg, M. (1964). 37 who saw murder didn't call the police. *The New York Times*.

Gold, N., & Sugden, R. (2007). Collective intentions and team agency. *The Journal of Philosophy, 104*(3), 109–137.

Goranko, V., Jamroga, W., & Turrini, P. (2013). Strategic games and truly playable effectivity functions. *Autonomous Agents and Multi-Agent Systems, 26*(2), 288–314.

Guala, F. (2016). *Understanding institutions: The science and philosophy of living together*. Princeton: Princeton University Press.

Herzig, A., & Schwarzentruber, F. (2008). Properties of logics of individual and group agency. In C. Areces, & R. Goldblatt (Eds.), *The Seventh Conference on Advances in Modal Logic* (pp. 133–149). College Publications.

Hetherington, S. (2003). Alternate possibilities and avoidable moral responsibility. *American Philosophical Quarterly, 40*(3), 229–239.

Hilpinen, R. (1971). *Deontic logic: Introductory and systematic readings*. Dordrecht: D. Reidel Publishing Company.

Horty, J. F. (1996). Agency and obligation. *Synthese, 108*(2), 269–307.

Horty, J. F. (2001). *Agency and deontic logic*. New York: Oxford University Press.

Horty, J. F., & Belnap, N. (1995). The deliberative stit: A study of action, omission, ability, and obligation. *Journal of Philosophical Logic, 24*(6), 583–644.
Kanger, S. (1971). New foundations for ethical theory. In R. Hilpinen (Ed.), *Deontic logic: introductory and systematic readings* (pp. 36–58). Dordrecht: D. Reidel Publishing Company.
Kenny, A. (1975). *Will, freedom and power*. Basil Blackwell.
Kenny, A. (1976). Human abilities and dynamic modalities. In J. Manninen & R. Tuomela (Eds.), *Essays on explanation and understanding* (pp. 209–232). D. Reidel Publishing Company.
Kohlberg, E., & Mertens, J.-F. (1986). On the strategic stability of equilibria. *Econometrica, 54*(5), 1003–1037.
Kooi, B., & Tamminga, A. (2008). Moral conflicts between groups of agents. *Journal of Philosophical Logic, 37*(1), 1–21.
Lewis, D. K. (1969). *Convention: A philosophical study*. Cambridge: Harvard University Press.
Luce, R. D., & Raiffa, H. (1957). *Games and decisions*. New York: Wiley.
McKenna, M. S. (1997). Alternative possibilities and the failure of the counterexample strategy. *Journal of Social Philosophy, 28*(3), 71–85.
Nash, J. F. (1950). Equilibrium points in n-person games. *Proceedings of the National Academy of Sciences of the United States of America, 36*(1), 48–49.
Nash, J. F. (1951). Non-cooperative games. *Annals of Mathematics, 54*, 286–295.
Okasha, S. (2016). On the interpretation of decision theory. *Economics & Philosophy, 32*(3), 409–433.
Osborne, M. J., & Rubinstein, A. (1994). *A course in game theory*. Cambridge: MIT Press.
Otsuka, M. (1998). Incompatibilism and the avoidability of blame. *Ethics, 108*(4), 685–701.
Pearce, D. G. (1984). Rationalizable strategic behavior and the problem of perfection. *Econometrica, 52*(4), 1029–1050.
Perea, A. (2012). *Epistemic game theory*. Cambridge: Cambridge University Press.
Perloff, M., & Belnap, N. (2011). Future contingents and the battle tomorrow. *The Review of Metaphysics, 64*(3), 581–602.
Prior, A. N. (1967). *Past, present and future*. Oxford: Clarendon Press.
Risse, M. (2000). What is rational about Nash equilibria? *Synthese, 124*(3), 361–384.
Savage, L. J. (1954). *The foundations of statistics*. New York: Wiley.
Savage, L. J. (1972). *The foundations of statistics* (2nd ed.). New York: Dover Publications.
Schelling, T. C. (1960). *The strategy of conflict*. Cambridge: Harvard University Press.
Schelling, T. C. (2010). Game theory: A practitioner's approach. *Economics & Philosophy, 26*(1), 27–46.
Selten, R. (1975). Reexamination of the perfectness concept for equilibrium points in extensive games. *International Journal of Game Theory, 4*(1), 25–55.
Tamminga, A. (2013). Deontic logic for strategic games. *Erkenntnis, 78*(1), 183–200.
Tamminga, A., & Duijf, H. (2017). Collective obligations, group plans and individual actions. *Economics & Philosophy, 33*(2), 187–214.
Tamminga, A., & Hindriks, F. (2020). The irreducibility of collective obligations. *Philosophical Studies, 177*(4), 1085–1109.
Thomason, R. H. (1970). Indeterminist time and truth-value gaps. *Theoria, 36*(3), 264–281.
Thomason, R. H. (1984). Combinations of tense and modality. In D. Gabbay & F. Guenthner (Eds.), *Handbook of philosophical logic* (Vol. 165, pp. 135–165). Dordrecht: Springer.
Turrini, P. (2012). Agreements as norms. In T. Ågotnes, J. M. Broersen, & D. Elgesem (Eds.), *Proceedings of the Eleventh International Conference on Deontic Logic in Computer Science* (pp. 31–45). Springer.
Vallentyne, P. (2008). Brute luck and responsibility. *Politics, Philosophy & Economics, 7*(1), 57–80.
Van De Putte, F., Tamminga, A., & Duijf, H. (2017). Doing without nature. In A. Baltag, J. Seligman, & T. Yamada (Eds.), *Proceedings of the Sixth International Workshop on Logic, Rationality, and Interaction* (pp. 209–223). Springer.
Van Inwagen, P. (1999). Moral responsibility, determinism, and the ability to do otherwise. *The Journal of Ethics, 3*(4), 341–350.

von Neumann, J., & Morgenstern, O. (1944). *Theory of games and economic behavior*. Princeton: Princeton University Press.

von Wright, G. H. (1951). Deontic logic. *Mind, 60*(237), 1–15.

Wyma, K. D. (1997). Moral responsibility and leeway for action. *American Philosophical Quarterly, 34*(1), 57–70.

Xu, M. (2015). Combinations of stit with ought and know. *Journal of Philosophical Logic, 44*(6), 851–877.

Chapter 3
Collective Obligations, Group Plans, and Individual Actions

Of the major disciplines concerned with social behaviour, game theory alone, it seems, has eschewed, and got along to date without, group notions.

Bacharach (2006, p. 72)

3.1 Introduction

In the previous chapter, we started to explore the concepts of moral responsibility and responsibility voids and gaps by considering the agency of individuals and groups. In this chapter, I will further develop the study of responsibility voids and gaps by examining the responsibility system that is based on dominance theory. The guiding idea of this chapter is that one can be held morally responsible only if one fails to fulfil one of their obligations. The converse need not hold, since there may be reasons for exculpating such failures. However, in the absence of such exculpating factors, the failure to fulfil one's obligations entails that one can be held morally responsible. I will adopt Horty's (2001) theory of obligations and propose that an agent fulfils her obligations if and only if she performs one of her deontically admissible actions.

I will first illustrate that individual and collective obligations do not match: the fulfilment of a collective obligation is neither necessary nor sufficient for the fulfilment of individual obligations.[1] It may be problematic when a collective failure to fulfil a collective obligation cannot be attributed to a member's failure to fulfil her

This chapter is largely based on published work with Allard Tamminga (Tamminga & Duijf, 2017), reprinted with permission of Cambridge University Press.

[1] This observation is not new. I refer the interested reader to (Horty, 2001, Sect. 6.2) and (Horty, 2011) and references therein.

© The Author(s), under exclusive license to Springer Nature Switzerland AG 2022

H. Duijf, *The Logic of Responsibility Voids*, Synthese Library 456,
https://doi.org/10.1007/978-3-030-92655-7_3

individual obligation. This opens the possibility for gaps between individual and collective responsibility. If group members aim to fulfil a collective obligation, they must act in such a way that the composition of their individual actions amounts to a group action that fulfils the collective obligation.

The central aim of the chapter is to study whether a group can prevent responsibility voids and gaps in cases where the group's members are able to communicate and agree on a group plan to fulfil their collective obligation. To do so, I will study a strong sense of joint action in which the members of a group, using team reasoning, design and then publicly adopt a group plan. I will give conditions under which a group plan that is designed to fulfil a collective obligation is a *good plan*, that is, conditions under which a group plan guarantees that if every group member fulfils her member obligation specified by the plan, then the group itself fulfils its collective obligation.

The chapter is set out as follows. In Sect. 3.2, I define individual and collective obligations in terms of deontically admissible actions in deontic games involving a single deontic ideality function. I illustrate that the fulfilment of a collective obligation is neither necessary nor sufficient for the fulfilment of individual obligations. In Sect. 3.3, I define a *group plan* as a set of group actions that are available to the group as a whole, and I introduce the notion of a *member obligation* specified by the plan. I model the public adoption of a group plan as an update of the deontic ideality of the action profiles in a deontic game. In Sect. 3.4, I give conditions under which a group plan is a *good plan*, that is, conditions under which a group plan guarantees that if every group member fulfils her member obligation specified by the plan, then the group itself fulfils its collective obligation. Although individual and member obligations can be distinct, I prove that individual and member obligations align whenever a good plan has been adopted in Sect. 3.4.3. In Sect. 3.5, I discuss collective deontic admissibility and so-called good* plans, where a group plan is good* if and only if after publicly adopting the group plan it holds that whenever every group member fulfils her individual obligation in the updated decision context, then the group fulfils its collective obligation. In the concluding section, I use my formal analysis of collective obligations, group plans, and individual actions to study some logical aspects of the problem of responsibility voids and gaps.

3.2 Individual and Collective Obligations

I use *deontic games* to study relations between collective obligations, group plans, and obligations of individual agents. Recall that a deontic game is a particular type of game (see Definition 2.3 and Sect. 2.2 for a more detailed introduction to the theory of games and further notational conventions). Deontic games involve a deontic ideality function which can be taken to represent a single moral code or to reflect a simple preference ordering of agents who classify action profiles unanimously as 'good' or 'bad'.

In the context of deontic games, the dominance theory (see Sect. 2.2) can be straightforwardly extended to group actions.[2] I follow Horty's (1996, 2001) deontic logic of agency and analyse a group's collective obligations in terms of its admissible group actions that are in turn defined using a dominance ordering of the group actions that are available to the group. Intuitively, group action $a_{\mathcal{G}}$ *simply dominates* group action $a'_{\mathcal{G}}$ in deontic game S (notation: $a_{\mathcal{G}} \succeq_S a'_{\mathcal{G}}$) if and only if $a_{\mathcal{G}}$ promotes deontic ideality in S at least as well as $a'_{\mathcal{G}}$, regardless of what the group's non-members do.[3]

Definition 3.1 (Dominance) Let $S = \langle N, (A_i), d \rangle$ be a deontic game. Let $\mathcal{G} \subseteq N$ be a group of agents. Let $a_{\mathcal{G}}, a'_{\mathcal{G}} \in A_{\mathcal{G}}$ be actions available to group $\mathcal{G}$. Then

$a_{\mathcal{G}} \succeq_S a'_{\mathcal{G}}$ iff for all $a''_{-\mathcal{G}} \in A_{-\mathcal{G}}$ it holds that $d(a_{\mathcal{G}}, a''_{-\mathcal{G}}) \geq d(a'_{\mathcal{G}}, a''_{-\mathcal{G}})$.

Weak dominance is defined in terms of simple dominance: $a_{\mathcal{G}} \succ_S a'_{\mathcal{G}}$ if and only if $a_{\mathcal{G}} \succeq_S a'_{\mathcal{G}}$ and $a'_{\mathcal{G}} \not\succeq_S a_{\mathcal{G}}$.

I define the set of *admissible group actions* that are available to a group $\mathcal{G}$ of agents in a deontic game S in terms of the dominance ordering of $A_{\mathcal{G}}$. A group action $a_{\mathcal{G}}$ in $A_{\mathcal{G}}$ is admissible if and only if it is not weakly dominated by any group action in $A_{\mathcal{G}}$:

Definition 3.2 (Admissible Actions) Let S be a deontic game. Let $\mathcal{G} \subseteq N$ be a group of agents. Then the set of $\mathcal{G}$'s *admissible actions in* S, denoted by $Admissible_S(\mathcal{G})$, is given by

$Admissible_S(\mathcal{G}) = \{a_{\mathcal{G}} \in A_{\mathcal{G}} :$ there is no $a'_{\mathcal{G}} \in A_{\mathcal{G}}$ such that $a'_{\mathcal{G}} \succ_S a_{\mathcal{G}}\}$.

Note that this definition implies that for every non-empty group of agents there is at least one admissible action (see Lemma B.1 in Appendix B). Since there always is at least one admissible action, in particular for any non-empty group and any of its non-empty subgroups, it makes sense to enquire about the relation between admissible group actions and admissible subgroup actions. First, note that an admissible group action is not necessarily composed of admissible subgroup actions. In the deontic game S_1 of Fig. 3.1 it holds that (a'_i, a'_j) is admissible for the group $\{i, j\}$, although a'_i is not admissible for agent i and a'_j is not admissible for agent j. (Notice the resemblance with the many-hands problem of Fig. 2.2.)

Second, the composition of admissible subgroup actions is not necessarily an admissible group action. Deontic game S_2 of Fig. 3.2 shows the deontic analogue of

[2] The following definitions are similar to the introductory Definitions 2.1, 2.3, 2.6 and 2.7 yet they concern deontic games and they cover admissible *group* actions. Unlike deontic games, games may involve individual agents with different utility functions; it is, therefore, not obvious how to define admissible group actions in games, more generally.

[3] Recall that my choice of terminology for 'weak dominance' follows standard practice in game and decision theory, but deviates from that of Horty (2001). My notion of 'simple dominance' is the same as Horty's notion of 'weak dominance' and my notion of 'weak dominance' is the same as his 'strong dominance'.

Fig. 3.1 Deontic game S_1

	a_j	a'_j	a''_j
a_i	1	1	1
a'_i	1	1	0
a''_i	1	0	0

Fig. 3.2 Deontic game S_2

	a_j	a'_j
a_i	1	0
a'_i	0	1

the driving game (Fig. 2.1). In S_2 it holds that a_i is admissible for agent i and a'_j is admissible for agent j, although (a_i, a'_j) is not admissible for the group $\{i, j\}$.

Finally, I submit that a group $\mathcal{G}$ fulfils its *collective obligation* in deontic game S if and only if it performs one of its admissible group actions. (Likewise, an agent i fulfils her *individual obligation* in deontic game S if and only if she performs one of her admissible individual actions.) The discussion of Figs. 3.1 and 3.2 shows that collective obligations and individual obligations do not match: the fulfilment of a collective obligation is neither necessary nor sufficient for the fulfilment of individual obligations. For example, this highlights that the driving game and the many-hands problem can give rise to cases where individual and collective obligations mismatch (Figs. 2.1 and 2.2). To fulfil its collective obligation the group's members must ensure that their individual actions amount to an admissible group action. The gap between collective obligations and individual agency is filled by *member obligations*. Intuitively, a member obligation is what a group member ought to do in order to help ensure that the group fulfils its collective obligation, that is, in order to help ensure that the group performs an admissible group action. In this chapter I consider member obligations as following from a collective obligation via a group plan.

3.3 Group Plans and Member Obligations

A group that aims to fulfil a collective obligation has a coordination problem: the group members must cooperate to ensure that the composition of their individual actions amounts to an admissible group action. In contrast to most coordination theorists, I assume that group members are able to communicate and to agree on a *group plan* to solve their coordination problem.[4] By agreeing on a group plan, it becomes common knowledge among the members of the group that the plan has been adopted. A group plan, once agreed upon, coordinates the individual actions of

[4] Coordination theorists typically address the following problem: given a one-shot two-player game where no communication between the agents is possible, how are we to explain an agent's ability to anticipate the other agent's actions? Schelling (1960, pp. 54–58), Lewis (1969), Gauthier (1975), Sugden (1993, 1995, 2003), and Bacharach (2006) all study this type of coordination problem, arguing that concepts like *salience*, *focal points*, or *framing* are the key to understanding the coordination abilities of non-communicating agents.

the members of the group: it allows them to act *simultaneously* and *unconditionally*, in the full belief that every group member acts according to plan. Group actions that are regulated by a group plan constitute a strong sense of joint action.[5] Raimo Tuomela calls this sense of acting together *proper joint action*:

> Acting together involves sociality in the relatively strong sense that such action must be based on joint intention or shared collective goal. This makes any case of acting together cooperative at least to the extent that the persons are collectively committed to making true a certain state of affairs. [...] In the strongest sense of acting together we require acting on a joint, agreed-upon plan. This I will call proper joint action. (Tuomela, 2000, p. 7)

To design a group plan the group members must discover which are the best courses of action they can take *as a group*. To do so, group members must abandon their individual perspective and reason from the standpoint of a group and the group actions that are available to it. This kind of reasoning is known as *team reasoning* (Bacharach, 1999, 2006; Sugden, 1993, 2000, 2003) or *we-reasoning* (Tuomela, 2013).[6]

I take it that team reasoning permits the group members to come up with and agree on a group plan.[7] Once adopted, a group plan provides "a filter on options that are potential solutions" (Bratman, 1987, p. 35) to a group's coordination problem. By filtering out group actions, a group plan specifies the remaining group actions and in consequence it highlights the individual actions that are the components of these highlighted group actions. Accordingly, a group plan specifies for each group member what she ought to do.

I intend to understand how a group plan gives rise to member obligations by way of Margaret Gilbert's account of joint commitments. I submit that by adopting a group plan, a group of agents enters a joint commitment to execute the plan.[8] After entering such a joint commitment, the group members "owe each other conformity to the commitment. Thus, they have obligations towards each other" (Gilbert, 2006a, p. 156). Such obligations of joint commitment are genuine obligations, Gilbert argues: they meet the condition that "one who has an obligation to perform some action will have sufficient reason for performing it, sufficient reason that is independent of his own inclinations or self-interest and that cannot be eradicated by his own fiat" (Gilbert, 2006a, p. 157). Nonetheless, obligations of joint commitment are social rather than moral obligations.

The relation between a joint commitment and its concomitant social obligations is, Gilbert claims, *a priori*: the mere fact of entering a joint commitment implies

---

[5] Weaker senses of joint action are explored by, for instance, Jackson (1987), Kutz (2000), and Chant (2007).

[6] Chapters 5 and 6 include more detailed discussions of team reasoning and we-reasoning.

[7] Similarly, Gold and Sugden (2007, p. 126) argue that "it is natural to regard the intentions that result from team reasoning as collective intentions".

[8] Compare Tuomela (2000, p. 8): "In general, the performance of a joint action can be regarded as agreement-based if the plan has been accepted by the participants and if they have communicated their acceptances appropriately to the others so that a joint commitment to perform the joint action has come about."

social obligations on the members of the group.[9] They "owe each other actions by virtue of their participation in the joint commitment *and that alone*. Consideration of what bad consequences might flow from violation of the commitment, for instance, is not relevant to the issue" (Gilbert, 1999, p. 151). A publicly adopted plan thus generates member obligations, regardless of whether or not the group members correctly assume that it is a good plan.[10] Robert Sugden concurs:

> To act as a member of the team is to act as a *component* of the team. It is to act on a concerted plan, doing one's allotted part in that plan without asking whether, taking other members' actions as given, one's own action is contributing towards the team's objective. [...] It must be sufficient for each member of the team that the plan itself is designed to achieve the team's objective: the objective will be achieved if everyone follows the plan. (Sugden, 1993, p. 86)[11]

I suggest that a *group plan* $P_{\mathcal{G}}$ of a group $\mathcal{G}$ in deontic game S be thought of as any subset of the set $A_{\mathcal{G}}$ of group actions that are available to $\mathcal{G}$ in S. By adopting a group plan, the group members enter a joint commitment to perform one of the group actions in the plan. Given an adopted group plan $P_{\mathcal{G}}$ and an individual group member i of $\mathcal{G}$, agent i fulfils her *member obligation* specified by the plan $P_{\mathcal{G}}$ if and only if she performs an action that is her component action of one of the group actions in the plan, that is, if and only if she performs an action from the set $\{a_i : a_{\mathcal{G}} \in P_{\mathcal{G}}\}$.[12]

3.3.1 Updating Deontic Games by Group Plans

I have argued that the adoption of a group plan generates member obligations and that these member obligations are specified by the group plan. There is, however,

---

[9] See also Tuomela (2005, p. 345): "If agreement making is in question, there will also be a publicly existing social (or, if you like, '*quasi*-moral') obligation to participate in joint action. This entailment of an obligation can be regarded as a conceptual truth about the notion of agreement." Bacharach (2006, p. 64—notation modified) is not so sure about the a priori character of this entailment relation: "[E]ven granted that an agent should decide that a certain profile a should be realized, why does this give her a reason to do her part in a?" Scanlon (1998, p. 317) argues against its a prioricity: "If a convention or social practice is taken to consist in the fact that people accept certain rules or norms and typically act in accordance with them, then we need a mediating moral principle to explain how such practices can be morally binding and generate specific obligations."

[10] See again Tuomela (2000, p. 207): "If some persons make an agreement to cooperate, that entails the obligation to cooperate, be cooperation rational or not. Accepting such an obligating agreement in a full sense entails for the participants a collective commitment to fulfil it."

[11] Compare Sugden (2003, p. 72): "A cooperative morality enjoins each individual to *do her part* in achieving outcomes that are good for all. [...] [T]he individual does not ask whether her own actions, considered in isolation, yield preferred outcomes."

[12] It may be useful to point out that this conception of member obligations naturally relates to important ideas in Chap. 4 (in particular, the discussion leading up to Theorem 4.4 and the characterization of collective know-how in Corollary 4.1) and Chap. 5 (in particular, the team-directed intentions discussed in Sect. 5.4.2).

a second way in which the adoption of a group plan generates obligations. The adoption of a group plan can also be understood as inducing a change of the deontic ideality of the action profiles in a deontic game.[13] Because a change in deontic ideality might affect the dominance ordering of an agent's set of actions, such a change might lead to a different set of actions with which an agent, whether individual or group, might fulfil her individual or its collective obligation.

Technically, I model the adoption of a group plan in deontic game S as an *update* of the deontic ideality function of the game's action profiles. I use $S{\uparrow}P_{\mathcal{G}}$ to denote the deontic game that results from updating deontic game S with a group plan $P_{\mathcal{G}}$. To keep the update of the deontic ideality function technically manageable, I require that the group plan be adopted *publicly*. We may hence assume that after the public adoption of a group plan it is *common knowledge* among the agents in the game, whether or not they are members of the group that adopts the plan, that the plan has been adopted. The public adoption of a group plan hence changes the decision context not only for group members, but also for agents who are not in the group. After the public adoption of a group plan each agent in the outgroup decides what to do, on the supposition that the group members act according to plan. To implement this in a simple way, I consider the update of the deontic ideality function to be uniform for all agents in the game.[14] Accordingly, updating a game with a group plan amounts to this: if an action profile is forbidden by the plan, its deontic ideality becomes 0; and if an action profile is permitted by the plan, its deontic ideality remains unchanged. Or equivalently, an action profile a is deontically ideal in $S{\uparrow}P_{\mathcal{G}}$ if and only if (1) the action profile a is deontically ideal in S; and (2) the group's component action $a_{\mathcal{G}}$ of the action profile a is a group action in $P_{\mathcal{G}}$[15]:

Definition 3.3 (Plan Updates) Let $S = \langle N, (A_i), d\rangle$ be a deontic game. Let $\mathcal{G} \subseteq N$ and let $P_{\mathcal{G}} \subseteq A_{\mathcal{G}}$. Then the update of S with $P_{\mathcal{G}}$, notation: $S{\uparrow}P_{\mathcal{G}}$, is the deontic game $S{\uparrow}P_{\mathcal{G}} = \langle N, (A_i), d^{\uparrow}\rangle$, where

$$d^{\uparrow}(a) = \begin{cases} d(a), & \text{if } a_{\mathcal{G}} \in P_{\mathcal{G}} \\ 0, & \text{if } a_{\mathcal{G}} \notin P_{\mathcal{G}}. \end{cases}$$

---

[13] Tuomela (2000, p. 210) makes a similar observation: "To be sure agreement making can well change more in the game than has been assumed above: Due to its institutional and *quasi*-moral character it can change the payoffs of defection in a way that changes the whole nature of the game."

[14] These idealizing assumptions are similar to those that underlie the logic of public announcements (Plaza, 1989). They were relaxed in the logic of epistemic actions (Baltag et al., 1998). Van Ditmarsch et al. (2007, Chs. 4 and 5) provide textbook presentations of these logics.

[15] Note that an update of a deontic game may be flat, that is, in the updated deontic game there may not be any deontically ideal action profile. It may therefore be helpful to foreshadow that if we update a deontic game with an optimal plan, then the updated deontic game is guaranteed to be non-flat (see Sect. 3.4.1 and, in particular, Lemma B.4).

Because an update of a deontic game with a group plan might change the deontic ideality of the game's action profiles, it might also change the dominance ordering of any group's group actions. There is one exception. Updating a deontic game with a group plan leaves the dominance ordering of the group actions in the plan unaffected (all claims are proved in Appendix B):

Observation 3.1 Let S be a deontic game. Let $\mathcal{G} \subseteq N$ and let $P_{\mathcal{G}} \subseteq A_{\mathcal{G}}$. Let $a_{\mathcal{G}}, a^*_{\mathcal{G}} \in P_{\mathcal{G}}$. Then

$a_{\mathcal{G}} \succeq_S a^*_{\mathcal{G}}$ iff $a_{\mathcal{G}} \succeq_{S \uparrow P_{\mathcal{G}}} a^*_{\mathcal{G}}$.

Although an update with a group plan does not change the dominance ordering of the group actions in the plan, it might change the dominance ordering of the individual actions that are component actions of the group actions in the plan. Ideally, an update with a group plan should change the dominance ordering of these individual actions in such a way that an individual action is a component of one of the group actions in the plan if and only if that individual action is an admissible individual action in the deontic game that results from updating the original deontic game with the plan. Not all group plans have this updating property. We show that if a group plan is a good plan (in the sense defined below), then it has this updating property.

3.4 Good Plans and Bad Plans

There are good plans and bad plans. A good plan guarantees that if every group member fulfils her member obligation specified by the plan, then the group itself fulfils its collective obligation.[16] Or equivalently, a good plan guarantees that if the group itself does *not* fulfil its collective obligation, then at least one group member does *not* fulfil her member obligation specified by the plan.[17] A bad plan fails to do so. By agreeing on a bad plan, even though it thereby becomes common knowledge that the plan has been adopted, the group members do not rule out the possibility that every group member fulfils her member obligation specified by the plan, while the composition of the group members' actions does not amount to a group action that fulfils their collective obligation. Accordingly, there are two conditions on fulfilling a collective obligation by way of a group plan: first, the group members must act

[16] Compare Regan (1980, p. 138—notation adapted): "If the members of $\mathcal{G}$ all do their part in the best pattern of behaviour for the members of $\mathcal{G}$ given the behaviour of non-members, it is clear that the members of $\mathcal{G}$ produce the best consequences possible as a group." We argue below that the truth of this conditional depends on the structure of the plan: if the plan is what we call 'optimal' and 'interchangeable', then the conditional is true.

[17] Bratman (2014, p. 34) claims that in basic cases "violations of these norms of social rationality will be constituted by violations, by one or more participants, of associated norms of individual planning agency". See also Jackson (1987, p. 107), who agrees with us that the conditional "If a group act is wrong, at least one of its constituent individual acts is wrong" is not a truth of logic.

according to plan, and second, the plan itself must be good. But what makes a group plan a good plan? I will argue that a plan is a good plan if and only if it is *optimal* and *interchangeable*.

This notion of good plan should not be confused with another one. Since the adoption of a group plan also generates obligations by changing the decision context, another natural notion of a good plan would be that it guarantees that if each group member fulfils her individual obligation in the updated decision context, then the group itself fulfils its collective obligation. To avoid ambiguity, let us refer to this second notion as *good* plans*. Since some group plans are such that the member obligations are distinct from the individual obligations in the updated decision context, the conditions under which a group plan is a good plan may be distinct from the conditions under which a group plan is a good* plan. I will focus on the notion of good plans first and discuss good* plans in Sect. 3.5.

3.4.1 Optimal Plans

The aim of a group plan is to fulfil a collective obligation. A group fulfils its collective obligation if and only if it performs an admissible group action. A good plan should hence be designed such that if all group members act according to plan, then the composition of their actions amounts to an admissible group action. The first design requirement of a good plan therefore is that the plan only consists of admissible group actions (as we shall see below, this is a necessary but not a sufficient condition). We say that a group plan is *optimal* if and only if it is a non-empty subset of the group's admissible group actions:

Definition 3.4 (Optimal Plans) Let S be a deontic game. Let $\mathcal{G} \subseteq N$ and let $P_{\mathcal{G}} \subseteq A_{\mathcal{G}}$. Then $P_{\mathcal{G}}$ is *optimal* if and only if $P_{\mathcal{G}} \neq \emptyset$ and $P_{\mathcal{G}} \subseteq \mathit{Admissible}_S(\mathcal{G})$.

What happens if we update a deontic game with such an optimal plan? An update of a deontic game with an optimal plan does not introduce admissible group actions that were not in the plan and does not eliminate admissible group actions that were in the plan. The set of admissible group actions in the deontic game that results from updating a deontic game with an optimal plan equals the set of group actions in the plan:

Observation 3.2 Let S be a deontic game. Let $\mathcal{G} \subseteq N$ and let $P_{\mathcal{G}} \subseteq A_{\mathcal{G}}$ be optimal. Then

$$\mathit{Admissible}_{S\uparrow P_{\mathcal{G}}}(\mathcal{G}) = P_{\mathcal{G}}.$$

This observation implies that every group action that is admissible in the deontic game $S\uparrow P_{\mathcal{G}}$ that results from updating a deontic game S with an optimal plan $P_{\mathcal{G}}$ is an admissible group action in the original deontic game S, that is, $\mathit{Admissible}_{S\uparrow P_{\mathcal{G}}}(\mathcal{G}) \subseteq \mathit{Admissible}_S(\mathcal{G})$. Accordingly, an update with an optimal plan highlights particular admissible group actions in the original deontic game.

However, it is not sufficient to require of a good plan that it be optimal. Indeed, if a plan consists of several admissible group actions and if each group member does her share of an admissible group action in the plan, then the composition of the group members' actions need not be an admissible group action. Writing on action profiles in games with individual utility functions rather than on group actions in games with a deontic ideality function, David Gauthier (1975, p. 201) observes: "If each person performs an action which has a best equilibrium as a possible outcome, and if there are several best equilibria, then the outcome need not be a best equilibrium." Because of this, coordination theorists standardly assume that a solution to a coordination problem consists in singling out a unique action profile:

> Several best equilibria are too many of a good thing. [...] What we need is a way to restructure our conception of the situation so that we are left with but one. We must restrict the possible actions which we consider, in such a way that we convert our representation of the situation into one with but one best equilibrium. (Gauthier, 1975, p. 210)[18]

In the present setting, we do not need this methodological assumption. To tackle the current problem of specifying the conditions under which a group plan successfully coordinates the actions of group members, we do not have to assume that the agents must somehow agree on a unique group action. I show that it suffices to require of good plans not only that they be optimal, but also interchangeable.

3.4.2 Interchangeable Plans

The second design requirement of a good plan is that the plan be closed under component individual actions. We say that a group plan is *interchangeable* if and only if for any two group actions in the plan it holds that the composition of a group member's contribution to the first group action and the joint contribution of all other group members to the second group action amounts to a group action that is also in the plan:[19]

Definition 3.5 (Interchangeable Plans) Let S be a deontic game. Let $\mathcal{G} \subseteq N$ and let $P_\mathcal{G} \subseteq A_\mathcal{G}$. Then $P_\mathcal{G}$ is *interchangeable* if and only if for all $a_\mathcal{G}, a'_\mathcal{G} \in P_\mathcal{G}$ and all $i \in \mathcal{G}$ it holds that $(a_i, a'_{\mathcal{G}-i}) \in P_\mathcal{G}$.[20]

A few examples: in deontic game S_3 of Fig. 3.3 the plan $\{(a_i, a_j)\}$ is interchangeable (as is every plan consisting of a single group action). Likewise,

[18] Compare Harsanyi and Selten (1988, p. 13): "Clearly a theory telling us no more than that the outcome can be any one of these equilibrium points will not give us much useful information. We need a theory selecting one equilibrium point as the solution of the game."

[19] The concept of interchangeability goes back to Nash (1951, p. 290).

[20] Observation 4.5 in Chap. 4 provides a logical characterization of interchangeability.

Fig. 3.3 Deontic game S_3

	a_j	a'_j	a''_j
a_i	1	1	0
a'_i	0	0	1
a''_i	0	1	0

$\{(a_i, a_j), (a_i, a'_j), (a_i, a''_j)\}$ is interchangeable. The plan $\{(a_i, a_j), (a_i, a'_j), (a'_i, a_j)\}$ is not, because (a'_i, a'_j) is not in it. Finally, $\{(a_i, a_j), (a_i, a''_j), (a'_i, a_j), (a'_i, a''_j)\}$ is interchangeable.

This definition implies that a plan is interchangeable if and only if for any two group actions in the plan it holds that the composition of a subgroup's contribution to the first group action and the joint contribution of all other group members to the second group action amounts to a group action that is also in the plan:

Observation 3.3 Let S be a deontic game. Let $\mathcal{G} \subseteq N$ and let $P_{\mathcal{G}} \subseteq A_{\mathcal{G}}$. Then $P_{\mathcal{G}}$ is interchangeable if and only if for all $a_{\mathcal{G}}, a'_{\mathcal{G}} \in P_{\mathcal{G}}$ and all $\mathcal{F} \subseteq \mathcal{G}$ it holds that $(a_{\mathcal{F}}, a'_{\mathcal{G}-\mathcal{F}}) \in P_{\mathcal{G}}$.

I have argued above that a group plan does not need to single out a unique group action to successfully coordinate the individual actions of the group members. To make this clear, consider again the deontic game S_3 of Fig. 3.3. To solve their coordination problem, group members i and j must agree on a plan that successfully coordinates their actions. Even though it consists of several group actions, the optimal and interchangeable plan $\{(a_i, a_j), (a_i, a'_j)\}$ does the job. The plan specifies the following member obligations on agents i and j: agent i ought to perform action a_i and agent j ought to perform one of the actions a_j and a'_j. The plan hence gives some leeway to agent j. Nonetheless, the plan ensures that if both group members act according to plan, they perform an admissible group action and hence the group itself fulfils its collective obligation.

This point can be made fully general: an optimal and interchangeable plan *guarantees* that if every group member fulfils her member obligation specified by the plan, then the group itself fulfils its collective obligation. Let us see why this is so. If every group member fulfils her member obligation specified by an optimal and interchangeable plan, then every group member performs an action that is a component action of one of the group actions in the plan. Because the plan is interchangeable, the combination of the actions performed by the group members must also be in the plan. Because the plan is optimal, it only contains admissible group actions, and hence this combination of group member actions is an admissible group action. The group members hence perform an admissible group action and thus fulfil the group's collective obligation. Therefore, if every group member acts according to an optimal and interchangeable plan, then the group itself fulfils its collective obligation.

3.4.3 Updates with Optimal and Interchangeable Plans

My central theorem concerns what happens if we update a deontic game with an optimal and interchangeable group plan. I show that if we update a deontic game with such a plan, then for any subgroup of this group it holds that an action of that subgroup is an admissible subgroup action in the deontic game that results from updating the original deontic game with the plan if and only if that subgroup action is a component subgroup action of one of the group actions in the plan:

Theorem 3.1 *Let S be a deontic game. Let $\mathcal{F} \subseteq \mathcal{G} \subseteq N$ and let $P_{\mathcal{G}} \subseteq A_{\mathcal{G}}$ be optimal and interchangeable. Then*

$$Admissible_{S\uparrow P_{\mathcal{G}}}(\mathcal{F}) = \{a_{\mathcal{F}} : a_{\mathcal{G}} \in P_{\mathcal{G}}\}.$$

This theorem shows that updates of deontic games with optimal and interchangeable plans relate collective obligations to individual obligations. Indeed, by setting $\mathcal{F} = \{i\}$ for any individual member i of $\mathcal{G}$ we obtain $Admissible_{S\uparrow P_{\mathcal{G}}}(i) = \{a_i : a_{\mathcal{G}} \in P_{\mathcal{G}}\}$. Accordingly, if we update a deontic game with an optimal and interchangeable group plan, then for every group member it holds that she fulfils her member obligation specified by the plan if and only if she fulfils her individual obligation in the deontic game that results from updating the original deontic game with the plan. Consequently, under the given assumptions, a group member acts according to plan if and only if she performs an admissible individual action in the changed decision context. It follows that, under the given assumptions, if every group member performs an admissible individual action in the changed decision context, then the group itself performs an admissible group action.

If we think of acting rationally as performing those actions that best promote deontic ideality, then we could say that an individual action is *individually rational* if and only if it is an admissible individual action, and that a group action is *collectively rational* if and only if it is an admissible group action. Within the narrow confines of my idealizing assumptions, Theorem 3.1 would then relate collective rationality to individual rationality and thereby give a tentative answer to Bratman's questions:

> Are there norms that are in some way fundamental to shared agency? If so, how precisely are they related to shared agency, and how are they related to norms of individual rationality? (Bratman, 2014, p. 4)

The answer runs as follows. A group action is collectively rational if and only if it is an admissible group action. To perform an admissible group action, the group members must adopt a good plan to ensure that the combination of their actions is an admissible group action. After the public adoption of such a plan, a group member's action is rational with respect to the group's objective of performing an admissible group action if and only if this action is permitted by the plan.[21] Moreover, when

[21] Compare (Gold, 2012, p. 185): "The basic idea is that, when an individual reasons as a member of a team, she considers which *combination* of actions by members of the team would best promote the team's objective, and then performs her part of that combination. The rationality of each

the plan has been publicly adopted and thereby changed the context in which agents make a decision about what to do, an individual action is individually rational if and only if it is an admissible individual action in the changed decision context. My theorem shows that, under the given assumptions, a group member's action is rational with respect to the group's objective of performing an admissible group action if and only if that action is individually rational in the decision context that results from the public adoption of the plan. It follows that, under the given assumptions, if every group member performs an individually rational action in the changed decision context, then the group itself performs a collectively rational group action. Therefore, if we think of acting rationally as performing those actions that best promote deontic ideality, the theorem would establish a connection between collective rationality and individual rationality.

3.5 Good* Plans and Collective Deontic Admissibility

In the preceding sections, I have studied the conditions under which a group plan is a *good plan*, that is, conditions under which a group plan guarantees that if each group member fulfils her member obligation specified by the plan, then the group itself fulfils its collective obligation. In this section, I will briefly investigate which conditions are necessary and sufficient for a group plan to be a good* plan, that is, conditions under which a group plan guarantees that if each group member fulfils her individual obligation in the updated decision context, then the group itself fulfils its collective obligation.

It should be noted that good* plans need neither be optimal nor interchangeable. To see this, reconsider deontic game S_1 of Fig. 3.1 and consider the group plan $P_{i,j}$ given by $\{(a_i, a'_j), (a'_i, a''_j)\}$. Note that $P_{i,j}$ is not optimal since it contains (a'_i, a''_j) and it is also not interchangeable since it excludes (a'_i, a'_j). Nonetheless, the group plan $P_{i,j}$ is a good* plan: Note that updating S_1 with $P_{i,j}$ results in the deontic game $S_1 \uparrow P_{i,j}$ of Fig. 3.4. It is easy to verify that the deontically admissible individual actions in $S_1 \uparrow P_{i,j}$ are a_i for agent i and a'_j for agent j. It follows that if each member of $\mathcal{G} = \{i, j\}$ fulfils her individual obligation in the updated decision context $S_1 \uparrow P_{i,j}$, then the group performs group action (a_i, a'_j) and thereby fulfils its collective obligation.

So, what are necessary and sufficient conditions for a group plan to be a good* plan? Although I regret that I will not be able to fully answer this question here, let me add a few remarks. First, any optimal and interchangeable plan is a good* plan. After all, Theorem 3.1 and the fact that optimal and interchangeable plans are good plans jointly entail that after the public adoption of an optimal and interchangeable

individual's action derives from the rationality of the joint action of the team." Sugden (1993, p. 87), Anderson (2001, pp. 28–30), and Bacharach (2006, p. 136) defend similar notions of group member rationality.

Fig. 3.4 Deontic game $S_1 \uparrow P_{i,j}$

	a_j	a'_j	a''_j
a_i	0	1	0
a'_i	0	0	0
a''_i	0	0	0

plan it holds that if every group member performs an admissible individual action in the updated decision context, then the group performs an admissible group action. In other words, interchangeability and optimality are *jointly sufficient* conditions under which group plans are good*.

Second, instead of investigating how the decision context could be updated so that individual and collective obligations match, we could aim to characterize desirable output. That is, we would try to carve out the subclass of deontic games where individual and collective obligations match. Then, we may be able to reverse engineer the necessary and sufficient conditions for a group plan to have the updating property of a good* plan. From this perspective, I'd like to discuss some recent developments in the logical investigation of individual and collective obligations. To do so, let me first present a logical framework. Let us use $\star_i$ and $\star_{\mathcal{G}}$ to formalize the statements that 'individual i performs a deontically admissible action' and 'group $\mathcal{G}$ performs a deontically admissible group action', respectively. In particular, $\neg\star_i$ and $\neg\star_{\mathcal{G}}$ express that agent i and group $\mathcal{G}$, respectively, failed to fulfil their obligation. In this chapter, we have observed that a combination of admissible individual actions may not constitute an admissible group action. From a logical perspective, this means that the following formula is falsifiable:

$$\bigwedge_{i \in \mathcal{G}} \star_i \rightarrow \star_{\mathcal{G}}.$$

One may ask whether there exist other statements about individuals that would guarantee that the group performs a deontically admissible group action. To address this question, consider the following multi-modal deontic logic of agency $\mathcal{L}_{ind}$ which models every conceivable combination of actions, omissions, abilities, obligations, prohibitions, and permissions of finitely many *individual* agents:

$$\varphi := q \mid \neg\varphi \mid \varphi \wedge \varphi \mid \Box\varphi \mid [i \text{ stit}]\varphi \mid \star_i,$$

where q ranges over a fixed set of propositional letters $\mathcal{P}$ and i ranges over a fixed, finite set of agents N. I will call $\mathcal{L}_{ind}$ the *individualistic language*, since it does not include the collective statements formalized by $\star_{\mathcal{G}}$ nor those formalized by $[\mathcal{G} \text{ stit}]\varphi$.

Let me proceed with mentioning two recent findings. First, one may ask whether the statement of collective deontic admissibility ($\star_{\mathcal{G}}$) can be expressed by a statement in this individualistic language. That is, one may ask whether there exists an individualistic statement that is *logically equivalent* to the statement that group $\mathcal{G}$ performs an admissible group action. This turns out to be impossible (Tamminga et al., 2021). In a slogan: collective deontic admissibility does not logically reduce to any statement about the actions and obligations of individual agents.[22] Hence, the necessary and sufficient conditions under which a group fulfils its collective obligation cannot be characterized in this individualistic language.

Finally, one may ask whether there is any individualistic statement that would guarantee that the group fulfils its collective obligation. That is, one may ask whether there exists a statement in the individualistic language such that its fulfilment would guarantee that the group performs an admissible group action. This is also impossible (Duijf et al., 2021): the sufficient conditions under which a group fulfils its collective obligation cannot be expressed in the individualistic language.[23]

3.6 Discussion: Objective Responsibility System Based on Dominance Theory

What are the conditions for the existence of responsibility voids and gaps from the perspective of this chapter? What, if anything, does my account of collective obligations, group plans, and individual actions tell us about the concept of collective blameworthiness, that is, backward-looking collective moral responsibility? The complexity of this concept has led some to argue that formal methods are of hardly any use in the study of collective moral responsibility. Margaret Gilbert, for example, writes:

> What does the blameworthiness of the collective's act imply about the personal blameworthiness of any one member of that collective? From a logical point of view, the short answer is: *nothing*. Everything depends on the details of a given member's particular situation. (Gilbert, 2006b, p. 109)[24]

Gilbert notes that some members of a blameworthy collective might have authorized others to decide and that this may make a difference to the attribution of blame to those members. At present, my formal analysis is too coarse to capture these structural aspects of collective moral responsibility. Nonetheless, even my relatively simple formalization of the relation between collective obligations, group plans, and individual actions brings to the fore some central aspects of the logic of backward-looking collective responsibility.

I take it that the concept of backward-looking individual responsibility supports the claim that not fulfilling an obligation is a necessary condition for being individually blameworthy: if an individual agent is individually blameworthy, then

[22] More formally, there exists no statement ψ in $\mathcal{L}_{ind}$ such that $\models \psi \leftrightarrow \star_{\mathcal{G}}$.

[23] More formally, there exists no statement ψ in $\mathcal{L}_{ind}$ such that $\not\models \neg\psi$ and $\models \psi \rightarrow \star_{\mathcal{G}}$. In (Duijf et al., 2021), we explore the ramifications of logical impossibility results for the debate on methodological individualism.

[24] Likewise, Isaacs (2011, p. 24) argues that "claims about collective moral responsibility neither entail nor are derivable from claims about individual moral responsibility".

she has failed to fulfil an obligation. The converse does not hold, because she might have a plausible excuse for not doing what she ought to do. Analogously, I submit that not fulfilling a collective obligation is a necessary, but not a sufficient condition for being collectively blameworthy. We thus obtain the following implication: if a group is collectively blameworthy, then it does not fulfil a collective obligation.

My account of the relation between collective obligations, group plans, and individual actions brought to light that a good plan has two key characteristics. First, a good plan guarantees that if every group member fulfils her member obligation specified by the plan, then the group itself fulfils its collective obligation. Second, if the group members, aiming to fulfil a collective obligation, publicly adopt a good plan to coordinate their individual actions, then for any group member it holds that if she fulfils her individual obligation in the decision context that results from publicly adopting the plan, then she fulfils her member obligation specified by the plan. We thus obtain a second implication: given that the group members, aiming to fulfil a collective obligation, publicly adopt a good plan to coordinate their individual actions, it holds that their failure to fulfil the collective obligation *logically implies* that at least one of them failed to fulfil her member obligation specified by the plan, which in turn entails that at least one group member failed to fulfil her individual obligation in the changed decision context.[25]

Combining the two implications, we can conclude: given that the group members, aiming to fulfil a collective obligation, publicly adopt a good plan to coordinate their actions, it holds that the collective blameworthiness of the group *logically implies* that at least one of the group members failed to act according to plan, which in turn entails that at least one group member failed to fulfil her individual obligation in changed decision context.[26]

I end with summarizing the implications for the study of responsibility voids and gaps. Since the dominance theory ignores mental features, this chapter naturally relates to the *causal* or *objective* responsibility system. In other words, this discussion can be taken to focus on the group members' conduct rather than the mental states that accompany it. Nonetheless, there are three distinct perspectives—collective, individual, and group member—which can be specified as follows: a group should perform a group action that fulfils its collective obligation; an individual agent should perform an individual action that fulfils its individual obligation; and, in case a group plan has been adopted, a group member should perform an individual action that fulfils its member obligation.

Can responsibility voids and gaps arise when we concentrate on this causal responsibility system? If we assume that a failure to fulfil an obligation entails blameworthiness, then there is no responsibility void nor gap when agreement is unproblematic and communication unrestricted. That is, under these assumptions,

[25] In joint work (Tamminga & Duijf, 2017, Sect. 5), we show that this implication also holds for a broader range of games that we call 'zero-preserving cooperation games'.

[26] Again, a group member's failure to fulfil her obligations does not entail that she is personally blameworthy—she may have had good reasons not to fulfil her obligations.

the group members should adopt a *good* plan to regulate their group action. Or, conversely, if responsibility voids or gaps are to exist, agreement must be problematic or communication must be restricted. Note that a good plan is always available, since there always exists an admissible group action. One could, however, worry that such a good plan cannot be expressed or communicated by the agents. More formally, given a formal language interpreted on deontic games, one may ask whether there is always a formula that expresses the good plan in question.[27] In any case, if, for some reason or other, the group members fail to agree on a group plan or if they agree on a bad plan, then it is not so clear how being collectively blameworthy relates to the failure of individuals to fulfil their obligations. In the subsequent chapters I will explore the connection, if any, between collective blameworthiness and individual blameworthiness by considering responsibility systems based on knowledge, intentions, and practical reasoning.

Appendix B: Collective Obligations, Group Plans, and Individual Actions

Lemma B.1 (Horty, 2001, p. 74) *Let S be a deontic game. Let $\mathcal{G} \subseteq N$ be a non-empty group of agents. Then*

$Admissible_S(\mathcal{G}) \neq \emptyset$.

Proof Assume that $Admissible_S(\mathcal{G}) = \emptyset$. By definition of S, it holds that $A_\mathcal{G}$ is finite and non-empty. Then for all $a'_\mathcal{G} \in A_\mathcal{G}$ there is an $a_\mathcal{G} \in A_\mathcal{G}$ such that $a_\mathcal{G} \succ_S a'_\mathcal{G}$. Because $A_\mathcal{G}$ is finite, there must be a cycle $a^n_\mathcal{G} \succ_S a^{n-1}_\mathcal{G} \succ_S \ldots \succ_S a^2_\mathcal{G} \succ_S a^1_\mathcal{G} = a^n_\mathcal{G}$ with all members $a^k_\mathcal{G}$ in $A_\mathcal{G}$. Because $\succ_S$ is transitive, it holds that $a^n_\mathcal{G} \succ_S a^n_\mathcal{G}$, that is, $a^n_\mathcal{G} \succeq_S a^n_\mathcal{G}$ and $a^n_\mathcal{G} \not\succeq_S a^n_\mathcal{G}$. Contradiction. Therefore, $Admissible_S(\mathcal{G}) \neq \emptyset$. □

Lemma B.2 (Kooi & Tamminga, 2008) *Let S be a deontic game. Let $\mathcal{F} \subseteq \mathcal{G} \subseteq N$. Let $a_\mathcal{F}, a'_\mathcal{F} \in A_\mathcal{F}$ and let $a''_{\mathcal{G}-\mathcal{F}} \in A_{\mathcal{G}-\mathcal{F}}$. Then*

If $a_\mathcal{F} \succeq_S a'_\mathcal{F}$, then $(a_\mathcal{F}, a''_{\mathcal{G}-\mathcal{F}}) \succeq_S (a'_\mathcal{F}, a''_{\mathcal{G}-\mathcal{F}})$.

Proof Assume $a_\mathcal{F} \succeq_S a'_\mathcal{F}$. Let $a''_{\mathcal{G}-\mathcal{F}} \in A_{\mathcal{G}-\mathcal{F}}$. Suppose $a'''_{-\mathcal{G}} \in A_{-\mathcal{G}}$. Then $(a''_{\mathcal{G}-\mathcal{F}}, a'''_{-\mathcal{G}}) \in A_{-\mathcal{F}}$. Hence, by our assumption it must be that $d(a_\mathcal{F}, a''_{\mathcal{G}-\mathcal{F}}, a'''_{-\mathcal{G}}) \geq d(a'_\mathcal{F}, a''_{\mathcal{G}-\mathcal{F}}, a'''_{-\mathcal{G}})$. Therefore, for all $a'''_{-\mathcal{G}} \in A_{-\mathcal{G}}$ it holds that $d(a_\mathcal{F}, a''_{\mathcal{G}-\mathcal{F}}, a'''_{-\mathcal{G}}) \geq d(a'_\mathcal{F}, a''_{\mathcal{G}-\mathcal{F}}, a'''_{-\mathcal{G}})$. Hence, $(a_\mathcal{F}, a''_{\mathcal{G}-\mathcal{F}}) \succeq_S (a'_\mathcal{F}, a''_{\mathcal{G}-\mathcal{F}})$. □

Lemma B.3 *Let S be a non-flat deontic game. Let $\mathcal{G} \subseteq N$. Then*

If $a_\mathcal{G} \in Admissible_S(\mathcal{G})$, then there is an $a'_{-\mathcal{G}} \in A_{-\mathcal{G}}$ such that $d(a_\mathcal{G}, a'_{-\mathcal{G}}) = 1$.

[27] I would like to thank an anonymous reviewer for making me aware of this research avenue.

Proof Suppose that $a_{\mathcal{G}} \in Admissible_S(\mathcal{G})$. Suppose that for every $a'_{-\mathcal{G}} \in A_{-\mathcal{G}}$ it holds that $d(a_{\mathcal{G}}, a'_{-\mathcal{G}}) = 0$. Because S is non-flat, there is an $a^* \in A$ such that $d(a^*) = 1$. Consider $a^*_{\mathcal{G}}$. It holds that $a^*_{\mathcal{G}} \succ_S a_{\mathcal{G}}$, that is (1) $a^*_{\mathcal{G}} \succeq_S a_{\mathcal{G}}$ and (2) $a_{\mathcal{G}} \not\succeq_S a^*_{\mathcal{G}}$. We have (1), because for every $a'_{-\mathcal{G}} \in A_{-\mathcal{G}}$ it holds that $d(a_{\mathcal{G}}, a'_{-\mathcal{G}}) = 0$. We have (2), because $d(a_{\mathcal{G}}, a^*_{-\mathcal{G}}) = 0$ and $d(a^*_{\mathcal{G}}, a^*_{-\mathcal{G}}) = d(a^*) = 1$. Hence, $a_{\mathcal{G}} \notin Admissible_S(\mathcal{G})$. Contradiction. □

Observation 3.1 Let S be a deontic game. Let $\mathcal{G} \subseteq N$ and let $P_{\mathcal{G}} \subseteq A_{\mathcal{G}}$. Let $a_{\mathcal{G}}, a^*_{\mathcal{G}} \in P_{\mathcal{G}}$. Then

$a_{\mathcal{G}} \succeq_S a^*_{\mathcal{G}}$ iff $a_{\mathcal{G}} \succeq_{S\uparrow P_{\mathcal{G}}} a^*_{\mathcal{G}}$.

Proof It is given that $a_{\mathcal{G}}, a^*_{\mathcal{G}} \in P_{\mathcal{G}}$. By construction of $S\uparrow P_{\mathcal{G}}$, for every $a'_{-\mathcal{G}} \in A_{-\mathcal{G}}$ it holds that $d(a_{\mathcal{G}}, a'_{-\mathcal{G}}) = d^{\uparrow}(a_{\mathcal{G}}, a'_{-\mathcal{G}})$ and $d(a^*_{\mathcal{G}}, a'_{-\mathcal{G}}) = d^{\uparrow}(a^*_{\mathcal{G}}, a'_{-\mathcal{G}})$. Then the following four statements are equivalent: (1) $a_{\mathcal{G}} \succeq_S a^*_{\mathcal{G}}$; (2) for every $a'_{-\mathcal{G}} \in A_{-\mathcal{G}}$ it holds that $d(a_{\mathcal{G}}, a'_{-\mathcal{G}}) \geq d(a^*_{\mathcal{G}}, a'_{-\mathcal{G}})$; (3) for every $a'_{-\mathcal{G}} \in A_{-\mathcal{G}}$ it holds that $d^{\uparrow}(a_{\mathcal{G}}, a'_{-\mathcal{G}}) \geq d^{\uparrow}(a^*_{\mathcal{G}}, a'_{-\mathcal{G}})$; and (4) $a_{\mathcal{G}} \succeq_{S\uparrow P_{\mathcal{G}}} a^*_{\mathcal{G}}$. □

Lemma B.4 *Let* $S = \langle N, (A_i), d\rangle$ *be a deontic game. Let* $\mathcal{G} \subseteq N$ *and let* $P_{\mathcal{G}}$ *be optimal. Then*

If S *is non-flat, then* $S\uparrow P_{\mathcal{G}}$ *is non-flat.*

Proof Suppose that S is non-flat. Because $P_{\mathcal{G}}$ is optimal, there is an $a_{\mathcal{G}} \in P_{\mathcal{G}}$ such that $a_{\mathcal{G}} \in Admissible_S(\mathcal{G})$. By Lemma B.3 there is an $a'_{-\mathcal{G}} \in A_{-\mathcal{G}}$ such that $d(a_{\mathcal{G}}, a'_{-\mathcal{G}}) = 1$. By the construction of $S\uparrow P_{\mathcal{G}}$, it must be that $d^{\uparrow}(a_{\mathcal{G}}, a'_{-\mathcal{G}}) = 1$. Therefore, $S\uparrow P_{\mathcal{G}}$ is non-flat. □

Observation 3.2 Let S be a deontic game. Let $\mathcal{G} \subseteq N$ and let $P_{\mathcal{G}} \subseteq A_{\mathcal{G}}$ be optimal. Then

$Admissible_{S\uparrow P_{\mathcal{G}}}(\mathcal{G}) = P_{\mathcal{G}}$.

Proof ($\subseteq$) Suppose that $a_{\mathcal{G}} \in Admissible_{S\uparrow P_{\mathcal{G}}}(\mathcal{G})$. By Lemma B.4, $S\uparrow P_{\mathcal{G}}$ is non-flat. By Lemma B.3, it must be that there is an $a'_{-\mathcal{G}} \in A_{-\mathcal{G}}$ such that $d^{\uparrow}(a_{\mathcal{G}}, a'_{-\mathcal{G}}) = 1$. By construction of $S\uparrow P_{\mathcal{G}}$, it must be that $a_{\mathcal{G}} \in P_{\mathcal{G}}$.

($\supseteq$) Suppose that $a_{\mathcal{G}} \in P_{\mathcal{G}}$. It is given that $a_{\mathcal{G}} \in Admissible_S(\mathcal{G})$ and that S is non-flat. Suppose that $a_{\mathcal{G}} \notin Admissible_{S\uparrow P_{\mathcal{G}}}(\mathcal{G})$. Then there is an $a^*_{\mathcal{G}} \in Admissible_{S\uparrow P_{\mathcal{G}}}(\mathcal{G})$ such that $a^*_{\mathcal{G}} \succ_{S\uparrow P_{\mathcal{G}}} a_{\mathcal{G}}$. By the first part of this proof, $a^*_{\mathcal{G}} \in P_{\mathcal{G}}$. By Observation 3.1, it must be that $a^*_{\mathcal{G}} \succ_S a_{\mathcal{G}}$. Hence, $a_{\mathcal{G}} \notin Admissible_S(\mathcal{G})$. Contradiction. Therefore, $a_{\mathcal{G}} \in Admissible_{S\uparrow P_{\mathcal{G}}}(\mathcal{G})$. □

Observation B.3 Let S be a deontic game. Let $\mathcal{G} \subseteq N$ and let $P_{\mathcal{G}} \subseteq A_{\mathcal{G}}$. Then $P_{\mathcal{G}}$ is interchangeable if and only if for all $a_{\mathcal{G}}, a'_{\mathcal{G}} \in P_{\mathcal{G}}$ and all $\mathcal{F} \subseteq \mathcal{G}$ it holds that $(a_{\mathcal{F}}, a'_{\mathcal{G}-\mathcal{F}}) \in P_{\mathcal{G}}$.

Proof By straightforward induction on the number of members of $\mathcal{F}$. □

Theorem 3.1 *Let S be a deontic game. Let $\mathcal{F} \subseteq \mathcal{G} \subseteq N$ and let $P_{\mathcal{G}} \subseteq A_{\mathcal{G}}$ be optimal and interchangeable. Then*

$$Admissible_{S\uparrow P_{\mathcal{G}}}(\mathcal{F}) = \{a_{\mathcal{F}} : a_{\mathcal{G}} \in P_{\mathcal{G}}\}.$$

Proof ($\subseteq$) Suppose that $a_{\mathcal{F}} \in Admissible_{S\uparrow P_{\mathcal{G}}}(\mathcal{F})$. By Lemma B.3, there is an $a'_{-\mathcal{F}} \in A_{-\mathcal{F}}$ such that $d^{\uparrow}(a_{\mathcal{F}}, a'_{-\mathcal{F}}) = 1$. By the construction of $S\uparrow P_{\mathcal{G}}$, it must be that $(a_{\mathcal{F}}, a'_{\mathcal{G}-\mathcal{F}}) \in P_{\mathcal{G}}$. Therefore, $a_{\mathcal{F}} \in \{a_{\mathcal{F}} : a_{\mathcal{G}} \in P_{\mathcal{G}}\}$.

($\supseteq$) Suppose that $a_{\mathcal{F}} \in \{a_{\mathcal{F}} : a_{\mathcal{G}} \in P_{\mathcal{G}}\}$. Then there is an $a'_{\mathcal{G}-\mathcal{F}} \in A_{\mathcal{G}-\mathcal{F}}$ such that $(a_{\mathcal{F}}, a'_{\mathcal{G}-\mathcal{F}}) \in P_{\mathcal{G}}$. Suppose that $a_{\mathcal{F}} \notin Admissible_{S\uparrow P_{\mathcal{G}}}(\mathcal{F})$. Then there is an $a^*_{\mathcal{F}} \in Admissible_{S\uparrow P_{\mathcal{G}}}(\mathcal{F})$ such that $a^*_{\mathcal{F}} \succ_{S\uparrow P_{\mathcal{G}}} a_{\mathcal{F}}$. Then there must be an $a^{**}_{-\mathcal{F}} \in A_{-\mathcal{F}}$ such that $d^{\uparrow}(a^*_{\mathcal{F}}, a^{**}_{-\mathcal{F}}) > d^{\uparrow}(a_{\mathcal{F}}, a^{**}_{-\mathcal{F}})$. Let $a'' = (a^*_{\mathcal{F}}, a^{**}_{-\mathcal{F}})$. Then $d^{\uparrow}(a'') = 1$. By construction of $S\uparrow P_{\mathcal{G}}$, it must be that $a''_{\mathcal{G}} = (a''_{\mathcal{F}}, a''_{\mathcal{G}-\mathcal{F}}) = (a^*_{\mathcal{F}}, a''_{\mathcal{G}-\mathcal{F}}) \in P_{\mathcal{G}}$. By Observation 3.3, it must be that $(a_{\mathcal{F}}, a''_{\mathcal{G}-\mathcal{F}}) \in P_{\mathcal{G}}$. Because $a^*_{\mathcal{F}} \succeq_{S\uparrow P_{\mathcal{G}}} a_{\mathcal{F}}$ and Lemma B.2, it must be that $(a^*_{\mathcal{F}}, a''_{\mathcal{G}-\mathcal{F}}) \succeq_{S\uparrow P_{\mathcal{G}}} (a_{\mathcal{F}}, a''_{\mathcal{G}-\mathcal{F}})$. Because it holds that $d^{\uparrow}(a^*_{\mathcal{F}}, a''_{\mathcal{G}-\mathcal{F}}, a''_{-\mathcal{G}}) = d^{\uparrow}(a^*_{\mathcal{F}}, a^{**}_{-\mathcal{F}}) = 1$ and $d^{\uparrow}(a_{\mathcal{F}}, a''_{\mathcal{G}-\mathcal{F}}, a''_{-\mathcal{G}}) = d^{\uparrow}(a_{\mathcal{F}}, a^{**}_{-\mathcal{F}}) = 0$, we have $(a_{\mathcal{F}}, a''_{\mathcal{G}-\mathcal{F}}) \not\succeq_{S\uparrow P_{\mathcal{G}}} (a^*_{\mathcal{F}}, a''_{\mathcal{G}-\mathcal{F}})$. Then it must be that $(a^*_{\mathcal{F}}, a''_{\mathcal{G}-\mathcal{F}}) \succ_{S\uparrow P_{\mathcal{G}}} (a_{\mathcal{F}}, a''_{\mathcal{G}-\mathcal{F}})$. By Observation 3.1, it must be that $(a^*_{\mathcal{F}}, a''_{\mathcal{G}-\mathcal{F}}) \succ_S (a_{\mathcal{F}}, a''_{\mathcal{G}-\mathcal{F}})$. Then $(a_{\mathcal{F}}, a''_{\mathcal{G}-\mathcal{F}}) \notin Admissible_S(\mathcal{G})$ which contradicts the fact that $(a_{\mathcal{F}}, a''_{\mathcal{G}-\mathcal{F}}) \in P_{\mathcal{G}}$. Therefore, $a_{\mathcal{F}} \in Admissible_{S\uparrow P_{\mathcal{G}}}(\mathcal{F})$. □

References

Anderson, E. (2001). Unstrapping the straitjacket of 'preference': A comment on Amartya Sen's contributions to philosophy and economics. *Economics & Philosophy, 17*(1), 21–38.

Bacharach, M. (1999). Interactive team reasoning: A contribution to the theory of co-operation. *Research in Economics, 53*(2), 117–147.

Bacharach, M. (2006). *Beyond individual choice: Teams and frames in game theory*, N. Gold & R. Sugden (Eds.). Princeton: Princeton University Press.

Baltag, A., Moss, L. S., & Solecki, S. (1998). The logic of public announcements, common knowledge, and private suspicions. In I. Gilboa (Ed.), *Proceedings of the Seventh Conference on Theoretical Aspects of Rationality and Knowledge* (pp. 43–56). Morgan Kaufmann Publishers.

Bratman, M. E. (1987). *Intention, plans, and practical reason*. Cambridge: Harvard University Press.

Bratman, M. E. (2014). *Shared agency: A planning theory of acting together*. Oxford: Oxford University Press.

Chant, S. R. (2007). Unintentional collective action. *Philosophical Explorations, 10*(3), 245–256.

van Ditmarsch, H., van der Hoek, W., & Kooi, B. (2007). *Dynamic epistemic logic*. Dordrecht: Springer.

Duijf, H., Tamminga, A., & Van De Putte, F. (2021). An impossibility result on methodological individualism. *Philosophical Studies, 178*(12), 4165–4185.

Gauthier, D. (1975). Coordination. *Dialogue, 14*(2), 195–221.

Gilbert, M. (1999). Obligation and joint commitment. *Utilitas, 11*(2), 143–163.

Gilbert, M. (2006a). *A theory of political obligation: Membership, commitment, and the bonds of society*. Oxford: Clarendon Press.

Gilbert, M. (2006b). Who's to blame? Collective moral responsibility and its implications for group members. *Midwest Studies in Philosophy, 30*(1), 94–114.
Gold, N. (2012). Team reasoning, framing and cooperation. In S. Okasha & K. Binmore (Eds.), *Evolution and rationality: decisions, co-operation and strategic behaviour* (pp. 185–212). Cambridge: Cambridge University Press.
Gold, N., & Sugden, R. (2007). Collective intentions and team agency. *The Journal of Philosophy, 104*(3), 109–137.
Harsanyi, J. C., & Selten, R. (1988). *A general theory of equilibrium selection in games*. Cambridge: MIT Press.
Horty, J. F. (1996). Agency and obligation. *Synthese, 108*(2), 269–307.
Horty, J. F. (2001). *Agency and deontic logic*. New York: Oxford University Press.
Horty, J. F. (2011). Perspectival act utilitarianism. In P. Girard, O. Roy, & M. Marion (Eds.), *Dynamic formal epistemology* (pp. 197–221). Dordrecht: Springer.
Isaacs, T. (2011). *Moral responsibility in collective contexts*. New York: Oxford University Press.
Jackson, F. (1987). Group morality. In P. Pettit, R. Sylvan, & J. Norman (Eds.), *Metaphysics and morality: Essays in honour of J.J.C. Smart* (pp. 91–110). Oxford: Blackwell.
Kooi, B., & Tamminga, A. (2008). Moral conflicts between groups of agents. *Journal of Philosophical Logic, 37*(1), 1–21.
Kutz, C. (2000). *Complicity: ethics and law for a collective age*. Cambridge: Cambridge University Press.
Lewis, D. K. (1969). *Convention: A philosophical study*. Cambridge: Harvard University Press.
Nash, J. F. (1951). Non-cooperative games. *Annals of Mathematics, 54*, 286–295.
Plaza, J. (1989). Logic of public communications. In M. L. Emrich, M. S. Pfeifer, M. Hadzikadic, & Z. W. Ras (Eds.), *Proceedings of the Fourth International Symposium on Methodologies for Intelligent Systems: Poster Session Program*, Charlotte (pp. 201–216). Oak Ridge National Laboratory.
Regan, D. (1980). *Utilitarianism and co-operation*. New York: Oxford University Press.
Scanlon, T. (1998). *What we owe to each other*. Cambridge: The Belknap Press.
Schelling, T. C. (1960). *The strategy of conflict*. Cambridge: Harvard University Press.
Sugden, R. (1993). Thinking as a team: Towards an explanation of nonselfish behavior. *Social Philosophy and Policy, 10*(1), 69–89.
Sugden, R. (1995). A theory of focal points. *The Economic Journal, 105*(430), 533–550.
Sugden, R. (2000). Team preferences. *Economics & Philosophy, 16*(2), 175–204.
Sugden, R. (2003). The logic of team reasoning. *Philosophical Explorations, 6*(3), 165–181.
Tamminga, A., & Duijf, H. (2017). Collective obligations, group plans and individual actions. *Economics & Philosophy, 33*(2), 187–214.
Tamminga, A., Duijf, H., & Van De Putte, F. (2021). Expressivity results for deontic logics of collective agency. *Synthese, 198*(9), 8733–8753.
Tuomela, R. (2000). *Cooperation: A philosophical study*. Number 82 in Philosophical Studies Series. Dordrecht: Kluwer Academic Publishers.
Tuomela, R. (2005). We-intentions revisited. *Philosophical Studies, 125*(3), 327–369.
Tuomela, R. (2013). *Social ontology: Collective intentionality and group agents*. New York: Oxford University Press.

Chapter 4
Guilty Minds and Collective Know-how

The "epistemic condition" corresponds to the excuse of ignorance. It captures the intuition that an agent is responsible only if he both knows the particular facts surrounding his action, and acts with the proper sort of beliefs and intentions.

Fischer and Ravizza (1998, p. 13)

4.1 Introduction

Many philosophers agree that moral responsibility often includes an epistemic requirement (Fischer & Ravizza, 1998; Ginet, 2000; Zimmerman, 1997, 2008).[1] In the previous chapter I have focused on the causal or objective perspective on moral responsibility: an agent can be held morally responsible if and only if she failed to fulfil an obligation or, equivalently, if and only if she did not perform a deontically admissible action. However, often times, it seems unjust to hold an agent morally responsible for certain harms if she did not know that her actions would bring them about. Simply stated, in this chapter, I will focus on the idea that an agent ought to perform an action if and only if it is the best option given her information or

Parts of this chapter draw from (Duijf et al., 2021).

[1] For example, Fischer and Ravizza (1998) write: "The first condition, which may be termed the 'epistemic condition,' corresponds to the excuse of ignorance. It captures the intuition that an agent is responsible only if he both knows the particular facts surrounding his action, and acts with the proper sort of beliefs and intentions. . . . The second condition of moral responsibility corresponds to the excuse of force; it pertains not so much to cognitive matters but affective, volitional, and executive features. We shall call the second condition, the 'freedom-relevant condition,' or perhaps the 'control condition.'"

© The Author(s), under exclusive license to Springer Nature Switzerland AG 2022
H. Duijf, *The Logic of Responsibility Voids*, Synthese Library 456,
https://doi.org/10.1007/978-3-030-92655-7_4

epistemic state.[2] From this informational or epistemic perspective, it is important to investigate the practical knowledge of the agents.

Two clarifications are in order. First, epistemic or informational responsibility is distinct from the topic of responsibility for beliefs. Rather, it is the idea that there is an epistemic condition for moral responsibility for actions or for certain outcomes. For example, this includes the requirement that an agent cannot be held responsible for a given outcome if that agent did not know that her actions could have led to that outcome. Second, there is a distinction between doing what one believes to be best and doing what is best given one's evidence. They come apart in situations where one's beliefs fail to track the evidence. Although I am inclined to think that the latter requirement would often make more sense for the allocation of moral responsibility, the framework presented in this chapter is neutral on this issue and can be used to model either one of these ideas.

To formalize informational responsibility systems, I will investigate the practical knowledge of individuals and groups. More precisely, I will use stit theory, extended with epistemic notions, to study the concepts of individual and collective *know-how* and their interrelation. My conceptual analysis of knowing-how relies on the concepts of action hierarchies, knowingly doing, and—in the case of collective knowing-how—effective divisions. We have seen in the previous chapter that in case communication is possible and agreement unproblematic, then responsibility voids and gaps can be circumvented by adopting a good group plan. It is therefore important to highlight that I will proceed with focusing on cases where communication is impossible and agreement is problematic.[3] Coordination problems illustrate an important way in which collective know-how may be undermined, since it may be impossible for a group to know how to coordinate (see, for example, Fig. 2.1). With a focus on these coordination problems and action hierarchies, my central definitions will clarify the complex concepts of individual and collective know-how. My central theorems concern the *characterization* of both individual and collective knowing-how.

Before outlining the chapter's contents, a preliminary remark on its methodology may be helpful. The analysis in this chapter is carried out partly in terms of the formal language rather than the semantics. Let me explain by contrasting two exemplars. In the previous chapter, I have explicated a theory of obligations in terms of the semantics: in a given deontic game, we say that an agent fulfils her individual obligations if and only if she performs one of her deontically admissible individual actions. In this chapter, I will explicate a theory of individual know-how where,

---

[2] Zimmerman (2008, pp. 2, 5, and 19) distinguishes between the objective, subjective and prospective views: "*The Objective View (first formulation)*: An agent ought to perform an act if and only if it is the best option that he (or she) has. ... *The Subjective View (first and only formulation)*: An agent ought to perform an act if and only if he believes that it is the best option that he has. ... *The Prospective View (second formulation)*: An agent ought to perform an act if and only if it is the prospectively best option that he has."

[3] At the end of Sect. 4.5 I briefly discuss some implications of my theory of collective know-how for cases where agreement is unproblematic and communication is possible.

simply stated, in a given model, we say that an individual agent knows how to φ if and only if there exists a refinement ψ that satisfies certain conditions. Instead of spelling out these conditions in terms of the semantics, I will use the formal language to explicate these conditions. In this way, I aim to follow the natural language of philosophers working on ability and know-how more closely.

The chapter is vast, so it is of utmost importance to be guided by a discussion of its outline. The central ideas and results are developed and presented in Sects. 4.2, 4.3, 4.5, and 4.7; the other two sections are helpful and important but optional (Sects. 4.4 and 4.6). In Sect. 4.2, I will present an epistemic extension of the basic stit framework that will be the backbone for my theory of know-how and I provide a complete axiomatization for an epistemic stit language. Those familiar with stit theory and epistemic stit theory may decide to skip this preliminary section. In Sect. 4.3, I will present my analysis of individual know-how: I will discuss action hierarchies in light of the philosophical literature on action individuation (Sect. 4.3.1), present the concept of knowingly doing (Sect. 4.3.2), and, then, define implicit and explicit individual knowing-how and prove the central theorems on individual knowing-how: individual knowing-how can be characterized in my formalism, despite the fact that the distinction between so-called implicit and explicit knowing-how cannot be characterized (Sect. 4.3.3). In an *optional* section, Sect. 4.4, I will explore some relations to work in economics, computer science, and philosophy. In Sect. 4.5, I will proceed with the analysis of collective know-how, present a definition of it motivated by these discussions, and prove that it can be characterized. There follows a discussion highlighting a connection with the previous chapter: the concept of collective know-how includes an interchangeable group plan. In a second *optional* section, Sect. 4.6, I will survey some connections to work in artificial intelligence research. In the concluding section, I will use my formalism to study aspects of subjective obligations and collective backward-looking responsibility.

4.2 Epistemic Stit Models

To characterize my views concerning collective know-how in a simple way, I will use an epistemic extension of atemporal stit models. (See Sects. 2.3–2.4 for a more detailed introduction to the basic, non-epistemic, stit framework and a discussion of its connections to game theory.) The framework I put forward here is a standard epistemic extension of the simple stit models discussed in Sect. 2.3 and, more specifically, it is related to and inspired by the framework developed by Broersen (2011). The aim of this section is to introduce this formal framework and to present a completeness result. A discussion of the interpretation of the formal framework is postponed to the next section.

Epistemic stit models are best thought of as representing the possibilities, knowledge, and group actions at a single moment in time. One may think that an adequate theory of know-how requires a strategic context. That is, one may think that know-how needs to be situated in extensive form games or temporally extended action, rather than in one-shot games or instantaneous action. Although such a context may contribute to a theory of know-how, the additional complexity is unnecessary for the difficulties I presently raise and address. I do believe that my present study can be transferred to these scenarios.[4]

The modal language of epistemic stit theory includes four operators. The formulas in this language are evaluated at moment/history pairs—also called indices. It is important to note that such an index is taken to include the complete temporal evolution of the world. This means that the truth of, for instance, a temporal condition may depend on the exact index of evaluation. The logical language extends the language $\mathfrak{L}_{stit}$ presented in Chap. 2 with the epistemic operators $\mathsf{K}_i\varphi$ and $\mathsf{C}_{\mathcal{G}}\varphi$ which express that agent i knows that φ and that the group $\mathcal{G}$ commonly knows that φ.[5]

Definition 4.1 (Syntax) The formal language $\mathfrak{L}_{estit}$ is:

$$\varphi := q \mid \neg\varphi \mid \varphi \wedge \varphi \mid \Box\varphi \mid [\mathcal{G}\ \mathsf{stit}]\varphi \mid \mathsf{K}_i\varphi \mid \mathsf{C}_{\mathcal{G}}\varphi,$$

where q ranges over a given countable set of propositions P, i ranges over a given finite set of agents Ags, and $\mathcal{G}$ ranges over subsets of Ags.

I use standard abbreviations for duals of modal operators, i.e. $\Diamond\varphi \equiv \neg\Box\neg\varphi$, $\langle\mathcal{G}\ \mathsf{stit}\rangle\varphi \equiv \neg[\mathcal{G}\ \mathsf{stit}]\neg\varphi$, and $\hat{\mathsf{K}}_i\varphi \equiv \neg\mathsf{K}_i\neg\varphi$. $\mathsf{C}_{\mathcal{G}}$ is the standard common knowledge operator (see Fagin et al., 2003; Meyer & van der Hoek, 1995), and I abbreviate $\bigwedge_{i\in\mathcal{G}}\mathsf{K}_i\varphi$ by $\mathsf{E}_{\mathcal{G}}\varphi$, which is the standard operator for 'everybody in $\mathcal{G}$ knows φ'. Common knowledge $\mathsf{C}_{\mathcal{G}}\varphi$ intuitively corresponds to everybody in $\mathcal{G}$ knows φ, everybody in $\mathcal{G}$ knows that everybody in $\mathcal{G}$ knows φ, and so on ad infinitum.

An epistemic stit model includes indistinguishability relations $\sim_i$, one for each agent $i \in Ags$.[6] An agent may be uncertain about which actions are available to another agent, and she may be uncertain about some other aspects of the underlying stit model. To model these cases, epistemic stit models need to be flexible enough so as to include several epistemically possible moments.[7]

---

[4] See (Broersen & Herzig, 2015; Broersen et al., 2006; Duijf & Broersen, 2016; Herzig & Troquard, 2006) for work on strategic stit theory.

[5] Xu (2015) presents an excellent survey on stit theory and its epistemic extensions.

[6] In artificial intelligence research such indistinguishability relations are standardly used to represent an agent's knowledge (see Fagin et al., 2003; Meyer & van der Hoek, 1995). They straightforwardly correspond to partition structures that are commonly employed in game theory and economics to model the information states of the players (see Aumann, 1999).

[7] In other words, these models should not be solo, i.e. they should not be based on a single moment (see Sect. 2.4).

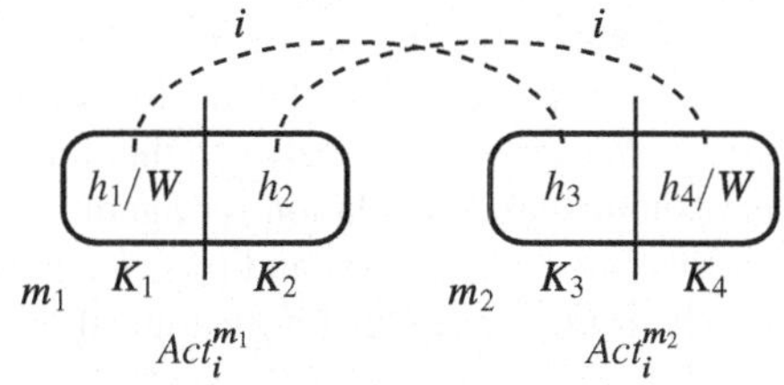

Fig. 4.1 A stit model that represents the coin example

Definition 4.2 (Epistemic Stit Models) An *epistemic stit frame* is a tuple $\langle M, H, Ind, Ags, (Act_{\mathcal{G}}), (\sim_i)\rangle$, involving a stit model and for each agent $i \in Ags$ an epistemic indistinguishability relation $\sim_i$, satisfying the following:

- $\langle M, H, Ind, Ags, (Act_{\mathcal{G}})\rangle$ is a stit frame (see Definition 2.12);
- for every $i \in Ags$ the epistemic indistinguishability relation $\sim_i$ is an equivalence relation on the set of indices *Ind*.

For each group $\mathcal{G}$, we let $\sim^*_{\mathcal{G}}$ denote the reflexive transitive closure of the union of the relations $\{\sim_i \mid i \in \mathcal{G}\}$, which will be used to interpret the common knowledge operator.

Such an epistemic stit frame is extended to an *epistemic stit model* by supplementing a valuation $V : \mathcal{P} \to 2^{Ind}$, which assigns to each atomic proposition q the set of indices $V(q)$ in which it is true.

To illustrate epistemic stit models, consider the following example depicted in Fig. 4.1.[8] An agent, called j, first places a coin on the table either heads up or tails up. Afterwards the other agent, called i, is offered the option to bet on whether agent j put the coin heads up or tails up. The bet happens at either moment m_1 or moment m_2, depending on agent j's choice. If agent j chooses to place the coin heads up, then the resulting moment will be m_1 and agent i bets heads by selecting K_1 and bets tails by selecting K_2. If agent j chooses to place the coin tails up, then the resulting moment will be m_2 and agent i bets heads by selecting K_3 and bets tails by selecting K_4. For simplicity's sake, we only model four possible histories h_1 through h_4, each associated with one action token. If we let W denote the state of affairs where agent i bets correctly, then we see that W holds at m_1/h_1 and m_2/h_4, and it is false at the other indices.

In this example, agent i does not know whether the coin has been placed heads up or tails up. This indistinguishability relation associated with a given agent is represented in the figures by a dashed line between indices which is labelled by that agent. It may be helpful to point out a few conventions for interpreting the figures: the indistinguishability relation is closed under reflexivity, transitivity, and symmetry; and, unless stated otherwise, we assume that an agent's information sets

[8] This example closely resembles the second coin example in (Horty & Pacuit, 2017, pp. 623–625, Figure 4), yet my modelling is in line with (Duijf et al., 2021).

can be viewed as unions of her action tokens.[9] Accordingly, the uncertainty of agent i is represented by the fact that agent i cannot distinguish between the indices m_1/h_1 and m_2/h_3 nor between the indices m_1/h_2 and m_2/h_4. In other words, the indistinguishability relation for agent i in the example is given by the equivalence classes $\{m_1/h_1, m_2/h_3\}$ and $\{m_1/h_2, m_2/h_4\}$.

The truth conditions for the logical operators are standard.

Definition 4.3 (Evaluation Rules) Let $\mathcal{M} = \langle M, H, Ind, Ags, (Act_{\mathcal{G}}), (\sim_i), V\rangle$ be an epistemic stit model. Then the truth of a formula φ at an index m/h in $\mathcal{M}$, notation: $\mathcal{M}, m/h \models \varphi$, is given by (suppressing the standard propositional clauses):

$\mathcal{M}, m/h \models \Box\varphi$	iff for every m'/h' satisfying $m = m'$ it holds that $\mathcal{M}, m'/h' \models \varphi$;
$\mathcal{M}, m/h \models [\mathcal{G}\ \mathsf{stit}]\varphi$	iff for every $h' \in Act^m_{\mathcal{G}}(h)$ it holds that $\mathcal{M}, m/h' \models \varphi$;
$\mathcal{M}, m/h \models \mathsf{K}_i\varphi$	iff for every index m'/h' satisfying $m/h \sim_i m'/h'$ it holds that $\mathcal{M}, m'/h' \models \varphi$;
$\mathcal{M}, m/h \models \mathsf{C}_{\mathcal{G}}\varphi$	iff for every index m'/h' satisfying $m/h \sim^*_{\mathcal{G}} m'/h'$ it holds that $\mathcal{M}, m'/h' \models \varphi$.

Validity on a model, notation: $\mathcal{M} \models \varphi$, validity on a frame, notation: $\mathcal{F} \models \varphi$, and general validity, notation: $\models \varphi$, are defined as usual.

Given a model $\mathcal{M}$ and a moment $m \in M$, the *truth set* of a formula φ relative to $\mathcal{M}$ or to m, notation: $[\![\varphi]\!]_{\mathcal{M}}$ and $[\![\varphi]\!]_m$ respectively, is given by $\{m'/h' \in Ind \mid \mathcal{M}, m'/h' \models \varphi\}$ and $\{m'/h' \in Ind \mid \mathcal{M}, m'/h' \models \varphi \text{ and } m = m'\}$, respectively.

Let me briefly illustrate these truth conditions using the coin example depicted in Fig. 4.1. Notice that, at m_1/h_1 agent i sees to it that she wins the bet while she does not do so at m_2/h_3, i.e. $m_1/h_1 \models [i\ \mathsf{stit}]W$ and $m_2/h_3 \not\models [i\ \mathsf{stit}]W$. Since she cannot distinguish these indices, it follows that agent i sees to it that W even though she does not know that she does. More formally, we get $m_1/h_1 \models [i\ \mathsf{stit}]W \wedge \neg\mathsf{K}_i[i\ \mathsf{stit}]W$. In anticipation of the notion of knowingly doing presented in Sect. 4.3, this observation demonstrates that seeing to it that a given state of affairs obtains is logically distinct from *knowingly* doing it.

It is important to flag that I do not think of the indistinguishability relation as a relation between moments, rather it is vital to view it as a relation between indices, i.e. moment/history pairs. There are two main reasons for doing so: First, if we were to impose the restriction of viewing it as a relation between moments, then these restricted models would validate the schema $\mathsf{K}_i\varphi \rightarrow \mathsf{K}_i\Box\varphi$. Or, equivalently, these restricted models are incompatible with the satisfiability of any formula of the form $\mathsf{K}_i\varphi \wedge \neg\mathsf{K}_i\Box\varphi$. As a consequence, these restricted model can only be used to investigate knowledge about settled propositions. This restricted scope is unnecessary. Second, relatedly, in these restricted models it cannot be that an agent

[9] More precisely, this assumption boils down to the following: if $m/h' \in Act_i(m/h)$, then $m/h \sim_i m/h'$. Also see the discussion of the own-action condition in Sect. 4.3.2.

knows that she brings about φ—unless φ is unavoidable. The restriction, hence, appears to impede the study of modes of acting and, in particular, of knowingly doing. Given my focus on knowingly doing and knowing-how, it therefore seems imperative to avoid this restriction and to think of the indistinguishability relation as a relation between indices (see Sect. 4.4.2 for further discussion).

I would like to end this section by demonstrating that a complete logic is readily available for these epistemic stit models, because they constitute a fusion of stit logic and standard epistemic logic.[10] This complete logic is important for two main reasons: (1) it helps my conceptual analysis, and clarifies the relations between the introduced modalities; (2) it enables artificial intelligent agents to reason about abilities, knowledge, and know-how, both individual and collective, using the logical system. (All claims are proved in Appendix C.)[11]

Theorem 4.1 (Completeness Epistemic stit) *The following axiom schemas, in combination with a standard axiomatization for propositional logic, and the standard rules (such as necessitation) for the normal modal operators, provide a complete Hilbert system for the validities on epistemic stit models:*

(S5 Historical Necessity)	S5 for $\Box$
(S5 Agency)	for each group $\mathcal{G}$: S5 for $[\mathcal{G}\ \mathsf{stit}]$
(Agent Monotonicity)	for all groups $\mathcal{F}$ and $\mathcal{G}$ satisfying $\mathcal{F} \subseteq \mathcal{G}$: $[\mathcal{F}\ \mathsf{stit}]\varphi \rightarrow [\mathcal{G}\ \mathsf{stit}]\varphi$
(Independence of Agency)	for all groups $\mathcal{F}$ and $\mathcal{G}$ satisfying $\mathcal{F} \cap \mathcal{G} = \emptyset$: $\Diamond[\mathcal{F}\ \mathsf{stit}]\varphi \wedge \Diamond[\mathcal{G}\ \mathsf{stit}]\psi \rightarrow \Diamond([\mathcal{F}\ \mathsf{stit}]\varphi \wedge [\mathcal{G}\ \mathsf{stit}]\psi)$
(S5 Knowledge)	for each $i \in Ags$: S5 for K_i
(Public Knowledge)	for each group $\mathcal{G}$: $\mathsf{C}_{\mathcal{G}}\varphi \rightarrow (\varphi \wedge \mathsf{E}_{\mathcal{G}}\mathsf{C}_{\mathcal{G}}\varphi)$
(Induction)	for each group $\mathcal{G}$: $\varphi \wedge \mathsf{C}_{\mathcal{G}}(\varphi \rightarrow \mathsf{E}_{\mathcal{G}}\varphi) \rightarrow \mathsf{C}_{\mathcal{G}}\varphi$

[10] Herzig and Schwarzentruber (2008) prove that group stit is non-axiomatizable, so this seems at odds with my axiomatization result. The key to my axiomatization is that, in contrast to Herzig and Schwarzentruber, I do not impose the intersection property (see Definition 2.14 in Sect. 2.4).

[11] Some comments on the logical system. For those unfamiliar with modal logic, it may be useful to point out that one of the basic results is that the S5 axioms (reflexivity: $\Box\varphi \rightarrow \varphi$, symmetry: $\varphi \rightarrow \Box\Diamond\varphi$, and transitivity: $\Box\varphi \rightarrow \Box\Box\varphi$) jointly correspond to an accessibility relation that is an equivalence relation. Moreover, an equivalence relation corresponds to a partitioning. I refer the reader to the standard textbook treatment of modal logic (Blackburn et al., 2001). The standard interpretation for the knowledge operator is as follows: (i) reflexivity, $\mathsf{K}_i\varphi \rightarrow \varphi$, requires that knowledge is factive, (ii) transitivity, $\mathsf{K}_i\varphi \rightarrow \mathsf{K}_i\mathsf{K}_i\varphi$, requires that knowledge is positively introspective, and (iii) euclidity, $\neg\mathsf{K}_i\varphi \rightarrow \mathsf{K}_i\neg\mathsf{K}_i\varphi$, requires that knowledge is negatively introspective.

This axiomatization of common knowledge is from the work of Meyer and van der Hoek (1995). Other axiomatizations of common knowledge rely on an induction rule such as $\varphi \rightarrow \mathsf{E}_{\mathcal{G}}(\varphi \wedge \psi) \mid \varphi \rightarrow \mathsf{C}_{\mathcal{G}}\psi$ (Fagin et al., 2003) or $\varphi \rightarrow \mathsf{E}_{\mathcal{G}}\varphi \mid \mathsf{E}_{\mathcal{G}}\varphi \rightarrow \mathsf{C}_{\mathcal{G}}\varphi$ (Lismont, 1993).

4.3 Individual Practical Knowledge

I proceed with developing my theory of individual know-how. I will start in Sect. 4.3.1 by explicating my views on action hierarchies in light of the philosophical literature on action individuation. In Sect. 4.3.2 I will develop an account of knowingly doing with an eye on the literature on formalisms of knowledge and action. Finally, in Sect. 4.3.3 I will discuss individual know-how, provide some impossibility results, and eventually give a characterization of individual know-how.

4.3.1 Action Hierarchies

Much ink has been spilled on the concepts of knowing-how, actions, and ability. To explicate my ideas and to illustrate my interpretation of stit theory, I will explain the concept of *action hierarchies* with reference to the relevant philosophical literature.[12] Elizabeth Anscombe, in her seminal work, writes:

> Are we to say that the man who (intentionally) moves his arm, operates the pump, replenishes the water-supply, poisons the inhabitants, is performing *four* actions? Or only one? (Anscombe, 1963, p. 45)[13]

Are there as many actions (and as many intentions) as there are such descriptions? I follow Anscombe (1963) and Davidson (1963) and submit that there is but one action which is described in various ways (albeit perhaps not by a definite description).[14] In a stit model, it is obviously true that at each index m/h an agent is only performing one particular action, viz. the action represented by $Act_i(m/h)$. It is best to interpret the expression $[i\ \mathsf{stit}]\varphi$ as describing agent i's action as one that guarantees φ.[15] Having clarified this distinction, I should point out that I occasionally conflate $[i\ \mathsf{stit}]\varphi$ as an act description and as a φ-action.

---

[12] In Sect. 4.6 I will briefly elaborate on connections between my view on action hierarchies and the view in the artificial intelligence literature on planning. More specifically, I will point out that my framework naturally relates to hierarchical planning (Sect. 4.6.1).

[13] Anscombe (1963, p. 46) answers her question as follows: "In short, the only distinct action of his that is in question is this one, A. For moving his arm up and down with his finger round the pump handle is, in these circumstances, operating the pump; and, in these circumstances, it is replenishing the house water-supply; and, in these circumstances, it is poisoning the household."

[14] This way of answering the question makes me a so-called 'coarse-grained theorist'. Goldman (1971) is a classic example of the opposite 'fine-grained theorist', who, among other things, maintains that the man in the example performs more than one action.

[15] This entails that someone who considers the semantical framework as primary will be a coarse-grained theorist, while someone who takes the syntactical framework as primary may be open to the fine-grained theory of action individuation. In traditional stit theory, a semantical fine-grained theory may be formalized by letting $Act_i(m/h)$ be a *collection* of subsets of moment/history pairs rather than a subset of moment/history pairs. In fact, in stit theory Broersen (2009) pioneered this way of modelling strategic action: a strategy is equated with the set of histories compatible with it; and a certain history may be compatible with multiple strategies.

Often, the expression $[i \text{ stit}]\varphi$ applies to multiple acts rather than to a definite unique action. This means that various descriptions, such as $[i \text{ stit}]\varphi$ and $[i \text{ stit}]\psi$, may pick out different *sets* of acts. In the example from Anscombe, for instance, it seems natural to say that the man is pumping the water by moving his arm, yet the converse does not hold. How should we interpret the by-relation between these particular two act descriptions?[16] In such a case I submit that the man's arm-movement is a *refinement* of his water-pumping. The example thus gives rise to an action hierarchy which contains several refinements (or granularities) of act descriptions.[17]

What is the by-relation between act descriptions? There are various guises that are standardly distinguished in philosophy, e.g. causal, intentional, teleological, constitutional, etc.[18] My formalism grants a conception of the by-relation that is based on historical necessity: relative to a given index m/h, we say that agent i is φ-ing by ψ-ing if and only if agent i sees to it that ψ and it is historically necessary that, whenever agent i sees to it that ψ, then agent i also sees to it that φ.[19] Semantically, this means that the actions in Act_i^m that guarantee ψ also guarantee φ. Or, equivalently, $[\![[i \text{ stit}]\psi]\!]_m \subseteq [\![[i \text{ stit}]\varphi]\!]_m$.[20] We say that this is a refinement because every way for agent i to see to it that ψ is a way for her to see to it that φ.

Definition 4.4 (Refinements & Action Hierarchies) Let $\mathcal{M}$ be an epistemic stit model, let $\mathcal{G} \subseteq Ags$ be a group, and let m/h be an index. Then we say that, relative to m/h, *ψ is a refinement of φ for $\mathcal{G}$* if and only if it is historically necessary that if $\mathcal{G}$ sees to it that ψ then $\mathcal{G}$ sees to it that φ, that is,

$$\mathcal{M}, m/h \vDash \Box([\mathcal{G} \text{ stit}]\psi \rightarrow [\mathcal{G} \text{ stit}]\varphi).$$

---

[16] Anscombe (1963, see p. 45) associates these descriptions with the man's intentions. I will not do so; instead my proposal is best viewed in terms of agency-causation. That is, $[i \text{ stit}]\varphi$ means that agent i causes φ rather than agent i intentionally φs. Intentions are studied in Chap. 5.

[17] Feinberg (1970, pp. 119–151) has referred to this, or a similar, idea as the "accordion effect". Davidson (1980, p. 53) explores the idea that "we may take the accordion effect as a mark of agency".

[18] On my view, this issue is connected to the literature on grounding (see the SEP entry by Bliss & Trogdon, 2016). Epstein (2015) gives a uniform framework for modelling all these senses of grounding. He convincingly shows that all these senses may be modelled as a necessary implication, although they may vary in the types of facts that ground this relation, for instance, some are grounded in frame conditions, others in model properties.

[19] Compare Wilson (1989), who presents a teleological account of intentionality, where 'agent i ψ'd in order to φ' is analysed as 'agent i ψ'd because he wanted to φ and believed that By(ψ, φ)'.

[20] Note the important difference with both $[\![\psi]\!]_m \subseteq [\![\varphi]\!]_m$ and $[\![[i \text{ stit}]\psi]\!]_{\mathcal{M}} \subseteq [\![[i \text{ stit}]\varphi]\!]_{\mathcal{M}}$. The former drops the $[i \text{ stit}]$-operator and therefore misses the fact that the by-relation applies to act descriptions. The latter expresses a global by-relation rather than a local by-relation, that is, it says that *whenever* agent i sees to it that ψ then she sees to it that φ rather than *at the current moment* if agent i sees to it that ψ then she sees to it that φ.

When the converse does not hold, then ψ is *a proper refinement* of φ for $\mathcal{G}$.[21]

It is important to add that this definition helps to give a treatment of a dyadic notion of ability: We say that a given agent has *the ability to see to it that φ by ψ-ing* if she has the ability to see to it that ψ and ψ-ing is a refinement of φ-ing.[22] In other words, if a given agent can φ by ψ-ing, then that agent is able to ψ and it is impossible for her to see to it that ψ without seeing to it that φ. In light of the above definition, this dyadic notion of ability can be characterized as follows:

$$\Diamond[i \text{ stit}]\psi \wedge \Box\big([i \text{ stit}]\psi \rightarrow [i \text{ stit}]\varphi\big). \qquad \text{(Dyadic Ability)}$$

I'd like to acknowledge that this definition of dyadic ability is vulnerable to concerns of irrelevance. Consider an example where Yuri rides his bike and talks to his friend. Since Yuri can surely also cycle without talking to his friend (and vice versa), my definition would suggest that Yuri has the dyadic ability to ride his bike by riding his bike *and* talking to his friend. However, this seems odd or wrong because his talking is irrelevant to his cycling.[23]

Nonetheless, I do believe that my condition is necessary: it would be odd to say that an agent has the ability to see to it that φ by ψ-ing if ψ is not a refinement of φ for that agent. One possible way to address the problem of irrelevance would be to ensure that ψ is relevant to agent i's φ-ing by putting additional constraints on the refinement ψ. Although this means that my analysis of dyadic ability could be further improved, one merit of my approach is that, by expressing the by-relation in the language, it opens up the question of what the relation between an act description and its refinement should be.[24]

It may be helpful to remark that there may be multiple ways in which she can bring about φ. This means that the converse need not hold: whenever an agent is able to φ by ψ-ing, then it need not entail that that agent is able to ψ by φ-ing. In fact, one might think that an agent is able to φ by ψ-ing *only if* the converse is false. From the perspective of my formalism, this view is represented by taking the agent's dyadic ability to φ by ψ-ing to include the requirement that seeing to it that ψ is a *proper* refinement of seeing to it that φ. Let us call this dyadic notion of ability *strong dyadic ability*; it can be characterized as follows:

$$\Diamond[i \text{ stit}]\psi \wedge \Box\big([i \text{ stit}]\psi \rightarrow [i \text{ stit}]\varphi\big) \wedge \neg\Box\big([i \text{ stit}]\varphi \rightarrow [i \text{ stit}]\psi\big).$$
(Strong Dyadic Ability)

---

[21] Note that the syntactical counterparts of $[\![\psi]\!]_m \subseteq [\![\varphi]\!]_m$ and $[\![[i \text{ stit}]\psi]\!]_{\mathcal{M}} \subseteq [\![[i \text{ stit}]\varphi]\!]_{\mathcal{M}}$, mentioned in the previous footnote, are $\mathcal{M}, m/h \vDash \Box(\psi \rightarrow \varphi)$ and $\mathcal{M} \vDash \Box([\mathcal{G} \text{ stit}]\psi \rightarrow [\mathcal{G} \text{ stit}]\varphi)$, respectively.

[22] The topic of dyadic ability has been rarely studied in the logic of action. Two exceptions are Elgesem (1993) and McNamara (2019), whose ideas are syntactically similar to my ideas yet differ semantically.

[23] I would like to thank an anonymous reviewer for bringing this issue to my attention.

[24] As far as I am aware, the issue of irrelevance has not been brought up before in other formalisms of ability and knowing-how such as other formalisms in the ATL tradition (Ågotnes et al., 2015) and the stit tradition (Horty & Belnap, 1995; Horty & Pacuit, 2017).

These ideas will be important for the semantics of knowing-how. But, first we need to introduce the concept of knowingly doing.

4.3.2 *Knowingly Doing*

My theory of know-how is cast against the background of a theory of *knowingly doing*. Broersen (2011, Sect. 3) was the first to present a logical treatment of knowingly doing, which I will largely follow. With the epistemic stit framework at play (Sect. 4.2), we can express that agent i *knowingly* sees to it that φ using the formula $\mathsf{K}_i[i\ \mathsf{stit}]\varphi$. The semantics of this expression are given in terms of epistemic indistinguishability relations on indices, i.e. moment/history pairs. An agent i knowingly does φ if the formula $[i\ \mathsf{stit}]\varphi$ holds at all indices in the epistemic equivalence set containing the index of evaluation. That is, an agent knowingly does φ if and only if the agent knows that she guarantees that φ holds, regardless of what the other agents do. Or, equivalently, φ is something that an agent knowingly does if and only if she is certain that the action she performs will result in φ.

To illustrate that knowingly doing φ is different from simply seeing to it that φ holds, consider the following simple example. Imagine a deck of cards, spread out face down on a table in front of Ann, and suppose she can only pick one card. Furthermore, imagine that Bob simultaneously selects a card by writing down the name of a card, for instance, 'ace of spades', on a piece of paper. Suppose that Bob writes down 'jack of hearts' and that Ann unwittingly picks the jack of hearts. Let p_m express that the card Ann picks *matches* what Bob selected, and let a and b stand for Ann and Bob, respectively. Moreover, from here on, propositions p and q are subscripted with, for instance, ♠ and J to make clear that I am referring to picking a spade and a jack. So $q_{\spadesuit A}$ and $q_{\heartsuit J}$ concern picking an ace of spades and a jack of hearts, respectively. A stit model of this scenario is depicted in Fig. 4.2, where any index $m/h_0 \in K_{\heartsuit J} \cap K'_{\heartsuit J}$ depicts the scenario where Ann unwittingly picks the jack of hearts and Bob selects the jack of hearts.

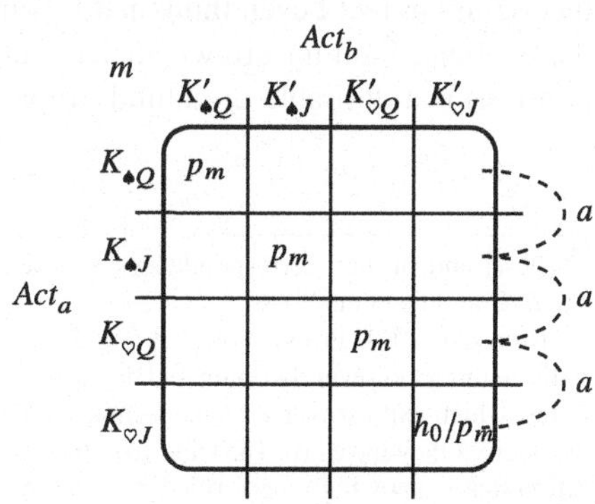

Fig. 4.2 A stit model that represents the scenario where Ann and Bob match cards

Let us consider Ann's epistemic state. Ann does not know which card she picks because she cannot distinguish, for instance, the jack of hearts from the queen of aces. I propose that her epistemic state can be represented by the fact that she cannot identify any of her available action tokens, in particular, $K_{\heartsuit J}$ and $K_{\spadesuit Q}$ are part of the same information set. In other words, her epistemic state can be represented by the epistemic indistinguishability relation $\sim_a$ given by $m/h \sim_a m/h'$ for all indices m/h and m/h'. Hence, her epistemic state is as depicted in Fig. 4.2—under the convention that her information sets can be viewed as unions of her action tokens.

Notice that Ann is, as a matter of fact, guaranteeing that she picks a jack of hearts. Formally, this is expressed by $m/h_0 \models [a \text{ stit}]q_{\heartsuit J}$. But, the model demonstrates that she does so unknowingly, as is expressed by $m/h_0 \models \neg \mathsf{K}_a[a \text{ stit}]q_{\heartsuit J}$. Finally, note that the card Ann picks matches what Bob writes down even though Ann does not knowingly do it and she also does not guarantee it. That is, p_m holds at m/h_0 even though $\mathsf{K}_a[a \text{ stit}]p_m$ and $[a \text{ stit}]p_m$ do not.

To highlight the flexibility and interpretation of my framework, let us now discuss two possible properties of knowledge and knowingly doing. These properties are in the Sahlqvist class, which means that they yield a complete logic. I will present them as axioms in the epistemic stit language (Definition 4.1) and give the corresponding first-order conditions on epistemic stit frames (Definition 4.2).[25]

Proposition 4.1

(OAC) *The* own-action condition, *schematically expressed by* $\mathsf{K}_i\varphi \rightarrow \mathsf{K}_i[i \text{ stit}]\varphi$, *corresponds to the condition:*
For all indices m/h, m'/h'_1, *and* m'/h'_2, *if* $m/h \sim_i m'/h'_1$ *and* $h'_2 \in Act_i(m'/h'_1)$ *then* $m/h \sim_i m'/h'_2$.

(Unif-H) *The* uniformity of historical possibility property, *schematically expressed by* $\Diamond \mathsf{K}_i\varphi \rightarrow \mathsf{K}_i\Diamond\varphi$, *corresponds to the confluency condition:*
For all indices m/h_1, m/h_2, *and* m'/h'_1, *if* $m/h_1 \sim_i m'/h'_1$ *then there is an index* m'/h'_2 *such that* $m/h_2 \sim_i m'/h'_2$.

Before discussing the interpretation of these conditions and their appeal, I would like to briefly point out whether my theories of individual and collective know-how depend on these conditions. The own-action condition plays no role in my theorizing; in fact I even think that it is undesirable (as will be hinted at below). At the moment, I am unsure whether the uniformity of historical possibility property (Unif-H) is a desirable or natural property to impose on the models. But, because

[25] These, and further, correspondences can be algorithmically checked using the SQEMA algorithm (Conradie et al., 2006).

Broersen (2011, Propositions 3.1 and 3.2) uses a stit logic about affecting *next* states, so-called Xstit, to model knowingly doing and discusses two additional properties: (i) knowledge about next states, which expresses that "agents cannot know more about next states than what is affected by the choices they have" (p. 145) and (ii) effect recollection, which expresses that "the effects of an action that is knowingly performed are known in the next state" (p. 145—it is a dynamic version of perfect recall).

game theorists seem to take it for granted, I will follow suit.[26] I will clearly indicate when (Unif-H) plays a role in proving a result.

It may be useful to add that, given that the necessitation-rule and both the transitivity- and the K-axiom hold for K_i, the own-action condition is equivalent to $\langle i\ \mathsf{stit}\rangle\varphi \rightarrow \hat{\mathsf{K}}_i\varphi$. The own-action condition therefore corresponds to the simple condition that for any indices $m/h, m/h'$ if $m/h' \in Act_i(m/h)$ then $m/h \sim_i m/h'$. That is, any information state in the partition induced by $\sim_i$ is a union of actions from Act_i.[27]

The own-action condition expresses the idea that an agent cannot know *more* than what she knows about what she herself brings about. Or, equivalently, when an agent does not know that she herself sees to it that φ then she also does not know that φ holds. In other words, agents can only know something if it is the result of an action they themselves knowingly perform. Conversely, an agent *unknowingly* does φ if and only if (i) she is performing an action that guarantees φ and (ii) she considers it possible that φ does not obtain. Jan Broersen writes:

> In general the things an agent does unknowingly vastly outnumber the things an agent *knows* it does. For instance, by sending an email, we may enforce many, many things we are not aware of, which are nevertheless the result of sending the email. All these things we do *unknowingly* by knowingly sending the email. (Broersen, 2011, p. 145)

We might say that the own-action condition is a consequence of the assumption that agents cannot know what actions other agents perform concurrently.[28] The independence-of-agency condition (see Definitions 2.10 and 2.12, and Theorem 4.1) guarantees that choices of agents always refine choices of other agents. So if an agent would know about the choices of other agents or about her own future choices, then she would violate the own-action condition.

The uniformity of historical possibility property expresses the idea that whenever it is possible for agent i to know φ then she knows that φ is possible. It is easy to see that the confluency condition also corresponds to $\mathsf{K}_i\Box\varphi \rightarrow \Box\mathsf{K}_i\varphi$, or, equivalently, $\Diamond\hat{\mathsf{K}}_i\varphi \rightarrow \hat{\mathsf{K}}_i\Diamond\varphi$.[29] This means that whenever an agent knows that φ is historically settled, then it is historically settled that she knows φ. Or, equivalently,

---

[26] An elaborate discussion of my worries has to be postponed to another occasion.

[27] In (Duijf et al., 2019), I point out that *intentions* conforming to the own-action condition form an important class of intentions, viz. those that are faithful to the intuition that "the subject of the intention is the subject of the intended activity" (Bratman, 2014, p. 13).

[28] It is questionable whether this property also holds under the assumption of common knowledge of rationality, which is standardly assumed in game theory. Under this assumption, it seems appropriate to say that an agent knows that her opponents are avoiding a ridiculous, yet possible, action. This would mean that she considers it impossible that her current action is compatible with such ridiculous actions of her opponents yet it is (historically) possible that her opponents perform these actions.

[29] This follows from the fact that $\Box$ is an S5 operator and K_i is a normal operator.

it rules out that agents know that a given proposition is historically settled in case it is possible that she does not know that proposition.[30]

4.3.3 Individual Know-how

The debates concerning practical knowledge are often ambiguous regarding the meaning of ability. So let me clarify what *I* mean by ability: the notion of ability adopted in my theorizing is based on causality. I submit that an agent is able to φ if and only if it is possible that she brings it about that φ. The logical characterization of 'group $\mathcal{G}$ is able to φ' is

$$\Diamond[\mathcal{G}\ \mathsf{stit}]\varphi.$$[31]

Note that this is importantly different from it being merely possible that φ, that is, $\Diamond\varphi$. After all, it is possible that I lift my arm at the same time as my neighbour blinks in front of the bathroom mirror, yet I certainly lack an ability to do so, in the sense that I cannot guarantee that this will happen. Ability is thus analysed as a nested modal operator: it is possible that the group performs an action that guarantees φ.[32]

There is an important distinction between being able to do φ and being able to knowingly do φ. That is, there is a distinction between $\Diamond[i\ \mathsf{stit}]\varphi$ and $\Diamond\mathsf{K}_i[i\ \mathsf{stit}]\varphi$. The distinction is best explained by considering an example. Reconsider the example of Ann, who considers a face-down deck of cards (see also Fig. 4.2). Ann is certainly able to pick a spade. That is, there is an action that she can perform which is, as a matter of fact, picking a spade, that is, letting a stand for Ann, $\Diamond[a\ \mathsf{stit}]q_\spadesuit$ holds. In contrast, Ann is not able to *knowingly* pick a spade. Indeed, there is no action available that she knows is an instantiation of her picking a spade, i.e. $\Diamond\mathsf{K}_a[a\ \mathsf{stit}]q_\spadesuit$ does not hold. Notice that this involves knowledge of her action, which is best viewed as *ex interim* knowledge (see Sect. 4.4.1 for more details on this terminology). In contrast, in this example Ann knows that she is able to pick a spade, that is, $\mathsf{K}_a\Diamond[a\ \mathsf{stit}]q_\spadesuit$. This knowledge concerns static properties: thirteen of these cards are spades, so she is able to pick one of them. She knows this. We thus obtain the following logical (in)validities:

---

[30] See my joint work (Duijf et al., 2021) for more discussion on the uniformity of historical possibility property and, in particular, its relation to, what we called, the condition of uniformity of available action types.

[31] Horty and Belnap (1995) propose a similar characterization for individual agents, although they rely on deliberative stit. They show that their characterization straightforwardly connects to Brown's (1988) proposal.

[32] It is certainly not my objective to give a thorough analysis of ability and all its complexities. Some think that knowing-how is merely a kind of ability, and my investigation of knowing-how proves a similar point.

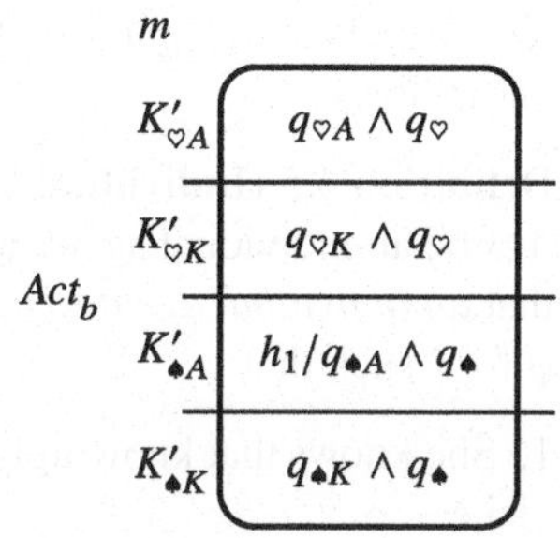

Fig. 4.3 An epistemic stit model that represents Bob's decision problem

Observation 4.2 (Properties of Knowledge and Ability) Let $i \in Ags$ be an agent. Assume (Unif-H). Then the following (schematic) validities and invalidities hold:

$\models \Diamond \mathsf{K}_i[i \text{ stit}]\varphi \rightarrow \mathsf{K}_i\Diamond[i \text{ stit}]\varphi$ (using **Unif-H**)
$\not\models \mathsf{K}_i\Diamond[i \text{ stit}]\varphi \rightarrow \Diamond \mathsf{K}_i[i \text{ stit}]\varphi$ (discussion above)
$\models \mathsf{K}_i\Diamond[i \text{ stit}]\varphi \rightarrow \Diamond[i \text{ stit}]\varphi$ (using the **T-axiom for** K_i)
$\not\models \Diamond[i \text{ stit}]\varphi \rightarrow \mathsf{K}_i\Diamond[i \text{ stit}]\varphi$ (discussion above)

My theory of knowing-how relies on refinements and on action hierarchies (Sect. 4.3.1). To illustrate, reconsider the example where Bob selects a card by writing down the card's name. In contrast to Ann, Bob does have the ability to knowingly select a spade. Why? Because there is a refinement, for instance selecting the ace of spades, which Bob knows is a refinement of selecting a spade. We say that this is a refinement because every way for him to select the ace of spades is a way for him to select a spade. And, furthermore, he knows that he is able to knowingly select the ace of spades.

Before presenting my conception of individual know-how, let us see how Bob's scenario can be modelled. A simplification of the scenario involving Bob is depicted by the stit model in Fig. 4.3, where b stands for Bob. In this simplification, Bob has four actions available to him: $K'_{\spadesuit A}$, $K'_{\spadesuit K}$, $K'_{\heartsuit A}$, and $K'_{\heartsuit K}$. Bob can distinguish all of his actions. Hence, his epistemic state can be represented by the epistemic indistinguishability relation $\sim_b$ given by $m/h \sim_b m/h'$ if and only if $m/h' \in Act_b(m/h)$.[33] The model indeed demonstrates that knowingly selecting the ace of spades is a refinement of knowingly selecting a spade for Bob. After all, any moment/history pair m/h supports $m/h \models \Box(\mathsf{K}_b[b \text{ stit}]q_{\spadesuit A} \rightarrow \mathsf{K}_b[i \text{ stit}]q_{\spadesuit})$.[34] Moreover, the model shows that, at m/h_1, Bob knowingly selects the ace of spades, since $m/h_1 \models \mathsf{K}_b[b \text{ stit}]q_{\spadesuit A}$. Hence, Bob knows that he is able to knowingly select the ace of spades. That is, $m/h \models \mathsf{K}_b\Diamond\mathsf{K}_b[b \text{ stit}]q_{\spadesuit A}$. These two conditions

[33] In line with the convention that her information sets can be viewed as unions of her action tokens, Fig. 4.3 does not show any dashed lines.

[34] In fact, the model shows that there are several distinct ways for Bob to pick a spade. After all, $m/h_1 \models \Box([b \text{ stit}]q_{\spadesuit K} \rightarrow [b \text{ stit}]q_{\spadesuit})$ while $m/h_1 \models \neg\Diamond(q_{\spadesuit A} \wedge q_{\spadesuit K})$.

respectively correspond to the two requirements in my definition of individual know-how.

Definition 4.5 (Individual Know-how) Let $\mathcal{M}$ be an epistemic stit model, let $i \in Ags$ be an individual agent, and let m/h be an index. Then we say, relative to m/h, that *an individual agent i knows how to* φ if and only if there is[35] a refinement ψ of φ for i such that

1. She knows that knowingly doing ψ is a refinement of knowingly doing φ for her, i.e.

$$\mathcal{M}, m/h \models \mathsf{K}_i\Box(\mathsf{K}_i[i \text{ stit}]\psi \rightarrow \mathsf{K}_i[i \text{ stit}]\varphi);$$

2. She knows that she is able to knowingly ψ, i.e.

$$\mathcal{M}, m/h \models \mathsf{K}_i\Diamond\mathsf{K}_i[i \text{ stit}]\psi.$$[36]

Both requirements are *necessary* for knowing-how. First, it is hard to imagine an agent who finds herself in a situation where there exists no statement that satisfies the second requirement. After all, this would imply that there is no statement ψ such that the agent knows that she can knowingly see to it that ψ. In any case, almost everyone would agree that such an agent does not possess any knowing-how. Second, notice that the first requirement is always satisfied: any statement ψ satisfying $\psi \equiv \varphi$ will satisfy the first requirement.

Are these requirements *jointly sufficient* for knowing-how, as well as individually necessary? I will assume that they are since, intuitively, any agent who satisfies both of them would be in a perfect position for knowing how to φ. There is a risk that further investigation shows that these two requirements turn out to not be jointly sufficient, *contra* my present intuitions. In fact, I welcome this risk and hope that the proposed framework facilitates other researchers to carefully identify errors or counterexamples.

---

[35] Unfortunately, this existential quantification cannot be captured in the current logic. This means that the concept of individual know-how is not straightforwardly characterizable in the current logic. Nevertheless, this section concludes with a central theorem that shows that individual know-how can be characterized.

[36] Compare Carr (1979, p. 402—notation adapted): "On the 'bring about' analysis of action descriptions our ability and knowing how contexts now expand as follows:

i is able to bring it about that φ.
i knows how to bring it about that φ.

It transpires on this analysis that the logical form suggested earlier, of sentences about knowing how and ability, was only the apparent form, for such sentences are really instances of one modal construction buried within another. Ability and know-how are thus seen to be concepts of third level (like e.g. the 'know' of self-knowledge, as it occurs in sentences like 'i knows that he knows that φ')." Accordingly, my notion of know-how would be a concept of fifth level.

Before exploring this characterization of knowing-how in further detail, it may be helpful to flag one possible objection to the idea that these requirements are jointly sufficient. Knowing-how is often equated with explainability and one might think that an agent who satisfies the two requirements need not be able to explain how she does it. In light of this objection, and to highlight how my framework can be used to accommodate additional requirements, let us distinguish between implicit and explicit knowing-how.

Implicit knowing-how concerns cases where one knows how to φ without having a proper refinement of φ-ing. An example might clarify this: an agent may know how to ride a bike without being able to explain how she does it. In this case, she knows how to ride a bike despite lacking knowledge of a *proper* refinement of her bike-riding. This is an instance of the above definition where φ expresses 'bike-riding' and $\psi \equiv \varphi$. (Since the formula in condition 1 then turns into a valid formula, her knowing-how amounts to condition 2, viz. $\mathsf{K}_i \Diamond \mathsf{K}_i [i \text{ stit}]\varphi$.) I submit that an agent implicitly knows how to φ if and only if she knows how to φ despite *lacking* knowledge of a *proper* refinement.

In contrast, *explicit knowing-how* concerns cases where one knows how to φ by having a proper refinement of φ-ing. An example may help to illustrate this: in the example of the face-up deck of cards, Bob knows that he can select a spade by selecting the ace of spades. In this way, he can explain that he knows how to select a spade by mentioning that he can do so by selecting the ace of spades. Although there may be multiple ways to select a spade, one witness suffices for him to know how to do so. This is an instance of the above definition where $\varphi \equiv q_{\spadesuit}$ and $\psi \equiv q_{\spadesuit A}$. Moreover, knowingly doing $q_{\spadesuit A}$ is a proper refinement of knowingly $q_{\spadesuit}$ for Bob, that is, $\Box(\mathsf{K}_b[b \text{ stit}]q_{\spadesuit A} \rightarrow \mathsf{K}_b[b \text{ stit}]q_{\spadesuit})$ holds while its converse does not (see Definition 4.4). I submit that an agent explicitly knows how to φ if and only if her knowing-how is witnessed by a *proper refinement* ψ.

The difference between implicit and explicit know-how is best expressed in terms of explainability. When an agent implicitly knows how to φ she is unable to explain how she does it. Conversely, when an agent explicitly knows how to φ she is able to explain how she does it. Although the agent knows how to φ in both cases, the difference is highlighted in my theory by the fact that her knowing-how may either exclude or include a proper refinement.

Although it is plausible that explainability requires knowledge of a proper refinement, I should note that it is likely that knowledge of a proper refinement is insufficient for explainability. One problem is that the particular proper refinement may be irrelevant. Recall the example where Yuri knows how to ride his bike by riding his bike *and* talking to his friend. Although riding and talking would be a proper refinement of riding, it seems odd to say that it constitutes an explanation of his riding because his talking is irrelevant to his cycling. Nonetheless, I believe that my notion of explicit knowing-how is a natural starting point, which could be refined in future work by adding further requirements on the proper refinement ψ.[37]

One might think that it is curious that whether an agent explicitly knows how to φ depends essentially on the truth of another formula that is *logically* unrelated to φ. Suppose we're considering a particular example in natural language and we ask whether the agent explicitly knows how to φ. Following my approach, one would construct a model (including an evaluation of propositions) that represents the example and then apply my analysis of explicit knowing-how. Although whether the agent explicitly knows how to φ depends on formulas that are logically unrelated to φ, I would say that it is plausible that it depends on propositions that are *situationally* related to φ, such as propositions concerning refinements of φ-ing.

Let me proceed with the question whether these notions can be logically characterized. It might be unsurprising (because of the existential quantification noted in Footnote 35) that neither explicit nor implicit know-how can be characterized:

Theorem 4.2 (Impossibility Results) *Implicit individual know-how and explicit individual know-how cannot be characterized in the current logic:*

1. *Given an agent i and a formula φ, there is* no *formula ψ such that for every model $\mathcal{M}$ and every index m/h it holds that, relative to m/h, agent i* implicitly *knows how to φ if and only if $\mathcal{M}, m/h \models \psi$.*
2. *Given an agent i and a formula φ, there is* no *formula ψ such that for every model $\mathcal{M}$ and every index m/h it holds that, relative to m/h, agent i* explicitly *knows how to φ if and only if $\mathcal{M}, m/h \models \psi$.*

Given this impossibility result, it may seem remarkable that individual know-how can be characterized as follows:

Theorem 4.3 (Characterization of Individual Know-how) *Individual know-how is characterized by*

$$\mathsf{K}_i \Diamond \mathsf{K}_i [i \ \mathsf{stit}]\varphi.$$

That is, for every model $\mathcal{M}$, every index m/h, every individual agent i, and every formula φ it holds that, relative to m/h, agent i knows how to φ if and only if $\mathcal{M}, m/h \models \mathsf{K}_i \Diamond \mathsf{K}_i [i \ \mathsf{stit}]\varphi$.

---

[37] As an anonymous reviewer has pointed out, it is plausible to think that the problem of irrelevance arises for my analysis because we expect that the agent in question is also aware of the formal language or can use it to describe their actions. I believe, however, that adding awareness will not address the problem of irrelevance. To see why, let's reconsider the example: Yuri knows how to ride his bike by riding his bike and talking to his friend. This is insufficient to conclude that Yuri explicitly knows how to ride his bike, since his talking is irrelevant to his riding. Could awareness address this problem? I think not. After all, since it is plausible that Yuri is aware of all the details mentioned in the example, he is aware that he can ride his bike by riding his bike and talking to his friend. In short: awareness of a proper refinement is insufficient for the relevance of that refinement. If this is correct, then it seems like adding awareness will not address the problem of irrelevance.

This subsection thus culminates in a neat characterization of individual know-how that addresses the raised concerns. This means that the current logical framework is powerful enough to express the concept of individual practical knowledge, despite being unable to express implicit and explicit knowledge. Among other things, this highlights that the complete system provided by Theorem 4.1 can be used to reason about individual practical knowledge.[38]

4.4 Related Research on Knowledge and Ability

I have presented a conceptual analysis of individual know-how using an epistemic extension of stit theory. In this section I will relate my formalism and analysis to several other lines of research:

- In Sect. 4.4.1, I will relate my formalism to the distinction from economics between three stages of decision-making: ex ante, interim, and ex post.
- In Sect. 4.4.2, I will relate my analysis to computer science logics and, in particular, the tradition of alternating-time temporal logic (ATL) by discussing uniform strategies and action types.
- In Sect. 4.4.3, I will elaborate on the implications of my characterization of knowing-how for the philosophical debates on intellectualism.

4.4.1 Ex Ante, Interim, and Ex Post Knowledge

It is useful to discuss the notions of knowledge and knowingly doing in my formalism in light of a distinction made by economists:

> Economists distinguish three stages in differential information environments. Ex ante, no one has any private information; in the interim, each agent has his private information only; ex post, all information is revealed to all. In our context, ex ante the protagonist knows only the belief system B—which is commonly known by all players; in the interim, each player knows his type, but not those of the others; ex post, each player knows the types of all players. (Aumann & Dreze, 2008, p. 80)[39]

---

[38] Nonetheless, it is unclear whether it is tractable to do so since I have not studied the complexity of either model-checking or satisfiability. For now, I wish to point to the relevant literature on this topic (Herzig & Schwarzentruber, 2008; van der Hoek & Wooldridge, 2003; Payette, 2014).

[39] Lorini et al. (2014, p. 1314) write: "Each type of knowledge is defined with respect to the time of the agent's choice: before one's choice (*ex ante* knowledge), after one's choice but before knowing the choices of others (*interim* knowledge), and after the choices of all agents have been made public (*ex post* knowledge)." Compare Horty and Pacuit (2017, pp. 31–32): "an agent's ex ante knowledge is the information available to the agent without taking into account any actions she is currently executing, while the agent's ex interim knowledge is information that does take into account whatever actions the agent is currently executing, along with the effects of these actions".

It thus seems natural to suppose that ex post knowledge refines interim knowledge, which in turn refines ex ante knowledge.[40] That is, whenever an agent knows φ ex ante then she knows φ ex interim, and, similarly, when an agent knows ψ ex interim then she knows ψ ex post.[41]

Since knowingly doing is characterized using the knowledge operator, the view on knowledge captured in my formalism is best interpreted as interim knowledge. That is, it is best viewed as interim knowledge because knowingly doing, expressed by $\mathsf{K}_i[i\ \mathsf{stit}]\varphi$, is a concept that clearly operates at the interim stage of decision-making. As mentioned before, whenever $\mathsf{K}_i[i\ \mathsf{stit}]\varphi$ holds at a moment/history pair m/h then it is the case that agent i knows that she ensures that φ holds, regardless of what the other agents do. Accordingly, $\mathsf{K}_i\varphi$ might be interpreted as expressing that agent i knows that φ holds, regardless of what *she thinks* the other agents might do. When the own-action condition is violated, knowingly doing φ may require that φ holds even at epistemically inaccessible indices. It thus seems appropriate to submit that $\mathsf{K}_i\varphi$ expresses that agent i interim knows φ.

The own-action condition should not be confused with a standard assumption in epistemic game theory: knowledge of one's own action. According to Pacuit and Roy (2017), knowledge of one's own action is "the trademark of ex-interim situations". It corresponds to the condition that for any indices m/h and m/h', if $m/h \sim_i m/h'$ then $m/h' \in Act_i(m/h)$. This means that an agent cannot be uncertain about which action she performs. In other words, an agent cannot know *less* than what she herself brings about.[42]

This reveals a conflicting assumption in game theory and my work on knowingly doing. I drop the standard assumption in game theory that an agent knows how to perform any of her available actions. To illustrate this, reconsider the face-down deck of cards example. On my account, it is impossible for Ann to knowingly pick the jack of hearts. It is, however, possible that she performs that action unwittingly, i.e. despite unknowingly doing so. This conflicts with the standard assumption in epistemic game theory. According to game theorists either (i) Ann cannot perform the action of picking the jack of hearts, or (ii) it is possible for Ann to knowingly do so. It is important to bear this conflict in mind.[43]

---

[40] Lorini et al. (2014, Sect. 2.2.2) model agent i's ex ante, interim, and ex post knowledge using accessibility relations $\mathcal{E}_i^{\bullet\circ\circ}$, $\mathcal{E}_i^{\circ\bullet\circ}$, and $\mathcal{E}_i^{\circ\circ\bullet}$, respectively. The idea that these are refinements is expressed by the inclusions $\mathcal{E}_i^{\bullet\circ\circ} \supseteq \mathcal{E}_i^{\circ\bullet\circ} \supseteq \mathcal{E}_i^{\circ\circ\bullet}$.

[41] The assumption that ex post knowledge refines ex ante knowledge is standardly referred to as 'perfect recall'.

[42] Aumann (1987, p. 8) writes: "Of course, a player always knows which decision he himself takes."

[43] It seems that Aumann had games of *perfect information* in mind, a term that became standard only after, and perhaps because of, his seminal works were published. A contemporary game theorist would reply to my worries expressed in the face-down deck of cards example by saying that the example is best modelled as a game of imperfect information. In games of imperfect information, an epistemic sense of ability is typically modelled using action types, rather than actions. We will discuss connections to action types shortly.

Agent i's knowledge that is independent of the actual action she performs is expressed by $\Box \mathsf{K}_i \psi$. It is, nonetheless, unclear whether this corresponds to ex ante knowledge.[44] The following two considerations may clarify why. First, because ex ante knowledge is not private knowledge it seems natural to equate it with common knowledge. Consequently, to express ex ante knowledge it seems necessary to use the common knowledge operator C_{Ags}. Second, ex ante knowledge is the available public information *before* making a choice. Although $\Box \mathsf{C}_{Ags}\varphi$ would capture that the knowledge is independent of the current actions, it is unclear whether this is equivalent to saying that it represents the information *before* any choices have been made. Perhaps some particular information is independent of the choice made yet only obtains after a choice is made (for instance, the information that a choice has been made).

Ex post knowledge is the knowledge that is attained after everyone acted. Since my simple epistemic stit models and language abstracted away from the temporal structure of branching-time agency models, it seems that this cannot be modelled appropriately. One could use more elaborate branching-time agency models and syntax, including a next operator X, to represent ex post knowledge by $\mathsf{XK}_i\varphi$. Alternatively, the sentence "ex post, all information is revealed to all" in the above quote suggests that one might model ex post knowledge as distributed knowledge: $\mathsf{D}_{Ags}\varphi$.[45]

These three types of knowledge help to clarify the interpretation of the kind of knowledge used in my formalism. The previous discussion is not meant to settle the correct interpretation of these three types of knowledge.[46] Rather, it is supposed to utilize my formalism to map a space of possible interpretations and ambiguities.

4.4.2 *Logics of Ability: Uniform Strategies and Action Types*

In an important contribution to stit theory, Horty and Pacuit (2017) give an analysis of, what they call, *epistemic ability*. Their analysis follows a by now

[44] Compare Horty and Pacuit (2017, p. 34—notation adapted): "if the agent has ex interim knowledge that φ no matter which of her available actions she happens to execute, this entails that she must have ex ante knowledge that φ".

[45] The distributed knowledge of a group, say $\mathcal{G}$, is typically modelled by a derived indistinguishability relation $\sim^{\mathsf{D}}_{\mathcal{G}} := \bigcap_{i \in \mathcal{G}} \sim_i$. The evaluation rule is as follows: $\mathcal{M}, m/h \models \mathsf{D}_{\mathcal{G}}\varphi$ if and only if for all m'/h' satisfying $m/h \sim^{\mathsf{D}}_{\mathcal{G}} m'/h'$ it holds that $\mathcal{M}, m'/h' \models \varphi$. (Which is equivalent to requiring that for all m'/h' satisfying $m/h \sim_i m'/h'$, for every $i \in \mathcal{G}$, it holds that $\mathcal{M}, m'/h' \models \varphi$.)

[46] This is unproblematic since the game-theoretical interpretation is also not settled: "At one extreme is the ex ante stage where no decision has been made yet. The other extreme is the ex post stage where the choices of all players are openly disclosed. In between these two extremes is the ex interim stage where the players have made their decisions, but they are still uninformed about the decisions and intentions of the other players. These distinctions are not intended to be sharp. Rather, they describe various stages of information disclosure during the decision-making process" (Pacuit & Roy, 2017).

standard approach to abilities under imperfect information (Horty & Pacuit, 2017, see the discussion in Sect. 5.2). Indeed, it relates naturally to computer science logics of knowledge and action, especially to the literature on alternating-time temporal logic (Alur et al., 2002), abbreviated to ATL, and its epistemic extension, standardly referred to as ATEL (see van der Hoek & Wooldridge, 2003; Jamroga & Ågotnes, 2007; Jamroga & van der Hoek, 2004; Schobbens, 2004). In these logical frameworks, the epistemic indistinguishability relations are usually thought of as a relation between states and *action types* are used to analyse epistemic ability. Simply stated, this tradition proposes that agent i is able, in an epistemic sense, to do φ if and only if there is an action type available to her that guarantees φ at every indistinguishable state.

In a similar way, Horty and Pacuit concede that their analysis of epistemic ability "makes most sense, and is most useful, when the indistinguishability relation ... can be thought of as a relation, not just between indices, but between moments themselves" (Horty & Pacuit, 2017, p. 631—condition C4). That is, they impose the restriction that agents cannot know more about the current moment/history pair than what is historically settled. This requirement can be characterized by the following semantic condition:

- for any agent i and for all $m/h, m'/h'_1$ if $m/h \sim_i m'/h'_1$, then for any m'/h'_2 it holds that $m/h \sim_i m'/h'_2$.

(Settled Knowledge)

This semantic condition can be characterized by an axiom scheme on epistemic frames:

Proposition 4.3 *Let $\mathcal{F}$ be an epistemic stit frame. Then, $\mathcal{F}$ satisfies the settled knowledge condition if and only if*

$\mathcal{F} \models \mathsf{K}_i\varphi \rightarrow \mathsf{K}_i\Box\varphi.$

It is important to flag that this condition aligns with existing frameworks in the computer science literature on knowledge and action. Models in the ATL tradition involve a set of states, and actions are thought of as transitions between such states. In light of the connections between stit theory and ATL (Broersen et al., 2006, 2007), a state in an ATL model can be thought of as a moment in a stit model. In the ATL tradition, imperfect information is usually modelled using an epistemic indistinguishability relation on states (see van der Hoek & Wooldridge, 2003), which hence corresponds to an epistemic indistinguishability relation on moments.

In my formalism, I emphasized that epistemic indistinguishability should be thought of as a relation between indices. So, what would a relation between indices correspond to in ATL models? An index involves a moment and a history and therefore includes a representation of the entire temporal evolution of the world. Since a stit theorist can think of a history as a set of linearly ordered moments, ATL theorists can think of a history as a set of linearly ordered states.[47] I postulate that an ATL theorist should think of an index in stit theory as a *dynamic state*, where a dynamic state involves the current state and the history of states that represent the temporal evolution of the world or system. (It is important to, once again, note a possible confusion: 'histories' are taken to include future states.) In contrast, I propose that a moment be thought of as a *static state*, which represents the current state but does not include a representation of the temporal evolution of the world or system.

Action types play a central role in the analysis of epistemic agency and ability by Horty and Pacuit (2017). They use new operators of the form $[i\ \mathsf{kstit}]\varphi$ to express that agent i epistemically sees to it that φ. Simply stated, they say that agent i epistemically sees to it that φ at a given index m/h if and only if agent i executes an action type that she knows to guarantee φ. Horty and Pacuit (2017) propose to use formulas of the form $\Diamond[i\ \mathsf{kstit}]\varphi$ to express epistemic abilities.[48] There is a connection with my analysis of knowing-how. In joint work (Duijf et al., 2021), we prove that these formulas naturally correspond to formulas of the form $\Diamond\mathsf{K}_i[i\ \mathsf{stit}]\varphi$ in the formalism of this chapter.

Given that Theorem 4.3 demonstrates that individual knowing-how is characterized by formulas of the form $\mathsf{K}_i\Diamond\mathsf{K}_i[i\ \mathsf{stit}]\varphi$, the aforementioned correspondence triggers the question of whether and why we would need to add the outermost K_i operator. In the formalism of Horty and Pacuit (2017), the aforementioned formulas of the form $\Diamond[i\ \mathsf{kstit}]\varphi$ are equivalent to formulas of the form $\mathsf{K}_i\Diamond[i\ \mathsf{kstit}]\varphi$, where the latter corresponds to $\mathsf{K}_i\Diamond\mathsf{K}_i[i\ \mathsf{stit}]\varphi$ in my formalism (Duijf et al., 2021).[49] So, one could say that from the perspective of (Horty & Pacuit, 2017) our analyses are logically equivalent. In contrast, from the perspective of my formalism, the two formulas $\Diamond\mathsf{K}_i[i\ \mathsf{stit}]\varphi$ and $\mathsf{K}_i\Diamond\mathsf{K}_i[i\ \mathsf{stit}]\varphi$ are equivalent when (Unif-H) holds (see Proposition 4.1). In other words, whether adding the outermost K_i operator is logically significant depends on whether one endorses (Unif-H).

Action types and *uniform strategies* play a key role in the analysis of epistemic ability in the computer science logic literature (see Herzig & Troquard, 2006; van der Hoek & Wooldridge, 2003; Jamroga & Ågotnes, 2007; Jamroga & van der Hoek, 2004; Schobbens, 2004). The concept of knowingly doing naturally relates to action types and uniform strategies. Following Herzig and Troquard (2006), in epistemic

---

[47] These are sometimes called paths or computations (for example, see van der Hoek & Wooldridge, 2003).

[48] The analysis of epistemic abilities by Horty and Pacuit (2017) is very similar to the analysis of knowing-how by Herzig and Troquard (2006, p. 214). The latter also use operators of the form $[i\ \mathsf{kstit}]\varphi$ to express a sense of epistemic agency, where the truth conditions are spelled out using action types. Moreover, they propose to use formulas of the form $\Diamond[i\ \mathsf{kstit}]\varphi$ to express that agent i knows how to φ. The main difference is the following: instead of introducing action labels into stit theory (Horty & Pacuit, 2017), Herzig and Troquard (2006, p. 214) introduce an indistinguishability relation, called R_{UC}, where "R_{UC_i} is the relation between indexes of identical choices lying in moments indistinguishable by agent i."

[49] This equivalence also holds in the formalism of Herzig and Troquard (2006).

stit models, I could define the epistemic indistinguishability relations on indices as follows: $m_1/h_1 \sim_i m_2/h_2$ if and only if agent i performs the same action type at these indices. That is, if and only if $Act_i(m_1/h_1)$ and $Act_i(m_2/h_2)$ are instances of the same action type. In this case, $\mathsf{K}_i[i\ \mathsf{stit}]\varphi$ would hold at a given index m/h if and only if the action type agent i performs at m/h ensures that φ obtains in every indistinguishable index, regardless of what the others do.[50] Accordingly, performing a uniform strategy that ensures that φ holds at every indistinguishable state in ATL models would correspond to knowingly doing φ in the associated epistemic stit model.[51]

The uniformity of historical possibility property (Unif-H) stated in Proposition 4.1 then relates to the concept of a *uniform strategy*. If we substitute $[i\ \mathsf{stit}]\varphi$ for φ, the (Unif-H) formula turns into $\Diamond\mathsf{K}_i[i\ \mathsf{stit}]\varphi \rightarrow \mathsf{K}_i\Diamond[i\ \mathsf{stit}]\varphi$.[52] This says that if it is possible for an agent to knowingly see to it that φ, then she knows there is an action available to her that ensures φ. Under the previously mentioned correspondence between knowingly doing and uniform strategies, the intuition that uniformity means that the same action types should be available at indistinguishable states follows from (Unif-H) and S5-axioms for K_i: $\Diamond\mathsf{K}_i[i\ \mathsf{stit}]\varphi \rightarrow \mathsf{K}_i\Diamond\mathsf{K}_i[i\ \mathsf{stit}]\varphi$.[53] This formula expresses the idea that when it is possible for an agent to knowingly ensure φ then she knows that there is an action available to her that she knows ensures φ. Or, equivalently, if she does not know that there is a way for her to knowingly ensure φ, then it is impossible for her to knowingly ensure φ.[54]

Lastly, I would like to emphasize an important connection between the frameworks discussed in this section and my formalism. In joint work (Duijf et al., 2021), we have shown that the analysis of epistemic ability by Horty and Pacuit (2017) can be simulated by the analysis of individual know-how presented in this chapter.[55] Moreover, it is highly likely that the analysis of epistemic abilities in the ATL

[50] It took a while for computer science logicians to successfully model this. Jamroga and Ågotnes (2007) were the first to do this using constructive knowledge. See also the brief discussion in (Duijf & Broersen, 2016, p. 24).

[51] Broersen et al. (2006) show that ATL can be embedded into stit theory. The central coalitional strategic ability operator of ATL, expressed by $\langle\langle \mathcal{G}\rangle\rangle\varphi$, corresponds to the strategic stit formula $\Diamond[\mathcal{G}\ \mathsf{sstit}]\varphi$. (Where $[\mathcal{G}\ \mathsf{sstit}]$ is a *strategic* stit operator, rather than the stit operator used in this book.)

[52] Broersen (2011) mistakenly thinks that this formula captures the intuition of uniform strategies. This is false because an agent may know that it is possible that she ensures that she picks an ace of spades from a face-down deck of cards ($\mathsf{K}_i\Diamond[i\ \mathsf{stit}]q_{\spadesuit A}$ holds), even though she does not know that it is possible for her to knowingly pick an ace of spades (she lacks a uniform strategy to ensure $q_{\spadesuit A}$). See the discussion surrounding Observation 4.2.

[53] This corresponds to the discussion of Herzig and Troquard (2006), more specifically Hypothesis 3 on page 212 and Property 2 on page 214.

[54] For more details and a more elaborate discussion, see (Duijf et al., 2021, Sect. 5.2).

[55] Horty and Pacuit (2017) argue that stit models *need to be extended with action types* to address certain puzzles about knowledge and action. I believe their argument is misguided due to their persistence that the indistinguishability relations are on moments. Engaging in this debate and working out the details would lead me too far astray.

tradition can also be simulated by the analysis of individual know-how presented in this chapter (without introducing action types) (Duijf et al., 2021; Kuncová et al., manuscript).

4.4.3 The Philosophical Debate on Intellectualism

Ever since Ryle (1949), philosophers have been divided into intellectualists, who think that knowing-how reduces to knowing-that, and anti-intellectualists, who resist such a reduction.[56] Recently, Stanley and Williamson (2001) have argued for the intellectualist position, a position that seems to be underpopulated. Theorem 4.3 shows that individual know-how is characterized by $\mathsf{K}_i\Diamond\mathsf{K}_i[i\ \mathsf{stit}]\varphi$, that is, by the fact that agent i knows that it is possible that she knowingly does φ. I will explain what this characterization establishes in light of this philosophical debate by highlighting four points.

First, the philosophical debate on intellectualism concerns the question of whether knowing-how *reduces to* knowing-that. A reduction can be thought of in different ways. My result applies most straightforwardly to the question of whether knowing-how *logically* or *semantically* reduces to knowing-that. That is, it concerns the question of whether any statement about knowing-how is logically equivalent to some statement about knowing-that. Or, equivalently, whether any statement about knowing-how can be translated into a statement about knowing-how such that these statements are true in exactly the same circumstances.

These philosophical considerations regarding the reducibility of knowing-how can be made precise by adopting a logical point of view. Let us use $\mathsf{H}_i\varphi$ to express that agent i knows how to φ. Consider the logical language $\mathcal{L}_{that}$ given by:

$$\varphi := q \mid \neg\varphi \mid \varphi \wedge \varphi \mid \Diamond\varphi \mid [i\ \mathsf{stit}]\varphi \mid \mathsf{K}_i\varphi,$$

where q ranges over a given set of propositions $\mathcal{P}$ and i ranges over a given set of agents Ags. I propose to think of $\mathcal{L}_{that}$ as including only statements about knowing-that. This logical perspective offers a *methodological* contribution to the debates on intellectualism. After all, the logical apparatus can be used to investigate whether intellectualism is tenable, since it gives us the means for determining whether knowing-that can be reduced to knowing-how. More precisely, if we wish to show that a particular statement about knowing how to φ cannot be reduced to a statement about knowing-that, it suffices to show that there is no statement ψ in $\mathcal{L}_{that}$ such that ψ and $\mathsf{H}_i\varphi$ are logically equivalent. Or, conversely, if we wish to show that any statement about knowing-how can be reduced to a statement about knowing-that, then it suffices to show that for any statement about knowing-how of the form $\mathsf{H}_i\varphi$,

[56] The debates usually depict two strands of anti-intellectualism: weak, which denies intellectualism, and strong, which embraces the prioricity of knowing-how over knowing-that.

there exists a statement ψ in $\mathcal{L}_{that}$ such that $\mathsf{H}_i\varphi$ and ψ are logically equivalent. In particular, it suffices to show that there exists a statement $\psi \in \mathcal{L}_{that}$ such that $\mathsf{H}_i q$ is logically equivalent to $\mathsf{K}_i\psi$.[57]

In light of these considerations, Theorem 4.3 is of great importance. After all, it vindicates intellectualism in that it proves that *any* statement about knowing-how *can be reduced to* a statement about knowing-that. More precisely, for any statement φ it holds that $\mathsf{H}_i\varphi$ is logically equivalent to $\mathsf{K}_i\Diamond\mathsf{K}_i[i\ \mathsf{stit}]\varphi$. Hence, where the philosophical debates mainly consists in clarifying the meaning and scope of intellectualism, Theorem 4.3 indicates that, by cashing the philosophical issue in logical terminology, we can precisely determine the situations under which intellectualism is tenable.

Second, it is useful to revisit the premises of the debate and clarify what is typically meant by knowing-how and knowing-that. Jeremy Fantl opens his paper on knowing-how by emphasizing different kinds of knowledge. He writes:

> Contemporary epistemology distinguishes among three kinds of knowledge: *propositional* knowledge, knowledge by *acquaintance*, and *practical* or *procedural* knowledge. Propositional knowledge is what is expressed by sentences relevantly similar to "Alex knows that George W. Bush is the U.S. president". ... Practical knowledge is what is expressed by sentences relevantly similar to "Callie knows how to ride a bicycle". (Fantl, 2008, p. 451)[58]

I propose to differentiate knowing-how and knowing-that on the basis of the kind of content they take: knowing-that takes a proposition as content, and knowing-how takes an action as content. Given the stit analysis of action (Sect. 2.3) and my views on action hierarchies (Sect. 4.3.1), act descriptions are expressed by locutions of the form 'agent i sees to it that φ'.[59] Although I am unsure whether this commonly qualifies as a proposition, such act descriptions are included in knowing-how, but not in knowing-that.[60] So, if one were to accept the statement 'it is possible that agent

---

[57] It is important to recognize that such a reduction should not be given by stipulation. It is hence important to see that my definition of knowing-how does *not* presuppose such a reduction (Definition 4.5). After all, the semantics of knowing-how include an existential quantification over ψ and this quantification is beyond the scope of the knowing-that operator.

[58] One's take on propositional knowledge may affect one's position in the intellectualism debate. For instance, Fantl (2008, pp. 452–453) argues that "[s]trong anti-intellectualism is most plausible if knowing that something is the case is essentially dispositional ... But if knowing that something is the case is not essentially dispositional, then it seems rather implausible for knowing-that to be reduced to or a species of knowing-how".

[59] Although David Carr so far agrees with my analysis, he eventually writes: "It appears to be the case that knowing how statements require as their objects, descriptions of actions construed in a much more sophisticated way [than descriptions of actions understood merely as instances of bringing about or agent-causation], as, in fact, *intentional actions*" (Carr, 1979, p. 409—emphasis added).

[60] Compare Glick (2011, p. 413—notation adapted): "Take, for instance, abilities. For any action of φ-ing, we could map i's ability to φ onto the proposition that $i\varphi$s, and instead of saying that i is able to φ, we could say that i 'ables that he φs'. If we had this linguistic convention, we might note that 'abling' is a relation to a proposition, but of course, by hypothesis, we would be talking about the same thing we actually talk about with ability attributions."

i knowingly does φ', expressed by $\Diamond \mathsf{K}_i[i\ \mathsf{stit}]\varphi$, into the realm of propositions then my characterization yields a reduction of knowing-how to knowing-that.

To understand the nature of propositions as used in my formalism it is vital to recall that they are evaluated at *moment/history pairs*, which include the temporal evolution of the world. Moreover, the valuation assigns to each proposition the set of such indices at which it holds. Since the temporal evolution of the world intuitively includes events and processes, propositions can depict various things: static states of affairs, temporal conditions, processes, activities, etc. Accordingly, practical knowledge can be viewed as a species of propositional knowledge.

Third, anti-intellectualists typically argue that knowing-that misses the crucial connection to skills and abilities that is akin to knowing-how.[61] It should be noted that my proposal for know-how (Definition 4.5) retains the connection to skills and abilities despite depicting knowing-how as a species of knowing-that. After all, whenever agent i knows how to φ, on my view, then she has the knowledge and skills to perform an action that guarantees φ.

In a similar way, some have rejected intellectualism because they take knowing-how to be demonstrable, that is, that one can express or explain her practical knowledge.[62] It is therefore important to emphasize that I distinguished between implicit and explicit knowing-how. Explicit knowing-how can be thought of as including the requirement that the agent is able to provide an explanation of her knowing-how. As a matter of fact, *if* one thinks that knowing-how is identical to explicit knowing-how, *then* Theorem 4.2 can be taken to show that it is not the case that any statement about knowing-how can be reduced to a statement about knowing-that. Hence, Theorem 4.2 can be used to indicate that intellectualists are logically committed to resist identifying knowing-how with explicit knowing-how.

Lastly, I would like to emphasize the methodological contribution once more by highlighting that my formalism might be adapted in order to refute intellectualism (i.e. contra Theorem 4.3). Let me give two examples of this strategy. First, one may contest some of the structural assumptions of the models. For example, one may object that knowledge is not properly modelled as a modal S5 operator. Of course, this objection is in itself not sufficient to disprove Theorem 4.3, but such objections may be used to prove that the theorem fails to hold in models that violate some of my structural assumptions.

Second, although I have argued that the semantics of knowing-how provided by Definition 4.5 is compelling, it is conceivable that some anti-intellectualists will contest this definition. Again, of course, merely contesting this definition is insufficient to disprove Theorem 4.3, but an alternative definition may be used

[61] Compare Stanley (2011, p. vii): "If it is surprising that knowledge of a fact can so immediately yield knowledge of how to swim, ride a bicycle, or play a piano, it is only so because of false assumptions about what it is to know a fact. . . . There are false assumptions about what it is to *act* on knowledge of facts, there are false assumptions about what it is to have *knowledge* of facts, and there are false assumptions about the *nature* of facts."

[62] Fodor (1968, p. 634) famously writes: "Certain of the anti-intellectualist arguments fail to go through because they confuse knowing that with being able to explain how."

to refute the reduction of knowing-how to knowing-that. In fact, I've already mentioned one such possibility: if one were to define knowing-how by way of my characterization of *explicit* knowing-how, then my formalism can be used to prove that this conception of knowing-how cannot be reduced to knowing-that.

4.5 Collective Know-how

Until now I have been mainly concerned with individual practical knowledge. I proceed with showing that these ideas can be fruitfully extended to the collective level. It is important to recall that my theory of collective know-how is designed for situations in which agreement is problematic and communication is hindered. One could therefore view my theory of a group's collective know-how as being somewhat *minimal*, that is, it seems plausible to say that the group's collective know-how expands if these restrictions are lifted. My starting point is that a group collectively knows how to achieve φ only if there is a (proper) refinement ψ which they collectively know is a way to achieve φ, and they collectively know that they are jointly able to knowingly ψ.

When does a group know that it is able to knowingly ψ? More specifically, which refinements justify this practical knowledge?[63] Let us reconsider the example of Ann and Bob to reveal some intuitions (Fig. 4.2). Recall that Ann is to draw a card from a face-down deck of cards and Bob is to select a card by writing down a card. Let $\mathcal{G}_1$ depict the group consisting of Ann and Bob. It is important to note that they are able to pick two spades. After all, there is a group action that they can perform which is, as a matter of fact, picking two spades. If we use $p_{\spadesuit\spadesuit}$ to denote the event where two spades are picked, then this can be verified by the fact that the model satisfies $\Diamond[\mathcal{G}_1 \text{ stit}]p_{\spadesuit\spadesuit}$.

Let us consider the epistemic states of Ann and Bob. Since Ann's deck is face down, Ann does not know how to pick a spade. However, notice that they commonly know that the only way for them to jointly pick two spades is by each picking a spade, that is, $\mathsf{C}_{\mathcal{G}_1}\Box([a \text{ stit}]q_{\spadesuit} \wedge [b \text{ stit}]q_{\spadesuit} \leftrightarrow [\mathcal{G}_1 \text{ stit}]p_{\spadesuit\spadesuit})$ holds. Nevertheless, since Ann does not know how to pick a spade, she *does not know how to play her part*. To my understanding, this entails that they do not collectively know how to pick two spades.

Let us proceed with considering an example where all cards are face up. Suppose there are two decks of cards face up on the table, one for Chris and one for Dee, and they simultaneously pick a card from their deck. A simplification of this scenario is depicted in the stit model of Fig. 4.4, where c and d stand for Chris and Dee

[63] Searle (1990, p. 410) writes: "I believe one of the keys to understanding collective intentionality is to see that in general the by and by-means-of relations for achieving the collective goal have to end in individual actions." My discussion of collective know-how, in terms of action hierarchies, relies on a similar intuition.

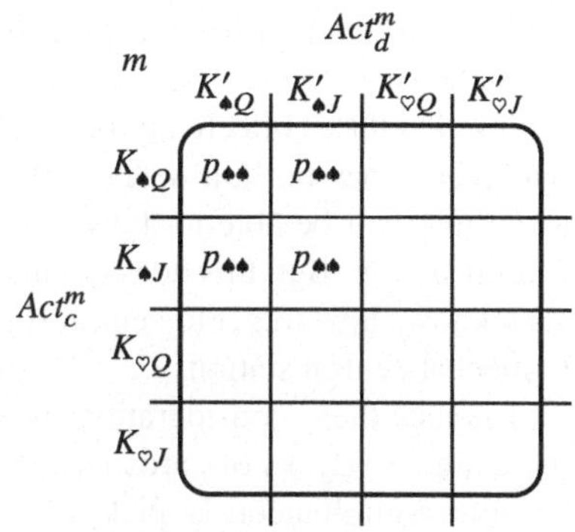

Fig. 4.4 A stit model that represents Chris and Dee's joint decision problem of picking two spades cards

respectively. Let $\mathcal{G}_2$ depict the group consisting of Chris and Dee. Note that, in line with our conventions, the epistemic indistinguishability relations $\sim_c$ and $\sim_d$ are given by $m/h \sim_c m/h'$ if and only if $m/h' \in Act_c(m/h)$ and by $m/h \sim_d m/h'$ if and only if $m/h' \in Act_d(m/h)$, respectively.[64] In contrast to the previous example of Ann and Bob, in this case there is a proper refinement of picking two spades, for instance Chris picking the ace of spades $q_{\spadesuit A}$ and Dee picking the jack of spades $q_{\spadesuit J}$, and they commonly know that is a way for them to pick two spades. More precisely, we have the following:

1. $\mathsf{C}_{\mathcal{G}_2}\Box([c \text{ stit}]q_{\spadesuit A} \wedge [d \text{ stit}]q_{\spadesuit J} \rightarrow [\mathcal{G}_2 \text{ stit}]p_{\spadesuit\spadesuit})$, that is, Chris and Dee commonly know that Chris picking the ace of spades and Dee picking the jack of spades is a way for them to pick two spades;
2. $\mathsf{C}_{\mathcal{G}_2}(\mathsf{K}_c\Diamond\mathsf{K}_c[c \text{ stit}]q_{\spadesuit A} \wedge \mathsf{K}_d\Diamond\mathsf{K}_d[d \text{ stit}]q_{\spadesuit J})$, that is, Chris and Dee commonly know that each of them knows how to carry out her part q_{-}.[65]

One may object that the 'common knowledge' requirement is too strong for an account of collective knowing-how. Although I think it is worthwhile to explore whether and how this requirement can be weakened, my present worries are complementary to such considerations. After all, an alternative account of collective knowledge could be implemented into my account of collective practical knowledge by augmenting the 'common knowledge' requirement accordingly.

To return to the last example, Chris and Dee both know that Chris's $q_{\spadesuit A}$-ing and Dee's $q_{\spadesuit J}$-ing jointly constitute a refinement of their picking two spades. In this example, they have exactly the same information. Chris, in particular, knows all the ways in which Dee can knowingly pick a spade. Since many everyday collaborations involve information asymmetry, a focus on symmetrical information states is too restrictive for a theory of collective know-how to encompass everyday collaborations.

[64] Note that Chris's and Dee's individual situation is similar to that of Bob, which is depicted in Fig. 4.3.

[65] Note that in the previous example of Ann and Bob, the first property holds. The problem with that example is that it violates the second property.

To investigate collective practical knowledge further, consider the following example. Suppose two agents want to meet and jointly decide to meet at central station. Do they collectively know how to meet at central station? In typical cases, one agent does not know about the other's exact whereabouts. In particular, one agent may not be able to draw a route on a city map for the other agent to get to central station. But, this does not matter: as long as the agents commonly know that each knows how to get to central station, I propose that they collectively know how to meet at central station.

To make these considerations precise, consider the following example. Suppose there are two decks of cards face down on the table, one for Edo and one for Fae, and they simultaneously pick a card from their deck. Before doing so, however, they each pick a pair of special glasses. These special glasses allow any agent to see through one particular suit. So, if an agent is wearing the hearts glasses, then she is able to see through hearts, that is, this allows her to identify the jack of hearts, the 2 of hearts, etc. Edo and Fae each take a pair of these glasses and put them on. As a matter of fact, Edo took the hearts glasses and Fae took the spades glasses. Suppose neither of them knows the other's particular type of special glasses.[66] Do Edo and Fae collectively know how to pick two jacks?

Figure 4.5 represents a simplified version of this complex scenario; let me explain the figure. We let e and f stand for Edo and Fae respectively, and let $\mathcal{G}_3$ depict the group consisting of Edo and Fae. In this simplified version, the face-down cards only include the jack and queen of hearts and spades, and the box of glasses only contains the pairs of glasses associated with spades or hearts. The stit model represents four possible moments m_1–m_4, each of which represents a particular distribution of the special glasses. For instance, m_1 represents the actual case where Edo wears the hearts glasses and Fae wears the spades glasses. At each moment, the figure depicts the actions available to each agent, for example, Edo is able to pick the queen of spades (since $K^k_{\spadesuit Q} \in Act_e^{m_k}$ for every m_k, where $k = 1, 2, 3,$ or 4). In addition, the figure explicitly states several histories. In particular, m_2/h_2 represents the scenario where both Edo and Fae wear the hearts glasses and where each of them picks the queen of hearts.

Let us consider the epistemic state of Edo in more detail. The epistemic indistinguishability of Edo is labelled by e and the one of Fae is labelled by f. Notice that Edo can distinguish moment m_1 from moment m_3: for all indices m_1/h and m_3/h' we have $m_1/h \not\sim_e m_3/h'$. Moreover, at m_1/h_1 Edo does not know that he is picking a jack: after all, $m_1/h_1 \sim_e m_2/h'_2$ and $m_2/h'_2 \in K^2_{\spadesuit Q}$.[67] This is formally expressed by the fact that $m_1/h_1 \not\models \mathsf{K}_e[e\ \mathsf{stit}]q_J$. It may help to add that the information set of Edo at index m_1/h_1 can be viewed as the

[66] Although it is a rather artificial example, it will point to a natural concern: even though my companion's implicit practical knowledge is opaque to me, this need not undermine our collective practical knowledge. The artificial example is meant to isolate this particular concern.

[67] Recall the conventions that the information sets can be viewed as unions of action tokens and that the indistinguishability relation is closed under transitivity.

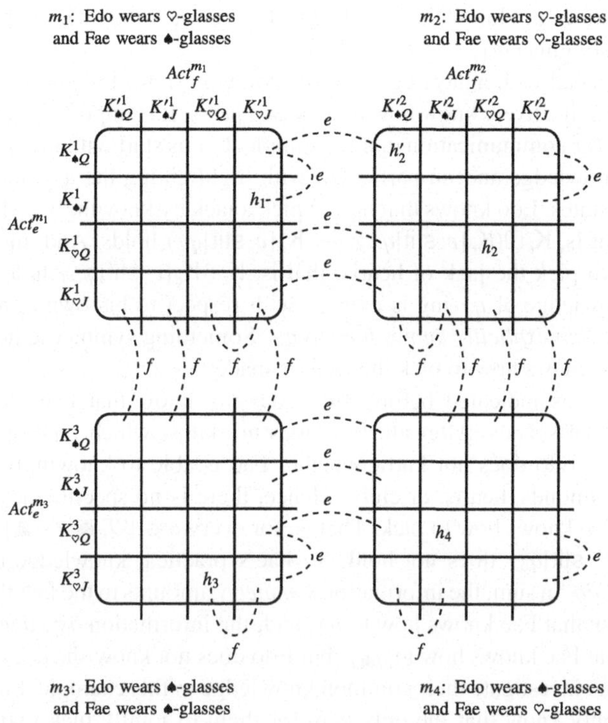

Fig. 4.5 A simplified epistemic stit model that represents Edo and Fae's joint decision problem

union $K^1_{\spadesuit J} \cup K^1_{\spadesuit Q} \cup K^2_{\spadesuit J} \cup K^2_{\spadesuit Q}$. In contrast, at m_2/h_2 Edo knows that he is picking a queen: his information set at m_2/h_2 is given by $K^1_{\heartsuit Q} \cup K^2_{\heartsuit Q}$. Therefore, we have $m_2/h_2 \vDash \mathsf{K}_e[e\ \mathsf{stit}]q_Q$. Hence, by similar reasoning, we get $m_1/h_1 \vDash \Diamond\mathsf{K}_e[e\ \mathsf{stit}]q_Q$.

Let us investigate the individual knowing-how in this example. Consider index m_1/h_1. Edo is wearing the hearts glasses and Fae is wearing the spades glasses. If we concentrate on Edo's epistemic uncertainty, the reasoning above demonstrates that Edo knows how to pick a queen. After all, we have $m_1/h_1 \vDash \mathsf{K}_e\Diamond\mathsf{K}_e[e\ \mathsf{stit}]q_Q$. In contrast, Edo does not know how to pick the jack of spades: since Edo cannot distinguish between indices m_1/h_1 and m_2/h'_2, it follows that Edo does not knowingly pick the jack of spades even though he does so unknowingly. In sum: at m_1/h_1 it is easy to verify that Edo knows how to pick the queen of hearts, yet he does not know how to pick the jack of spades.

Let us move on to higher-order knowledge. What does Edo know about Fae's individual knowing-how? By symmetry, similar reasoning as above demonstrates that at m_1/h_1 Fae knows how to pick the jack of spades, but does not know how to pick the jack of hearts. By analogy, at m_2/h'_2 the converse holds: Fae knows how to pick the jack of hearts but does not know how to pick the jack of spades. Hence, at

m_1/h_1, Edo does not know that Fae knows how to pick the jack of spades—since he cannot distinguish m_1/h_1 from m_2/h'_2.

Let us proceed with analysing *collective* knowing-how. I would like to say that Edo and Fae collectively know how to pick two jacks. It is important to note that we do not allow for communication in this example. Let us start with investigating their individual knowledge and, in particular, with highlighting the asymmetry in their information states. Edo knows that he can pick a jack by knowingly picking the jack of hearts, that is, $\mathsf{K}_e\Box(\mathsf{K}_e[e\ \mathsf{stit}]q_{\heartsuit J} \rightarrow \mathsf{K}_e[e\ \mathsf{stit}]q_J)$ holds. And, moreover, Edo knows how to pick the jack of hearts, that is, $\mathsf{K}_e\Diamond\mathsf{K}_e[e\ \mathsf{stit}]q_{\heartsuit J}$ holds. So, Edo's practical knowledge of q_J-ing is explicit with respect to his own knowledge. Or, equivalently, *Edo explicitly knows how* to q_J. Something symmetric holds for Fae: she explicitly knows how to pick the jack of spades.

In contrast, as indicated before, Edo does not know that Fae knows how to pick the jack of spades. After all, Edo does not know which type of glasses Fae is wearing, so Edo does not know whether Fae is able to knowingly pick a jack of spades, diamonds, hearts, or clubs. Hence, there is no specific jack which Edo knows that Fae knows how to pick. That is, for every $\circ \in \{\heartsuit, \spadesuit, \diamondsuit, \clubsuit\}$ the formula $\mathsf{K}_e\mathsf{K}_f\Diamond\mathsf{K}_f[f\ \mathsf{stit}]q_{\circ J}$ does not hold. So Fae's practical knowledge of q_J-ing is *implicit for Edo*. In sum, the information *symmetry* amounts to the fact that both Edo and Fae know that Fae knows how to q_J; and, the information *asymmetry* amounts to the fact that Fae knows how to $q_{\spadesuit J}$, but Edo does not know she does.

Now, let us investigate their common knowledge in this example. First, note that they commonly know that the only way for them to jointly pick two jacks is by each picking a jack. That is, $\mathsf{C}_{\mathcal{G}_3}\Box([e\ \mathsf{stit}]q_J \wedge [f\ \mathsf{stit}]q_J \leftrightarrow [\mathcal{G}_3\ \mathsf{stit}]p_{JJ})$ holds. This means that group $\mathcal{G}_3$ commonly knows that $[\mathcal{G}_3\ \mathsf{stit}]p_{JJ}$ divides into parts $[e\ \mathsf{stit}]q_J$ and $[f\ \mathsf{stit}]q_J$. Second, observe that it is commonly known that each of them knows how to play her part. That is, for example, $\mathsf{C}_{\mathcal{G}_3}\mathsf{K}_e\Diamond\mathsf{K}_e[e\ \mathsf{stit}]q_J$. After all, Fae knows that Edo is able to identify a jack, since she knows that he is wearing a pair of special glasses—despite not knowing which one.

We arrive at a complex picture of the refinements that justify collective know-how in this example:

Observation 4.4 In the discussed example, we say that group $\mathcal{G}_3$, consisting of e and f, knows how to φ because the following conditions hold:

1. $\mathsf{C}_{\mathcal{G}_3}\Box([e\ \mathsf{stit}]q_J \wedge [f\ \mathsf{stit}]q_J \leftrightarrow [\mathcal{G}_3\ \mathsf{stit}]p_{JJ})$: group $\mathcal{G}_3$ commonly knows that $[\mathcal{G}_3\ \mathsf{stit}]p_{JJ}$ divides into parts $[e\ \mathsf{stit}]q_J$ and $[f\ \mathsf{stit}]q_J$;
2. $\mathsf{C}_{\mathcal{G}_3}\mathsf{K}_e\Diamond\mathsf{K}_e[e\ \mathsf{stit}]q_J$, and similarly for f: group $\mathcal{G}_3$ commonly knows that each of its members knows how to carry out her part;
3. $\mathsf{K}_e\Box(\mathsf{K}_e[e\ \mathsf{stit}]q_{\heartsuit J} \rightarrow \mathsf{K}_e[e\ \mathsf{stit}]q_J)$: Edo knows that there is a proper refinement $q_{\heartsuit J}$ of his part q_J (and something similar holds for f and $q_{\spadesuit J}$);
4. $\mathsf{K}_e\Diamond\mathsf{K}_e[e\ \mathsf{stit}]q_{\heartsuit J}$: Edo knows how to perform his $q_{\heartsuit J}$ (and something similar holds for f and $q_{\spadesuit J}$).

The action hierarchy in this definition has *three* levels, the collective action (given by $[\mathcal{G}_3\ \mathsf{stit}]p_{JJ}$), the division (jointly expressed by $[e\ \mathsf{stit}]q_J$ and $[f\ \mathsf{stit}]q_J$), and the individual refinements (given by $[e \text{ stit}]q_{\heartsuit J}$ and $[f \text{ stit}]q_{\spadesuit J}$).[68] Group $\mathcal{G}_3$ commonly knows that $[e \text{ stit}]q_J \wedge [f \text{ stit}]q_J$ is a refinement of $[\mathcal{G}_3 \text{ stit}]p_{JJ}$, though not a proper refinement. This means that $\mathcal{G}_3$ collectively *implicitly* knows how to p_{JJ}. Each member knows that q_- is a proper refinement of her q_J and knows how to q_-. This means that each member *explicitly* knows how to play her own part q_J. In general this individual practical knowledge need not be explicit. Given the characterization of individual know-how (Theorem 4.3), we can simplify the concept of collective know-how to the following:

Definition 4.6 (Collective Know-how) To aid readability, I present my definition of collective know-how for a two-agent group $\mathcal{G} = \{i, j\}$. We say that $\mathcal{G}$ *knows how to* φ if and only if there are[69] φ_i and φ_j such that the following two conditions hold:

1. $\mathsf{C}_{\mathcal{G}}\Box([i \text{ stit}]\varphi_i \wedge [j \text{ stit}]\varphi_j \leftrightarrow [\mathcal{G} \text{ stit}]\varphi)$: group $\mathcal{G}$ commonly knows that $[\mathcal{G} \text{ stit}]\varphi$ divides into parts $[i \text{ stit}]\varphi_i$ and $[j \text{ stit}]\varphi_j$;
(Common Division)
2. $\mathsf{C}_{\mathcal{G}}\mathsf{K}_i\Diamond\mathsf{K}_i[i \text{ stit}]\varphi_i$ and $\mathsf{C}_{\mathcal{G}}\mathsf{K}_j\Diamond\mathsf{K}_j[j \text{ stit}]\varphi_j$: group $\mathcal{G}$ commonly knows that each member knows how to play her part.
(Part Know How)

One may ask whether the 'part know how' condition is necessary for collective knowing-how. To see that it is, reconsider the example of Ann and Bob (see Fig. 4.2). Recall that the 'common division' condition is met in this example, but Ann and Bob do not collectively know how to pick two spades. I argued that this is due to the fact that Ann does not know how to play her part and, as a consequence, Ann and Bob do not commonly know that each knows how to play her part. Or, equivalently, this means that if the 'part know how' condition is violated then the group does not collectively know how to pick two spades. Therefore, the 'part know how' condition is necessary for collective knowing-how.

One may think that the biconditional in the 'common division' condition is too strong. That is, one may think that the left-to-right implication suffices. Can this condition be relaxed accordingly? Suppose we would only require the left-to-right implication: $\mathsf{C}_{\mathcal{G}}\Box([i \text{ stit}]\varphi_i \wedge [j \text{ stit}]\varphi_j \rightarrow [\mathcal{G} \text{ stit}]\varphi)$. It is useful to briefly consider a standard coordination game: to stick with the chapter's type of examples, reconsider the example of Chris and Dee, where each draws a card from a face-up deck of cards. Do Chris and Dee know how to pick an identical face

---

68 It may be helpful to point out that I will present a hierarchical task network that represents these levels in Sect. 4.6.1.

69 It is important to note that this existential quantification cannot be captured in the current logic. This means that collective know-how is not straightforwardly characterizable in the current logic. In the remainder of this section it will be shown that, under the assumption that (Unif-H) holds, collective know-how is characterizable.

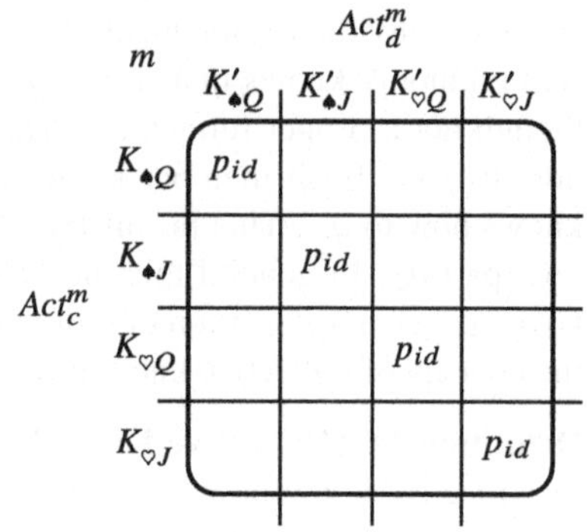

Fig. 4.6 A simplified epistemic stit model that represents Chris and Dee's joint coordination problem of picking an identical face card

card? (Recall that we do not allow for any communication.)[70] Figure 4.6 presents a simplified stit model of this example, where p_{id} expresses that they pick an identical face card.[71] Note that the left-to-right implication holds since Chris and Dee commonly know that if each would pick a jack, then they would be jointly picking an identical face card—formally, $\mathsf{C}_{\mathcal{G}_2}\Box([c \text{ stit}]q_J \wedge [d \text{ stit}]q_J \rightarrow [\mathcal{G}_2 \text{ stit}]p_{id})$ holds. Moreover, note that they commonly know that each knows how to pick a jack, which means that the 'part know how' condition holds. However, in this example, the group faces a coordination problem that typically cannot be solved without prior communication. The members are unable to effectively coordinate their individual actions.[72] Therefore, the group does not know how to pick an identical face card on my view. This coordination problem hence indicates that the one-way implication is insufficient for a theory of collective know-how that applies to cases where agreement is problematic and communication is hindered.[73]

It is important to note that this indicates a divergence from individual practical knowledge. In the example of the face-up deck of cards (Fig. 4.3), Bob knows how to pick a face card, even though there are multiple ways of realizing this. After all, for the individual case, we were satisfied with the implication of the form

---

[70] The game resembles the driving game discussed by Lewis (1969, pp. 6, 44–45—see also Sect. 2.2).

[71] Note that Chris's and Dee's individual situation is similar to that of Bob, which is represented in Fig. 4.3.

[72] Although Chris and Dee are not able to solve their coordination game without prior communication, people are often quite effective at solving such coordination problems. Game theorists typically argue that concepts such as *salience*, *focal points*, and *framing* are key to understanding the coordination abilities of non-communicating agents (see Bacharach, 2006; Gauthier, 1975; Lewis, 1969; Schelling, 1960; Sugden, 1993, 1995, 2003). My notion of collective know-how is best viewed as the ability of a group of non-communicating agents that does not rely on such additional concepts.

[73] It is unclear how ATL-based paradigms deal with this difficulty (Ågotnes et al., 2015; Jamroga & Ågotnes, 2007; with the possible exception of Hawke, 2017). I believe that this lacuna is an artefact of the fact that these formalisms only mention two levels: the goal φ and a (maximally specific) strategy s.

$\mathsf{K}_i\Box(\mathsf{K}_i[i\ \mathsf{stit}]\psi \rightarrow \mathsf{K}_i[i\ \mathsf{stit}]\varphi)$ instead of a biconditional (see Definition 4.5). The divergence is due to the fact that an individual agent is able to decide to pick the jack of spades and then execute this plan. In the absence of communication, a group may not be able to do this. (At the end of this section I will discuss how communication and agreements may help improve a group's abilities.)

Nonetheless, the problem with a one-way implication in the collective case is not that the collective act can be realized in *multiple* ways, although the problem does not arise if there is a unique way to realize the collective act. After all, in the example of two face-up decks of cards, Chris and Dee collectively know how to pick two spades cards, which can be realized in multiple ways. The crucial condition is that when each member of the group plays her alleged part then they jointly succeed in realizing the collective act. The difficulty emphasized in the coordination problem is that playing their alleged parts may not be enough to ensure that they pick an identical face card.[74]

This discussion brings us to the following question: what is a member's *part* in a collective action? There seem to be at least two ways to describe this.[75] Let $[\mathcal{G}\ \mathsf{stit}]\varphi$ be a collective act description. First, one may require that the collective action reduces to individual parts φ_i, one for each $i \in \mathcal{G}$. That is, $\mathcal{G}$ jointly brings about φ if and only if each member i plays her part φ_i—this is formally expressed by $\Box([\mathcal{G}\ \mathsf{stit}]\varphi \leftrightarrow \bigwedge_{i\in\mathcal{G}}[i\ \mathsf{stit}]\varphi_i)$. Second, one may simply say that a member i plays her part in the collective action if and only if she performs her component individual action of an instance of this collective action, that is, if and only if $\langle i\ \mathsf{stit}\rangle[\mathcal{G}\ \mathsf{stit}]\varphi$. Or, equivalently, playing one's part means refraining from obstructing the collective act. I prove that, under the assumption that (Unif-H) holds, when $\mathcal{G}$ collectively knows how to φ, these readings are equivalent:[76]

Theorem 4.4 *Let $\mathcal{M}$ be an epistemic stit model, and let m/h be an index. Assume that $\mathcal{M}$ satisfies (Unif-H). Suppose $\mathcal{G}$ collectively knows how to φ, as witnessed by $(\varphi_i)_{i\in\mathcal{G}}$. Then*

$$\mathcal{M}, m/h \models \mathsf{C}_{\mathcal{G}}\Box \bigwedge_{i\in\mathcal{G}}([i\ \mathsf{stit}]\varphi_i \leftrightarrow \langle i\ \mathsf{stit}\rangle[\mathcal{G}\ \mathsf{stit}]\varphi), \qquad (*)$$

and

$$\mathcal{M}, m/h \models \mathsf{C}_{\mathcal{G}}\Box \bigwedge_{i\in\mathcal{G}}(\mathsf{K}_i[i\ \mathsf{stit}]\varphi_i \leftrightarrow \mathsf{K}_i\langle i\ \mathsf{stit}\rangle[\mathcal{G}\ \mathsf{stit}]\varphi). \qquad (**)$$

[74] This observation aligns with my work in Chap. 3. The connections will be emphasized by Observation 4.5 below and the associated discussion.

[75] These ideas originate from my previous work Tamminga and Duijf (2017); see also Chap. 3 and, more specifically, Sects. 3.3–3.4. In Chap. 5 I develop a more demanding account of participation.

[76] To be precise, (Unif-H) is used to prove (∗∗) below.

Given these equivalences, it can be proven that collective know-how can be characterized. The final picture of the refinements that justify collective know-how can be simplified accordingly:

Corollary 4.1 (Characterization of Collective Know-how) *To aid readability, I present this corollary on the characterization of collective know-how for a two-agent group* $\mathcal{G} = \{i, j\}$. *Assume (Unif-H). Then group* $\mathcal{G}$ *knows how to* φ *if and only if the following two conditions hold:*

1. $\mathsf{C}_{\mathcal{G}}\Box(\langle i \text{ stit}\rangle[\mathcal{G} \text{ stit}]\varphi \wedge \langle j \text{ stit}\rangle[\mathcal{G} \text{ stit}]\varphi \leftrightarrow [\mathcal{G} \text{ stit}]\varphi)$*: group* $\mathcal{G}$ *commonly knows that* $[\mathcal{G} \text{ stit}]\varphi$ *divides into parts;*

(Effectivity)

2. $\mathsf{C}_{\mathcal{G}}\mathsf{K}_i\Diamond\mathsf{K}_i\langle i \text{ stit}\rangle[\mathcal{G} \text{ stit}]\varphi$*, and similarly for* j*:* $\mathcal{G}$ *commonly knows that each of them knows how to carry out her part.*

(Part Know-how)

It is important to highlight that the problematic existential quantification of my initial definition of collective know-how has disappeared (see Footnote 69). The theorem establishes that when a group commonly knows that the group action $[\mathcal{G} \text{ stit}]\varphi$ divides into parts, then these parts can be simply expressed by $\langle i \text{ stit}\rangle[\mathcal{G} \text{ stit}]\varphi$, and no reference to the initial division, that is, $(\varphi_i)_{i\in\mathcal{G}}$, is needed.

The corollary highlights that my epistemic stit logic is able to characterize collective know-how. By providing the formal framework, I aim to contribute to theories of collective know-how by clarifying and specifying particular elements needed to overcome the discussed conceptual difficulties. Moreover, my current logic is able to express the complex notion of collective know-how that I defended, despite it being unable to express the distinction between explicit and implicit practical knowledge.

It may be useful to explain why the first condition has been renamed 'effectivity' when it was previously called 'common division'. In light of Theorem 4.4, given collective know-how, each member's part is clear: it is characterized by $\langle i \text{ stit}\rangle[\mathcal{G} \text{ stit}]\varphi$. This means that the common division is also evident. This observation suggests that the first condition means that the group commonly knows that if each member carries out her alleged part, then they will jointly *succeed* in guaranteeing φ. Because it is important that this common distribution is effective, it seems apt to rename the condition 'effectivity'. Under this interpretation, the first condition does not require a common division but it does require common knowledge of *effectivity*: the group commonly knows that its members can effectively ensure that together they guarantee φ by each member playing her part.

The characterization of collective know-how can be used to show that there are several ways in which a group may lack practical knowledge. It naturally reveals ways in which communication and agreements may help to improve a group's abilities; I will briefly discuss four of these opportunities. First, the group may lack an effective common division. This means that there are multiple ways in which the group may achieve its goal φ and that these constitute a coordination problem. In the absence of communication, the group fails to collectively know how to φ. In Chap. 3

I studied cases in which communication is possible and agreement unproblematic. We saw that in such cases there are good plans and bad plans. One of the critical conditions of a good plan is that it is interchangeable (recall Sects. 3.3–3.4, more specifically, Definition 3.5). It can be proven that the effectivity condition relates to interchangeability:

Observation 4.5 (Interchangeability & Effectivity) Let S be a game model, let $\mathcal{G}$ be a group of agents, and let φ be a formula. The following are equivalent:

1. $S \vDash \Box([\mathcal{G}\ \mathsf{stit}]\varphi \leftrightarrow \bigwedge_{i\in\mathcal{G}}\langle i\ \mathsf{stit}\rangle[\mathcal{G}\ \mathsf{stit}]\varphi)$;
2. $P_{\mathcal{G}} := \{a_{\mathcal{G}} \in A_{\mathcal{G}} \mid S, a \vDash [\mathcal{G}\ \mathsf{stit}]\varphi\}$ is interchangeable.

To solve its coordination problem the group should agree on a good group plan to achieve its goal. As argued in Sect. 3.3, a group plan, once agreed upon, coordinates the individual actions of the members of the group: it allows them to act *simultaneously* and *unconditionally*, in the full belief that every group member acts according to the plan. An interchangeable and optimal group plan *guarantees* that if every group member acts according to the plan, then the group itself fulfils its collective obligation (see the end of Sect. 3.4.2 for an informal proof of this conditional and the role of interchangeability). The above correspondence implies that when group $\mathcal{G}$ collectively knows how to φ then the group plan expressed by $[\mathcal{G}\ \mathsf{stit}]\varphi$ is interchangeable. More specifically, collective know-how requires that it be commonly known that the corresponding group plan is interchangeable. So, when the group lacks an effective common division, it can solve this by agreeing on an effective and interchangeable group plan.

Second, the group may lack *common knowledge* of the fact that the division is effective. Or, equivalently, the collective action $[\mathcal{G}\ \mathsf{stit}]\varphi$ might, as a matter of fact, depict an interchangeable plan, yet this fact may not be commonly known. Besides agreeing on a good group plan, to retain common knowledge of effectivity the group could refine its public knowledge through communication. By sharing their private information the group members may learn that the effectivity condition is satisfied. In this way the group retains common knowledge of effectivity without agreeing on a good group plan.

Third, one or more group members may lack the relevant individual know-how. This means that the 'part know-how' condition is violated. This failure can be overcome by improving a group member's individual know-how. While the previous break-downs required communication or agreement, this failure could be overcome without any communication, for instance by practising in solitude. Communication and agreement may, nonetheless, help to address this issue. The defective group member may learn from others, through communication, how to carry out her part.

Fourth, all members might have the relevant individual know-how, yet together they may lack common knowledge that this is the case (even if the effectivity condition is satisfied). This defect is typically resolved by publicly announcing one's capacities and individual know-how. In this way the group retains common knowledge of part know-how without improving any member's individual know-how.

A study of when and how agents can effectively jointly communicate to adopt these improvement mechanisms has to be left for another occasion.

4.6 Related Artificial Intelligence Research

I have presented a conceptual analysis of collective know-how using an epistemic extension of stit theory. The key elements of my conceptual analysis are refinements, action hierarchies, knowledge, knowingly doing, and abilities. In short, my theory of a group's collectively knowing how to φ amounts to this: (1) they commonly know that φ divides into members' parts; and (2) they commonly know that each of them knows how to play her part. In this section I will relate my work to research in artificial intelligence.

4.6.1 AI Planning and Hierarchical Planning

One of the subfields of artificial intelligence is concerned with automated planning (see the textbook by Ghallab et al., 2004). My ideas on action hierarchies naturally relate to one of the subfields of automated planning, viz. *hierarchical* planning.[77] Wikipedia contributors write:

> Planning problems are specified in the *hierarchical task network* approach by providing a set of tasks, which can be:
>
> 1. primitive tasks, which roughly correspond to the actions of STRIPS;
> 2. compound tasks, which can be seen as composed of a set of simpler tasks;
> 3. goal tasks, which roughly correspond to the goals of STRIPS, but are more general.[78]
>
> ...Constraints among tasks are expressed in the form of networks, called task networks. A task network is a set of tasks and constraints among them. Such a network can be used as the precondition for another compound or goal task to be feasible. (Wikipedia Contributors, 2017, emphasis added)

Primitive tasks are actions that can be executed, compound tasks are composed of sequences of actions, and goal tasks are tasks that are done to satisfy a condition. A stit-formula $[i \text{ stit}]\varphi$ can best be compared to a goal task that needs to be done

[77] Other subfields include conformant planning, (partially observable) Markov decision processes, and multi-agent planning.

[78] STRIPS, short for STanford Research Institute Problem Solver, is a problem-solving program that has been designed "to find some composition of operators that transforms a given initial world model into one that satisfies some stated goal condition" (Fikes & Nilsson, 1971). One particular formalism that has been widely used to represent hierarchical task networks is TAEMS (Decker, 1995; Horling et al., 1999).

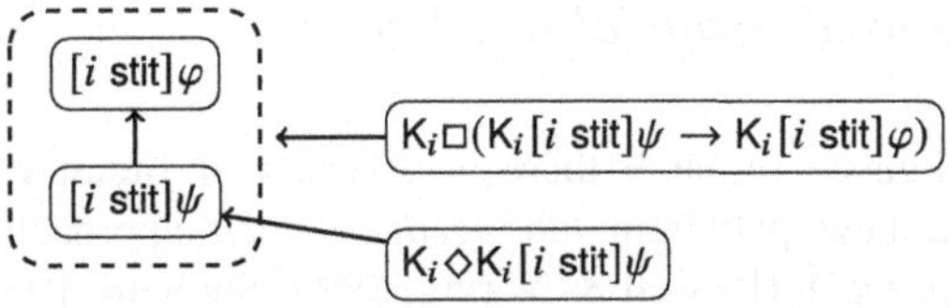

Fig. 4.7 A goal-based hierarchical task network depicting individual know-how

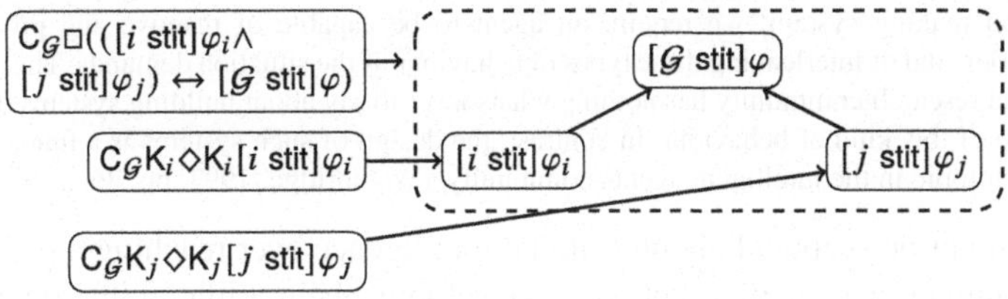

Fig. 4.8 A multi-agent goal-based hierarchical task network depicting collective know-how

for agent i to satisfy φ. My stit framework therefore naturally relates to goal-based hierarchical networks.

For individual know-how, the constraints of such a goal-based hierarchical network that I am mostly interested in are refinements (Sects. 4.3.1 and 4.3.3). That is, I am mostly interested in constraints between goal tasks $[i \text{ stit}]\varphi$ and $[i \text{ stit}]\psi$ that are of the following sort: guaranteeing ψ is a way to achieve φ. More specifically, to possess the relevant individual know-how, the agent is required to *know* that guaranteeing ψ is a way to achieve φ. So a goal-based hierarchical network that represents individual know-how consists of a network of goal tasks such that a link between two goal tasks signifies that the individual agent knows that the former goal task is a refinement of the latter goal task. Figure 4.7 depicts a goal-based hierarchical network for individual know-how.

My discussions of collective know-how highlighted that a corresponding multi-agent goal-based hierarchical network could consist of several layers: (i) a collective goal $[\mathcal{G} \text{ stit}]\varphi$, (ii) a division $([i \text{ stit}]\varphi_i)_{i\in\mathcal{G}}$, and (iii) a collection of refinements $[i \text{ stit}]\psi_i$ (Sect. 4.5). The constraints between these layers vary: it should be commonly known that $[\mathcal{G} \text{ stit}]\varphi$ divides into $([i \text{ stit}]\varphi_i)_{i\in\mathcal{G}}$, each member i should know that $[i \text{ stit}]\psi_i$ refines $[i \text{ stit}]\varphi_i$, and each member i should be able to execute $[i \text{ stit}]\psi_i$. This means that collective know-how may be represented by such a complex multi-agent goal-based hierarchical network. Figure 4.8 depicts a simplified two-agent goal-based hierarchical task network for collective know-how, where the goal-based hierarchical task networks for the members' individual know-how are suppressed.

4.6.2 Agent-Based Artificial Intelligence

In artificial intelligence research there is a strand of literature that recognizes and argues for a new paradigm: an *agent-oriented* approach, rather than an object-oriented approach (Russell & Norvig, 1995; Shoham, 1993; Wooldridge & Jennings, 1995; Yu, 2001). Michael Wooldridge writes:

> But agents are not simply objects by another name. This is because an agent is a rational decision making system: we require an agent to be capable of reactive and pro-active behaviour, and of interleaving these types of behaviour as the situation demands. The object-oriented research community has nothing whatsoever to say about building systems that are capable of this kind of behaviour. In contrast, the design of such systems is a fundamental research topic in the intelligent agents community. (Wooldridge, 1997, pp. 26–27)[79]

One might be sceptical about artificial intelligence ever reaching a point equivalent to human-level agency, but recent developments in artificial intelligence have shown that it may well surpass human intelligence (at least in some domains).[80] It may therefore make sense to treat such artificial intelligent systems as agents, rather than objects. Regardless of these recent breakthroughs, an agent-based approach may help us *design* complex systems. Nicholas Jennings argues for two central claims:

> **The Adequacy Hypothesis.** Agent-oriented approaches can significantly enhance our ability to model, design and build complex, distributed software systems.
> **The Establishment Hypothesis.** As well as being suitable for designing and building complex systems, the agent-oriented approach will succeed as a mainstream software engineering paradigm. (Jennings, 2000, p. 278)

Issues concerning cooperation and competition are central to multi-agent systems. It is therefore vital for the agent-based approach to artificial intelligence to study action and knowledge in a precise and formal way. To highlight the impact of my characterization and discussion of collective know-how, I will briefly mention some implications for this agent-based approach.

First, when designing a multi-agent system, one typically uses model-checking techniques to check whether some property Q holds for the system (Alur et al., 2002; van der Hoek & Wooldridge, 2003). Perhaps you want to check whether adversaries collectively know how to break a user's encryption. To check for this, one constructs a model of the multi-agent system and then verifies whether the adversaries possess the relevant collective know-how. An adequate account of collective know-how is thus needed for such model-checking techniques, which is exactly what this chapter

[79] Compare Shoham (1993, p. 52): "Most often, when people in AI use the term 'agent', they refer to an entity that functions continuously and autonomously in an environment in which other processes take place and other agents exist. This is perhaps the only property that is assumed uniformly by those in AI who use the term. The sense of 'autonomy' is not precise, but the term is taken to mean that the agents' activities do not require constant human guidance or intervention."

[80] In recent years, artificial intelligence has surpassed humans in *Go* (Metz, 2016), something that was long thought practically impossible, in *Jeopardy!* (Markoff, 2011), and in *Poker* (Metz, 2017), which is relevant because it involves uncertainty.

is about: analysing the concept of collective know-how and accurately formalizing it.

Second, intelligent agents inside a multi-agent system are typically modelled using mental constructs such as beliefs, desires, and intentions.[81] This has given rise to several BDI-based[82] theories of intelligent agents (Cohen & Levesque, 1990; Rao & Georgeff, 1991, to cite a few). From the perspective of the members of a group of intelligent agents $\mathcal{G}$, it seems that an important condition for adopting a collective goal φ is that they collectively know how to φ. If a group of agents does not collectively know how to φ, then what do they gain from adopting φ as their collective goal? Even if collectively knowing how to φ is not a necessary condition for adopting the collective goal φ, it would be an important property. My characterization of collective know-how allows individual intelligent agents to reason about their joint capabilities (for instance, using the complete logical system of Theorem 4.1).

4.6.3 Logics of Knowledge and Action

I am certainly not the first person to present a formal theory of group knowledge and group action. The literature on group knowledge typically distinguishes between three types: everybody in $\mathcal{G}$ knows φ, typically expressed by $\mathsf{E}_{\mathcal{G}}\varphi$, distributed knowledge that φ, expressed by $\mathsf{D}_{\mathcal{G}}\varphi$, and common knowledge that φ, expressed by $\mathsf{C}_{\mathcal{G}}\varphi$ (Fagin et al., 2003; Meyer & van der Hoek, 1995). To situate my theory of collective know-how within the existing literature on logics of group action and group knowledge, next I discuss two dominant views in light of this standard distinction.

First, Herzig and Troquard (2006, p. 210) "assume that a coalition can ensure φ if by *sharing their knowledge* and acting together they can ensure φ". This is why their notion of collective know-how relies on *distributed* knowledge. This assumption is problematic for two reasons. First, taking distributed knowledge as a foundation implies that a coalition collectively knows how to φ if there is a way for its members to communicate such that they know how to φ afterwards. But the whole point of my theory of collective know-how is that its members are required to know this *before* communicating. After all, distributive knowledge merely marks the possibility, or potentiality, that the know-how will become actual, not that a coalition collectively knows how to φ here and now. Second, I agree with Ågotnes and Wáng (2016,

[81] Shoham (1993, p. 52) writes: "An agent is an entity whose state is viewed as consisting of mental components such as beliefs, capabilities, choices, and commitments. These components are defined in a precise fashion, and stand in rough correspondence to their common sense counterparts. In this view, therefore, agenthood is in the mind of the programmer: What makes any hardware or software component an agent is precisely the fact that one has chosen to analyse and control it in these mental terms."

[82] 'BDI' stands for 'beliefs, desires, and intentions'.

p. 31) that it is a mistake to think that "something is distributed knowledge in a group if the agents in the group could get to know it after some (perhaps unlimited) communications between them". So, it is even doubtful that distributed knowledge is the correct formalization of "sharing our knowledge".

Second, Ågotnes et al. (2015, p. 575–576) analyse the notion of "knowing how to play", for the collective case, by appealing to "several different 'modes' in which they can know the right uniform strategy", referring to mutual, distributed, or common knowledge. My conceptual analysis gives two reasons why this categorization is not refined enough. First, when a group collectively knows how to φ then its members commonly know that this divides into members' parts, but the group need not commonly know the exact uniform strategy that each member employs. So, it is not common knowledge of the right strategy that is essential, but common knowledge of *an effective division*. Second, although collectively knowing how to φ implies distributively knowing the right uniform strategy, the converse does not hold. (A case in which neither of us knows their own part, yet each knows the other's part, proves this point.) So, although collective know-how is a case of distributive knowledge, it is of a particular kind: each member is required to know how to carry out *her own part*. These observations jointly show that neither common nor distributed knowledge captures the intricacies of collective know-how.

In conclusion, justified by the discussions of various examples, I have proposed a characterization of collective know-how that contains elements that have not been recognized in the existing literature. First, my characterization uses action hierarchies. My final definition (Definition 4.6) refers to *three* levels in such action hierarchies: a collective goal, a refinement that specifies each members' part, and a set of individual refinements. In contrast, existing theories typically rely on two levels: the goal, and the strategy or action type. So, although collective practical knowledge has been investigated before in other formal frameworks, its interplay with action hierarchies has been given little weight or attention. I have shown that this emphasis is useful for the individual case and essential for the collective case. In the individual case, it gives a principled distinction between implicit and explicit practical knowledge. In the collective case, it is needed to distinguish between the members' individual practical knowledge and the collective practical knowledge. Second, existing accounts typically rely on either distributed or common knowledge. However, I argued that neither common nor distributed knowledge captures the intricacies of collective know-how.

Although my study adds to the existing literature, it still leaves interesting questions unanswered. First, what is the logic of collective know-how? My formalism can be used to uncover logical properties of collective know-how. For instance, in the next section I will show that the logic of collective know-how is not monotonic (cf. Wang, 2018). Second, although Theorem 4.1 provides a finite axiomatization of epistemic stit logic, it remains an open question whether this logic and the corresponding model-checking problem are decidable (important pointers include the work by Herzig & Schwarzentruber, 2008; van der Hoek & Wooldridge, 2003; and Payette, 2014).

4.7 Discussion: Informational Responsibilty System

The overall aim of this book is to shed light on the existence of responsibility voids and collective responsibility problems. As highlighted in Sect. 3.6, a theory of obligations, both individual and collective, is crucial for a theory of responsibility. In this final section I aim to briefly investigate individual and collective obligations and responsibility from the perspective of my theory of practical knowledge.

It is natural to distinguish between objective obligations and subjective obligations. Subjective obligations take into account the epistemic state of the agent: roughly stated, an agent fulfils her subjective obligations if and only if she performs an action that is the best option given her information or epistemic state.[83] The distinction is based on the intuition that an agent can only be subjectively obliged to do something if she possesses the relevant knowledge. Inspired by the dictum that 'ought implies can', my epistemic account of individual and collective ability gives rise to the requirement that if an agent has a subjective obligation to do φ then she has to know how to φ.[84] So practical knowledge is essential for subjective obligations. In this section I will explore the implications of my account of individual and collective know-how without developing a detailed account of subjective obligations.[85]

To showcase how my theory of individual know-how may shed light on individual *subjective obligations*, let us consider a well-known example: the miners' problem. Niko Kolodny and John MacFarlane write:

> Ten miners are trapped either in shaft A or in shaft B, but we do not know which. Flood waters threaten to flood the shafts. We have enough sandbags to block one shaft, but not both. If we block one shaft, all the water will go into the other shaft, killing any miners inside it. If we block neither shaft, both shafts will fill halfway with water, and just one miner, the lowest in the shaft, will be killed. (Kolodny & MacFarlane, 2010)[86]

[83] These should not be conflated with obligations regarding the epistemic state of the agent, which are guided by epistemic norms, such as belief consistency.

[84] The 'ought implies can' principle has often been ascribed to Immanuel Kant, although this attribution is debated. Vranas (2007) gives a defence of the principle, and writes: "I understand the claim that an agent can do something as the claim that the agent has both the ability and the opportunity to do the thing. The agent has the ability to do the thing in the sense of having the requisite skills, physical capacities, and knowledge" (p. 169).

[85] Horty (2019) and Ramírez Abarca and Broersen (2019a, 2019b) present a detailed account of subjective obligations for individual agents within stit theory. The main difference between these two formalisms is that the former relies on action types, whereas the latter does not. The latter also presents a complete logical system of objective and subjective obligations.

[86] Kolodny and MacFarlane (2010) take the example from Parfit (1988) who in turn credits Regan (1980, p. 265).

Regan (1980, p. 265) can be taken to say that if we assign equal subjective probabilities to the fact that the miners are trapped in shaft A rather than B, then act-utilitarianism requires us to block neither shaft, even though blocking neither shaft cannot possibly be the best act in the circumstances, given the actual location of the miners. Wherever the miners are located, there is an act which is preferable to blocking neither shaft. Regan (1980, p. 265—terminology adapted)

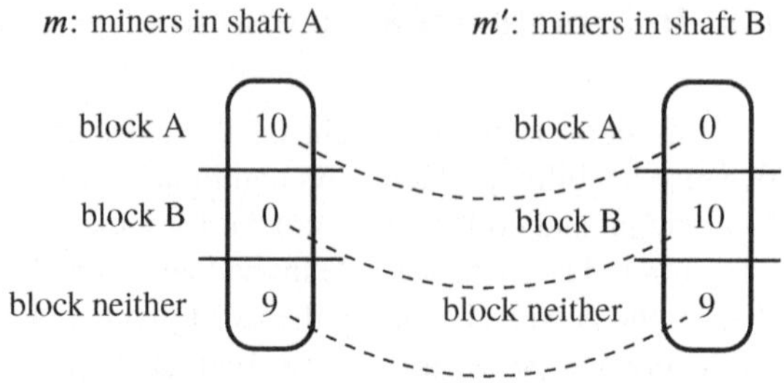

Fig. 4.9 An epistemic stit model of the miners' problem: the numbers represent the number of miners saved; the epistemic indistinguishability relation is represented by the dashed lines, that is, for instance, the agent cannot distinguish between blocking shaft A at m and blocking shaft A at m'

It is often assumed that the miners' problem warrants the following outcomes of deliberation:

1. We ought to block neither shaft.
2. If the miners are in shaft A, we ought to block shaft A.
3. If the miners are in shaft B, we ought to block shaft B.
4. Either the miners are in shaft A or they are in shaft B.
5. Either we ought to block shaft A or we ought to block shaft B.[87]

I will show how my account of individual practical knowledge, aided by the dictum of ought implies can, may help to dispel the apparent paradox in the miners' problem.[88] Figure 4.9 depicts the miners' problem in an epistemic stit model. The 'ought implies can' dictum entails that if an agent cannot do φ then she cannot possibly be obliged to do φ. It is not my aim to provide a theory of what the particular subjective obligation *is* in the miners' problem; rather, it is to investigate the practical knowledge of the individual agent in this model and then map a space for the *possible* subjective obligations.

To begin with, note that the agent obviously knows how to block shaft A, how to block shaft B, and how to block neither shaft. Does the agent know how to block shaft A if the miners are in shaft A? The answer is affirmative: she can ensure that she blocks shaft A if the miners are in shaft A by knowingly blocking shaft

concludes: "Still a reasonable approach to the [miners'] problem requires [us] to abandon all hope of producing the best consequences possible."

[87] Although the obligations expressed in 1–5 take 'we' as a subject, these obligations depict a general individual agent rather than a collective agent.

[88] Kolodny and MacFarlane (2010, p. 116), in contrast, argue that "the best way to resolve the paradox is to give a semantics for deontic modals and indicative conditionals that lets us see how the argument can be invalid even with its obvious logical form".

A.[89] In contrast, the problem with assumptions 2 and 3 above is that she does not know how to simultaneously perform the corresponding conditional actions. Let me explain why. Given 4, the only way for her to knowingly ensure that she blocks shaft A if the miners are in shaft A is by knowingly blocking shaft A. Something similar holds for shaft B. Formally, this observation translates to the formula $\mathsf{K}_i\Box(\mathsf{K}_i[i\ \mathsf{stit}](p_A \rightarrow [i\ \mathsf{stit}]A) \rightarrow \mathsf{K}_i[i\ \mathsf{stit}]A)$, where we let p_A stand for 'miners are in shaft A' and let $[i\ \mathsf{stit}]A$ stand for 'i blocks shaft A'.[90] Therefore, the only way for her to knowingly simultaneously (i) block shaft A if the miners are in shaft A and (ii) block shaft B if the miners are in shaft B is by knowingly blocking both shaft A and shaft B, which is impossible. She therefore does not know how to simultaneously perform the conditional actions that correspond to assumptions 2 and 3. Hence, assumptions 2 and 3 jointly lead to a conflict in the required practical knowledge.

In addition, notice that the agent knows that she is able to knowingly save nine miners, namely by knowingly blocking neither shaft. In contrast, she knows that knowingly blocking shaft A is a refinement of both (a) risking that all miners are killed and (b) taking the chance that all miners are saved. Something similar holds for shaft B. In particular, this means that there is no subjective normative difference between knowingly blocking shaft A and knowingly blocking shaft B. Hence, the subjective obligation is either: (i) to knowingly block neither shaft, (ii) to knowingly block one of the shafts, or (iii) to knowingly do anything.[91] Accordingly, I am sceptical that assumption 5 is warranted: we should not presuppose that obligations always determine one maximally specific course of action.

Note that this example highlights that individual objective and subjective obligations may differ. Suppose the miners are in shaft A. Then, it is plausible that the agent is objectively obliged to block shaft A. However, as noted above, my theory of individual practical knowledge suggests that the agent is not subjectively obliged to block shaft A.

It is interesting to note that this *single-agent* scenario indicates the possibility of responsibility voids: after all, irrespective of the agent's decision a morally undesirable outcome may result. After all, if she decides to block neither shaft, then one of the miners will be killed whereas this was avoidable by blocking the correct shaft; if she decides to block one of the shafts, then this may lead to the death of all miners. The agent may be held responsible if her beliefs turn out to be unjustified. In

---

[89] Note that, given that the agent does not know the location of the miners, this means that she knowingly blocks shaft A even if it turns out that the miners are located in shaft B. It may help to indicate that the agent does not know how to block shaft A *only if* the miners are in shaft A.

[90] A similar observation inspired my study of conditional strategies (Duijf, 2015; Duijf & Broersen, 2016).

[91] Ultimately, it seems plausible that the subjective obligations depend on the morally right risk attitude: (I) if she ought to be risk-averse, then she could be obliged to knowingly block neither shaft, (II) if she ought to be risk-seeking, then she could be obliged to knowingly block one of the shafts, or (III) if she ought to be risk-neutral, then she could be obliged to knowingly do anything.

case her beliefs are justified, I am inclined to think, however, that such a void would not be problematic, rather, it would be an unfortunate tragedy of the situation.

Next, we move on to a study of subjective *collective obligations*. For the *logical* study of subjective collective obligations, it may be interesting to note that collective know-how, unlike individual know-how, is not monotonic. That is, letting $\mathsf{H}_{\mathcal{G}}\varphi$ stand for '$\mathcal{G}$ collectively knows how to φ', it might be that $\models \varphi \rightarrow \psi$ while $\not\models \mathsf{H}_{\mathcal{G}}\varphi \rightarrow \mathsf{H}_{\mathcal{G}}\psi$. After all, recall the discussions of the coordination game (Fig. 4.6): when Chris and Dee independently pick cards from face-up decks of cards, they do not collectively know how to jointly pick an identical face card, despite collectively knowing how to pick two jacks. Since picking two jacks is a way for them to pick an identical face card, this example shows that collective know-how is not monotonic: in the model $\mathcal{M}$ of Fig. 4.6, it is the case that $\mathcal{M} \models p_{JJ} \rightarrow p_{id}$ while $\mathcal{G}_2$ collectively knows how to p_{JJ} despite not collectively knowing how to p_{id}. The intuitive reason is that it may be clear how a specific group action divides into members' parts, while this may be obscured by a more coarse-grained group action.

Under the assumption that 'ought implies can', this entails that it is plausible that subjective collective obligations are also not monotonic. That is, letting $\mathsf{SO}_{\mathcal{G}}\varphi$ stand for '$\mathcal{G}$ subjectively collectively ought to φ', it might be that $\models \varphi \rightarrow \psi$ while $\not\models \mathsf{SO}_{\mathcal{G}}\varphi \rightarrow \mathsf{SO}_{\mathcal{G}}\psi$. After all, the example of Fig. 4.6 could be extended with a deontic ideality function such that all and only those indices where two jacks are picked are deontically ideal. It seems plausible that the group is subjectively collectively obliged to jointly pick two jacks. Moreover, the example would validate that jointly picking two jacks logically entails jointly picking an identical face card. But, since the group does not collectively know how to jointly pick an identical face card, it is plausible that the group is also not subjectively collectively obliged to jointly pick an identical face card. The logic of subjective collective obligations therefore has to be non-standard.

What, if anything, does my theory of practical knowledge imply for the relation between collective and individual blameworthiness, that is, backward-looking moral responsibility? I take it that the concept of backward-looking moral responsibility supports the claim that not fulfilling a subjective obligation is a necessary condition for being individually blameworthy: if an individual agent is individually blameworthy, then she has failed to fulfil a subjective obligation. The converse does not hold, because she might have a plausible excuse for not doing what she ought to do. Analogously, I submit that not fulfilling a subjective collective obligation is a necessary, but not a sufficient, condition for being collectively blameworthy. We thus obtain the following implication: if a group is collectively blameworthy, then it does not fulfil a subjective collective obligation.

Suppose a group $\mathcal{G}$ is collectively blameworthy. According to the previously mentioned implication, this entails that the group failed to fulfil a subjective collective obligation. Under the assumption that ought implies can, this entails that the group collectively knew how to fulfil its subjective collective obligation. Say it would fulfil its subjective collective obligation if and only if it performs a group action that guarantees $p_{\checkmark}$. From the perspective of my theory of collective know-how, the 'effectivity' condition shows that the group commonly knew that they would have fulfilled their subjective collective obligation if and only if each member had played her part. Assuming that each member's individual action becomes public, this means that the group can identify the members who failed to play their part and hold them responsible to an appropriate degree.

Let us look more closely at the epistemic state of group members who fail to play their part. Suppose agent i fails to knowingly carry out her part in fulfilling a subjective collective obligation. In such a case, we get $\neg\mathsf{K}_i\langle i\ \mathsf{stit}\rangle[\mathcal{G}\ \mathsf{stit}]p_{\checkmark}$, or, equivalently, $\hat{\mathsf{K}}_i[i\ \mathsf{stit}]\neg[\mathcal{G}\ \mathsf{stit}]p_{\checkmark}$. This means that the agent considers it possible that she herself guarantees that the group fails to fulfil its subjective collective obligation.[92] Hence, she decided to perform an action which might implicate herself as *causing* the group's failure to fulfil its subjective collective obligation. In other words, she risked that she herself guarantees the group's failure to fulfil its subjective collective obligation.

Could she have avoided this risk? The 'part know-how' condition of collective know-how entails that she did know how to play her part, that is, $\mathsf{K}_i\Diamond\mathsf{K}_i\langle i\ \mathsf{stit}\rangle[\mathcal{G}\ \mathsf{stit}]p_{\checkmark}$ holds. In other words, she knew that it was possible for her to knowingly play her part. Or, equivalently, she knew that it was possible for her to knowingly prevent that she risks the group's failure. That is, she could have decided to knowingly guarantee that she does not see to it that the group fails to fulfil its collective obligation. After all, at such a moment, it is possible that $\mathsf{K}_i\neg[i\ \mathsf{stit}]\neg[\mathcal{G}\ \mathsf{stit}]p_{\checkmark}$ holds. Hence, she had the opportunity to knowingly guarantee that she cannot be implicated as *causing* the group's failure.

The 'causing', or $[i\ \mathsf{stit}]$-operator, above is essential.[93] That is, it could be that knowingly playing her part makes no difference to whether she knowingly risks a collective failure. For instance, she may doubt the collective success, because she is uncertain whether others will carry out their part. In such a case, it is unavoidable that she considers it possible that the group fails to fulfil its collective obligation. More precisely, we would have $\Box\hat{\mathsf{K}}_i\neg[\mathcal{G}\ \mathsf{stit}]p_{\checkmark}$. However, when she does not knowingly play her part, it follows that she knowingly risks that she *herself* is a cause of the collective failure. After all, we would have $\hat{\mathsf{K}}_i[i\ \mathsf{stit}]\neg[\mathcal{G}\ \mathsf{stit}]p_{\checkmark}$ (notice the $[i\ \mathsf{stit}]$-operator). Or, conversely, if she chooses to knowingly play her part she at least knows that she herself will not be causally responsible for the collective failure, despite the fact that she does not know that collective failure will be avoided.

A typical context in which a group member knows that the subjective collective obligation is not fulfilled, regardless of whether she herself knowingly plays her part, is when she knows that other group members will not comply. Because of the 'effectivity' condition, if she knows that some group member will not do her part, then she knows that the group will fail to fulfil its subjective collective obligation. To illustrate this possibility, consider the version of the prisoners' dilemma depicted

[92] Note that not knowingly carrying out her part is consistent with carrying out her part unknowingly.

[93] Causality has been a thorny issue in philosophy. For my current purposes, it is sufficient to assume that when an agent sees to it that φ, then she causes it.

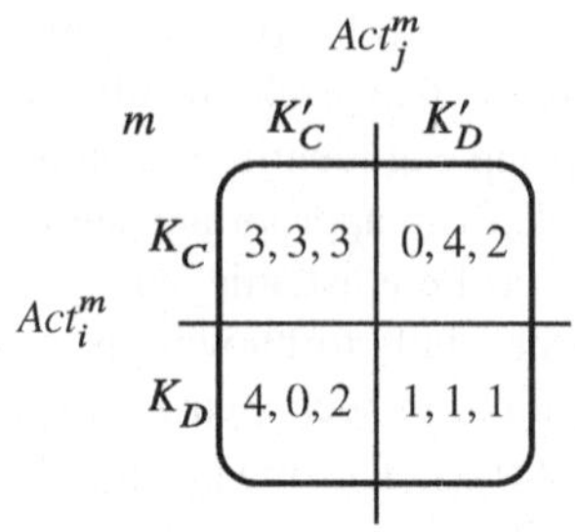

Fig. 4.10 A stit model of the prisoners' dilemma. The only difference with the standard prisoners' dilemma is that each action profile is assigned a triple of utilities: one for agent i, one for agent j, and one for the group $\mathcal{G} = \{i, j\}$, respectively, where $u_{\mathcal{G}}(m/h)$ is the average of $u_i(m/h)$ and $u_j(m/h)$

by the stit model in Fig. 4.10.[94] Although this model excludes the knowledge of the prisoners, it can be used to illustrate that an agent may know that the group fails to fulfil its subjective collective obligation, for example, because she knows that others are guided by their personal interests, rather than the collective good. The prisoners' dilemma is a standard game-theoretical example that highlights this worry: each prisoner promotes her personal interests (modelled by u_i or u_j), regardless of what the other prisoner does, only if she defects (modelled by K_D and K'_D). But if each defects, then this will lead to a worse outcome than if each had cooperated (modelled by K_C and K'_C). In fact, to jointly promote the collective good (modelled by $u_{\mathcal{G}}$) they both need to cooperate.

What kind of reasons might pardon a member from being responsible for not knowingly carrying out her part, which is necessary for the group to fulfil its subjective collective obligation? Why would a member decide against playing her part in jointly promoting the collective good? On the one hand, she may not be motivated to devalue her own personal interests for the collective good. In such cases, there is no individualistic reason for her to knowingly play her part. The individualistic motives of the members of a group may therefore undermine its collective performance.

On the other hand, the member would know that the subjective collective obligation will not be fulfilled if she knows that the others will not impair their personal interests. She would then know that she will not be the sole cause of the collective failure. Having partners in crime might alleviate her individual blameworthiness. However, Matthew Braham and Martin van Hees write:

> a person is an apposite target of censure and sanction for some state of affairs only if ... it was within her power to reasonably choose not to be an "author" (or "co-author" in the

[94] The stit model relates to what Tamminga and Duijf (2017) call a cooperation game.

presence of multiple causal conditions) of that state of affairs. (Braham & van Hees, 2012, p. 607)[95]

If we take it that authorship of agent i for χ is implied by $[i \text{ stit}]\chi$, then it intuitively seems that knowingly causing a collective failure makes one an appropriate target of blame or sanction for the collective failure. A group member may therefore value the fact that she knows that she is not an *author*, or co-author, of the group's failure to fulfil its subjective collective obligation, regardless of whether she knows that the group will fail to do so. Hence, if group members collectively know how to fulfil the group's subjective collective obligation and if they are motivated in this way, then it is guaranteed that the group will fulfil its subjective collective obligation. In other words, it is impossible for a group to fail to fulfil its subjective collective obligation if each group member values the fact that she knows that she is not an author of the group's failure.

In sum, a group's collective blameworthiness *logically implies* that at least one member knowingly risked that she herself causes the group's failure to fulfil its corresponding subjective collective obligation. In fact, it logically implies that every member who failed to knowingly play her part is so implicated. From the collective perspective, assuming that the members' individual actions become public, the group can identify the members who failed to play their part and hold them responsible to an appropriate degree. From the individualistic perspective, this means that at least one member knowingly risked that she is an author, or co-author, of the group's failure to fulfil its subjective collective obligation. I highlighted that individualistic reasons for this divergence may be epistemic, such as when she knows that some other members will also not do their part, or motivational, such as when she does not want to devalue her individual interests for the collective good.[96] In the absence of such exculpating factors, *responsibility gaps do not arise*: collective blameworthiness entails that at least one agent knowingly risked that she is a co-author of the group's failure.

It is important and interesting to develop a full-fledged theory of subjective obligations—individual and collective—and investigate the relation between subjective individual obligations and subjective collective obligations further. For now, I have to settle for these preliminary observations and leave such a study for another occasion.

[95] The details of our discussions differ substantially. Their framework includes subjective probabilities, relies on the NESS condition (which stands for 'Necessary Element of a Sufficient Set') to assess causal connections, and includes eligible options. Mine, in contrast, is non-probabilistic, relies on control (or α-effectivity) to assess causal connections, and does not include the eligibility of the available options.

[96] It remains to be studied whether these reasons *justify* the member's divergence and thereby alleviate her individual blameworthiness.

Appendix C: Guilty Minds and Collective Know-how

C.1 Epistemic Stit Theory

Theorem 4.1 (Completeness Epistemic Stit) *The following axiom schemas, in combination with a standard axiomatization for propositional logic, and the standard rules (such as necessitation) for the normal modal operators, provide a complete Hilbert system for the validities on epistemic stit models:*

(S5 Historical Necessity)	S5 for $\Box$
(S5 Agency)	for each group $\mathcal{G}$: S5 for $[\mathcal{G}\ \mathsf{stit}]$
(Agent Monotonicity)	for all groups $\mathcal{F}$ and $\mathcal{G}$ satisfying $\mathcal{F} \subseteq \mathcal{G}$: $[\mathcal{F}\ \mathsf{stit}]\varphi \to [\mathcal{G}\ \mathsf{stit}]\varphi$
(Independence of Agency)	for all groups $\mathcal{F}$ and $\mathcal{G}$ satisfying $\mathcal{F} \cap \mathcal{G} = \emptyset$: $\Diamond[\mathcal{F}\ \mathsf{stit}]\varphi \wedge \Diamond[\mathcal{G}\ \mathsf{stit}]\psi \to \Diamond([\mathcal{F}\ \mathsf{stit}]\varphi \wedge [\mathcal{G}\ \mathsf{stit}]\psi)$
(S5 Knowledge)	for each $i \in Ags$: S5 for K_i
(Public Knowledge)	for each group $\mathcal{G}$: $\mathsf{C}_{\mathcal{G}}\varphi \to (\varphi \wedge \mathsf{E}_{\mathcal{G}}\mathsf{C}_{\mathcal{G}}\varphi)$
(Induction)	for each group $\mathcal{G}$: $\varphi \wedge \mathsf{C}_{\mathcal{G}}(\varphi \to \mathsf{E}_{\mathcal{G}}\varphi) \to \mathsf{C}_{\mathcal{G}}\varphi$

Proof (Sketch) The epistemic stit logic is a so-called fusion of epistemic logic and non-epistemic stit theory. The complete logical system for epistemic stit theory is therefore given by the simple combination of the logical systems for epistemic logic and (non-epistemic) stit logic (see Carnielli & Coniglio, 2020, Sect. 4.1).

It is well-established that the non-epistemic fragment is complete with respect to stit models, for instance, by using Sahlqvist correspondence (see the standard textbook treatment of Blackburn et al. (2001)). The completeness of the epistemic logic is standard (see, e.g. Meyer & van der Hoek, 1995). (Broersen, 2011, Theorem 2.1 proves a similar result for Xstit, the difference is that his logic concerns Xstit and excludes common knowledge.) □

C.2 Individual Practical Knowledge

Proposition 4.1

(OAC) *The* own-action condition, *schematically expressed by* $\mathsf{K}_i\varphi \to \mathsf{K}_i[i\ \mathsf{stit}]\varphi$, *corresponds to the condition:*
For all indices m/h, m'/h'_1, *and* m'/h'_2, *if* $m/h \sim_i m'/h'_1$ *and* $h'_2 \in Act_i(m'/h'_1)$ *then* $m/h \sim_i m'/h'_2$.

(Unif-H) *The* uniformity of historical possibility property, *schematically expressed by* $\Diamond\mathsf{K}_i\varphi \to \mathsf{K}_i\Diamond\varphi$, *corresponds to the confluency condition:*

For all indices m/h_1, m/h_2, and m'/h'_1, if $m/h_1 \sim_i m'/h'_1$ then there is an index m'/h'_2 such that $m/h_2 \sim_i m'/h'_2$.

Proof These correspondences can be checked using the algorithm SQEMA (Conradie et al., 2006). □

Theorem 4.2 (Impossibility Results) *Implicit individual know-how and explicit individual know-how cannot be characterized in the current logic:*

1. *Given an agent i and a formula φ, there is* no *formula ψ such that for every model $\mathcal{M}$ and every index m/h it holds that, relative to m/h, agent i* implicitly *knows how to φ if and only if $\mathcal{M}, m/h \vDash \psi$.*
2. *Given an agent i and a formula φ, there is* no *formula ψ such that for every model $\mathcal{M}$ and every index m/h it holds that, relative to m/h, agent i* explicitly *knows how to φ if and only if $\mathcal{M}, m/h \vDash \psi$.*

Proof Implicit individual know-how would be characterizable in $\mathfrak{L}_{estit}$ if and only if, given an agent $i \in Ags$ and a formula φ, there is a formula ψ available such that for any model $\mathcal{M}$ and any index m/h it holds that $\mathcal{M}, m/h \vDash \psi$ iff i implicitly knows how to φ.

We argue by contradiction. Suppose ψ characterizes that agent i implicitly knows how to p. Let $P' \subset P$ denote the set of propositional variables occurring in either ψ or p, and let $q \notin P'$. Consider a model $\mathcal{M}$ and an index m/h in which agent i has two options, that is, Act_i^m contains two acts. Let the epistemic indistinguishability relation $\sim_i$ be given by $m_1/h_1 \sim_i m_2/h_2$ if and only if $m_2/h_2 \in Act_i(m_1/h_1)$. Consider the valuation function V which assigns to each propositional variable the set of all indices in the model. It is now easy to see that i implicitly knows how to p, because for every formula χ we have $\mathcal{M} \vDash \Box(p \leftrightarrow \chi)$ or $\mathcal{M} \vDash \Box(p \leftrightarrow \neg\chi)$. The assumption implies that $\mathcal{M}, \vDash \psi$ holds. See Fig. 4.11 for the initial model in which agent i implicitly knows how to p.

We can construct a countermodel $\mathcal{M}'$ from $\mathcal{M}$ by adjusting the propositional valuation to V' in the following way: one choice guarantees q, the other guarantees $\neg q$, and both guarantee any $p' \in P'$ (see the constructed model in Fig. 4.12). Note that V' only differs from V on q. It is easy to see that in $\mathcal{M}'$, i does not implicitly

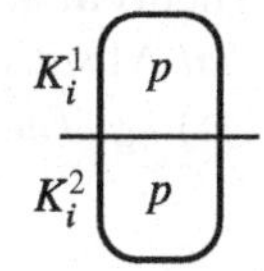

Fig. 4.11 The initial model $\mathcal{M}$

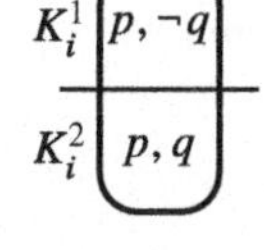

Fig. 4.12 The constructed model $\mathcal{M}'$

know how to p, because, in $\mathcal{M}'$, q is a proper refinement of p for agent i. However, because we did not alter the truth values of the propositions occurring in ψ, it is the case that ψ also holds in $\mathcal{M}'$. Contradiction.

In a similar way, one can prove that explicit knowledge is also not characterizable. □

Theorem 4.3 (Characterization of Individual Know-how) *Individual know-how is characterized by*

$$\mathsf{K}_i \Diamond \mathsf{K}_i [i \ \mathsf{stit}]\varphi.$$

That is, for every model $\mathcal{M}$, every index m/h, every individual agent i, and every formula φ it holds that, relative to m/h, agent i knows how to φ if and only if $\mathcal{M}, m/h \models \mathsf{K}_i \Diamond \mathsf{K}_i [i \ \mathsf{stit}]\varphi$.

Proof (**If.**) Follows immediately by letting $\psi := \varphi$ in Definition 4.5.

(**Only if.**) It is immediate for implicit know-how. For explicit know-how it follows from two facts. First, $\Box$ is monotonic: $\models \Box(\chi_1 \to \chi_2) \to (\Box\chi_1 \to \Box\chi_2)$, which entails $\models \Box(\chi_1 \to \chi_2) \to (\Diamond\chi_1 \to \Diamond\chi_2)$. Replacing χ_1 with $\mathsf{K}_i[i \ \mathsf{stit}]\psi$ and χ_2 with $\mathsf{K}_i[i \ \mathsf{stit}]\varphi$ yields

$$\models \Box(\mathsf{K}_i[i \ \mathsf{stit}]\psi \to \mathsf{K}_i[i \ \mathsf{stit}]\varphi) \to (\Diamond\mathsf{K}_i[i \ \mathsf{stit}]\psi \to \Diamond\mathsf{K}_i[i \ \mathsf{stit}]\varphi).$$

Second, by K_i-necessitation, and two applications of the K-axiom for K_i it holds that:

$$\models \mathsf{K}_i\Box(\mathsf{K}_i[i \ \mathsf{stit}]\psi \to \mathsf{K}_i[i \ \mathsf{stit}]\varphi) \to (\mathsf{K}_i\Diamond\mathsf{K}_i[i \ \mathsf{stit}]\psi \to \mathsf{K}_i\Diamond\mathsf{K}_i[i \ \mathsf{stit}]\varphi).$$

By assumption, both the antecedent of the principal implication and the antecedent of the subordinate implication obtain. Hence, $\mathsf{K}_i\Diamond\mathsf{K}_i[i \ \mathsf{stit}]\varphi$ holds, as desired. □

C.3 Collective Know-how

Theorem 4.4 *Let $\mathcal{M}$ be an epistemic stit model, and let m/h be an index. Assume that $\mathcal{M}$ satisfies (Unif-H). Suppose $\mathcal{G}$ collectively knows how to φ, as witnessed by $(\varphi_i)_{i\in\mathcal{G}}$. Then*

$$\mathcal{M}, m/h \models \mathsf{C}_{\mathcal{G}}\Box \bigwedge_{i\in\mathcal{G}}([i \ \mathsf{stit}]\varphi_i \leftrightarrow \langle i \ \mathsf{stit}\rangle[\mathcal{G} \ \mathsf{stit}]\varphi), \qquad (*)$$

and

$$\mathcal{M}, m/h \models \mathsf{C}_{\mathcal{G}}\Box \bigwedge_{i\in\mathcal{G}}(\mathsf{K}_i[i \ \mathsf{stit}]\varphi_i \leftrightarrow \mathsf{K}_i\langle i \ \mathsf{stit}\rangle[\mathcal{G} \ \mathsf{stit}]\varphi). \qquad (**)$$

Proof Assume all the stated assumptions. To clarify, the crucial assumptions are (1) $\mathsf{C}_{\mathcal{G}}\Box(\bigwedge_{i\in\mathcal{G}}[i\ \mathsf{stit}]\varphi_i \leftrightarrow [\mathcal{G}\ \mathsf{stit}]\varphi)$ and (2) $\mathsf{C}_{\mathcal{G}}\bigwedge_{i\in\mathcal{G}}\mathsf{K}_i\Diamond\mathsf{K}_i[i\ \mathsf{stit}]\varphi_i$. It is important to note that (2) entails (2') $\mathsf{C}_{\mathcal{G}}\bigwedge_{i\in\mathcal{G}}\Diamond[i\ \mathsf{stit}]\varphi_i$.

First, consider the following subformula of (1), which results from ignoring the outermost modality $\mathsf{C}_{\mathcal{G}}$: (1') $\Box(\bigwedge_{i\in\mathcal{G}}[i\ \mathsf{stit}]\varphi_i \leftrightarrow [\mathcal{G}\ \mathsf{stit}]\varphi)$. Let us take an arbitrary $j\in\mathcal{G}$. The right-to-left implication of (1') entails that at any index m/h where (1') obtains, we get that $m/h \vDash \langle j\ \mathsf{stit}\rangle[\mathcal{G}\ \mathsf{stit}]\varphi \rightarrow \langle j\ \mathsf{stit}\rangle[j\ \mathsf{stit}]\varphi_j$. Note that $\vDash \langle j\ \mathsf{stit}\rangle[j\ \mathsf{stit}]\varphi_j \rightarrow [j\ \mathsf{stit}]\varphi_j$ and, therefore, at any index m/h where (1') obtains, we get $m/h \vDash \langle j\ \mathsf{stit}\rangle[\mathcal{G}\ \mathsf{stit}]\varphi \rightarrow [j\ \mathsf{stit}]\varphi_j$. Since j was arbitrary, $\Box$ is an S5 modality and $\mathsf{C}_{\mathcal{G}}$ is a normal modality, it follows that (1) entails $\mathsf{C}_{\mathcal{G}}\Box\bigwedge_{i\in\mathcal{G}}(\langle i\ \mathsf{stit}\rangle[\mathcal{G}\ \mathsf{stit}]\varphi \rightarrow [i\ \mathsf{stit}]\varphi_i)$.

For the converse, consider the subformula of (2'), which results from ignoring the outermost modality $\mathsf{C}_{\mathcal{G}}$: (2") $\bigwedge_{i\in\mathcal{G}}\Diamond[i\ \mathsf{stit}]\varphi_i$. The independence of agency condition entails that at any index where (2") holds also $\Diamond\bigwedge_{i\in\mathcal{G}}[i\ \mathsf{stit}]\varphi_i$ obtains. Let us take an arbitrary $j\in\mathcal{G}$. Then, at any index m/h where (2") obtains, we get that $m/h \vDash [j\ \mathsf{stit}]\varphi_j \rightarrow \langle j\ \mathsf{stit}\rangle\bigwedge_{i\in\mathcal{G}}[i\ \mathsf{stit}]\varphi_i$. The left-to-right implication in (1') entails that at any index m/h where (1') obtains, we get that $m/h \vDash \langle j\ \mathsf{stit}\rangle\bigwedge_{i\in\mathcal{G}}[i\ \mathsf{stit}]\varphi_i \rightarrow \langle j\ \mathsf{stit}\rangle[\mathcal{G}\ \mathsf{stit}]\varphi$. Hence, at any index m/h where (2") and (1') hold, we get $m/h \vDash [j\ \mathsf{stit}]\varphi_j \rightarrow \langle j\ \mathsf{stit}\rangle[\mathcal{G}\ \mathsf{stit}]\varphi$. Since j was arbitrary and $\Box$ and $\mathsf{C}_{\mathcal{G}}$ are normal modalities, we have $\mathsf{C}_{\mathcal{G}}\Box\bigwedge_{i\in\mathcal{G}}([i\ \mathsf{stit}]\varphi_i \rightarrow \langle i\ \mathsf{stit}\rangle[\mathcal{G}\ \mathsf{stit}]\varphi)$, as desired.

Second, (**) follows from (*) and two facts. First, the fact that $\vDash \mathsf{C}_{\mathcal{G}}\chi \rightarrow \mathsf{C}_{\mathcal{G}}\mathsf{K}_i\chi$, for each $i\in\mathcal{G}$. Second, the fact that (Unif-H) entails that $\mathcal{M}\vDash \mathsf{K}_i\Box\chi \rightarrow \Box\mathsf{K}_i\chi$. □

Observation 4.5 (Interchangeability & Effectivity) Let S be a game model, let $\mathcal{G}$ be a group of agents, and let φ be a formula. The following are equivalent:

1. $S\vDash\Box([\mathcal{G}\ \mathsf{stit}]\varphi \leftrightarrow \bigwedge_{i\in\mathcal{G}}\langle i\ \mathsf{stit}\rangle[\mathcal{G}\ \mathsf{stit}]\varphi)$;
2. $P_{\mathcal{G}} := \{a_{\mathcal{G}}\in A_{\mathcal{G}} \mid S, a\vDash[\mathcal{G}\ \mathsf{stit}]\varphi\}$ is interchangeable.

Proof (1. ⇒ 2.) Assume 1. Let $b, c\in A$ be such that $b_{\mathcal{G}}, c_{\mathcal{G}}\in P_{\mathcal{G}}$, and let $i\in\mathcal{G}$. To prove 2., we take an arbitrary $d\in A$ such that $d_{\mathcal{G}} = (b_{\mathcal{G}-i}, c_i)$, and prove that $d_{\mathcal{G}}\in P_{\mathcal{G}}$. For any $j\in\mathcal{G}-i$ it holds that $S, d\vDash\langle j\ \mathsf{stit}\rangle[\mathcal{G}\ \mathsf{stit}]\varphi$, because $S, b\vDash[\mathcal{G}\ \mathsf{stit}]\varphi$ and $d_j = b_j$. Hence, $S, d\vDash\bigwedge_{j\in\mathcal{G}-i}\langle j\ \mathsf{stit}\rangle[\mathcal{G}\ \mathsf{stit}]\varphi$. In a similar way, we can prove that $S, d\vDash\langle i\ \mathsf{stit}\rangle[\mathcal{G}\ \mathsf{stit}]\varphi$ (note the 'i' here). By the right-to-left implication in 1. it follows that $S, d\vDash[\mathcal{G}\ \mathsf{stit}]\varphi$. Hence $d_{\mathcal{G}}\in P_{\mathcal{G}}$.

(2. ⇒ 1.) Assume 2. Take any $a\in A$. We need to show that $S, a\vDash[\mathcal{G}\ \mathsf{stit}]\varphi \leftrightarrow \bigwedge_{i\in\mathcal{G}}\langle i\ \mathsf{stit}\rangle[\mathcal{G}\ \mathsf{stit}]\varphi$. The left-to-right implication follows immediately from the fact that $[i\ \mathsf{stit}]$ is reflexive, i.e. satisfies $\vDash\chi\rightarrow\langle i\ \mathsf{stit}\rangle\chi$. To establish the right-to-left implication, assume $S, a\vDash\bigwedge_{i\in\mathcal{G}}\langle i\ \mathsf{stit}\rangle[\mathcal{G}\ \mathsf{stit}]\varphi$. That is, for every $i\in\mathcal{G}$ there is a $b^i_{\mathcal{G}}\in P_{\mathcal{G}}$ such that $b^i_i = a_i$. Using the fact that $P_{\mathcal{G}}$ is interchangeable, one can inductively show that for any subgroup $\mathcal{F}\subseteq\mathcal{G}$ there is a $b^{\mathcal{F}}_{\mathcal{G}}\in P_{\mathcal{G}}$ such that $b^{\mathcal{F}}_{\mathcal{F}} = a_{\mathcal{F}}$. Hence, $a_{\mathcal{G}} = b^{\mathcal{G}}_{\mathcal{G}}\in P_{\mathcal{G}}$ and therefore there is an $a'\in A$ such that $a'_{\mathcal{G}} = a_{\mathcal{G}}$ and $S, a'\vDash[\mathcal{G}\ \mathsf{stit}]\varphi$. Since $\vDash[\mathcal{G}\ \mathsf{stit}]\varphi\leftrightarrow[\mathcal{G}\ \mathsf{stit}][\mathcal{G}\ \mathsf{stit}]\varphi$ and $a'_{\mathcal{G}} = a_{\mathcal{G}}$, it holds that $S, a\vDash[\mathcal{G}\ \mathsf{stit}]\varphi$, as desired. □

References

Ågotnes, T., Goranko, V., Jamroga, W., & Wooldridge, M. (2015). Knowledge and ability. In H. van Ditmarsch, J. Y. Halpern, W. van der Hoek, & B. Kooi (Eds.), *Handbook of epistemic logic* (pp. 543–589). London: College Publications.

Ågotnes, T., & Wáng, Y. N. (2016). Resolving distributed knowledge. In R. Ramanujam (Ed.), *Proceedings of the Fifteenth Conference on Theoretical Aspects of Rationality and Knowledge* (pp. 37–46).

Alur, R., Henzinger, T. A., & Kupferman, O. (2002). Alternating-time temporal logic. *Journal of the ACM, 49*(5), 672–713.

Anscombe, G. E. M. (1963). *Intention*. Cambridge: Harvard University Press.

Aumann, R. J. (1987). Correlated equilibrium as an expression of Bayesian rationality. *Econometrica, 55*(1), 1–18.

Aumann, R. J. (1999). Interactive epistemology I: Knowledge. *International Journal of Game Theory, 28*(3), 263–300.

Aumann, R. J., & Dreze, J. H. (2008). Rational expectations in games. *The American Economic Review, 98*(1), 72–86.

Bacharach, M. (2006). *Beyond Individual choice: Teams and frames in game theory*, N. Gold & R. Sugden (Eds.). Princeton: Princeton University Press.

Blackburn, P., De Rijke, M., & Venema, Y. (2001). *Modal logic*. Cambridge: Cambridge University Press.

Bliss, R., & Trogdon, K. (2016). Metaphysical grounding. In E. N. Zalta (Ed.), *The stanford encyclopedia of philosophy*.

Braham, M., & M. van Hees (2012). An anatomy of moral responsibility. *Mind, 121*(483), 601–634.

Bratman, M. E. (2014). *Shared agency: A planning theory of acting together*. Oxford: Oxford University Press.

Broersen, J. (2009). A stit-logic for extensive form group strategies. In P. Boldi, G. Vizzari, G. Pasi, & R. Baeza-Yates (Eds.), *Proceedings of the International Joint Conference on Web Intelligence and Intelligent Agent Technology* (Vol. 3, pp. 484–487). Washington: IEEE Computer Society.

Broersen, J. (2011). Deontic epistemic stit logic distinguishing modes of mens rea. *Journal of Applied Logic, 9*(2), 137–152.

Broersen, J., & Herzig, A. (2015). Using STIT theory to talk about strategies. In J. van Benthem, S. Ghosh, & R. Verbrugge (Eds.), *Models of strategic reasoning* (pp. 137–173). Springer.

Broersen, J., Herzig, A., & Troquard, N. (2006). Embedding alternating-time temporal logic in strategic logic of agency. *Journal of Logic and Computation, 16*(5), 559–578.

Broersen, J., Herzig, A., & Troquard, N. (2007). A normal simulation of coalition logic and an epistemic extension. In D. Samet (Ed.), *Proceedings of the Eleventh Conference on Theoretical Aspects of Rationality and Knowledge* (pp. 92–101). ACM.

Brown, M. A. (1988). On the logic of ability. *Journal of Philosophical Logic, 17*(1), 1–26.

Carnielli, W., & Coniglio, M. E. (2020). Combining logics. In E. N. Zalta (Ed.), *The Stanford Encyclopedia of Philosophy* (Fall 2020 ed.). Metaphysics Research Lab, Stanford University.

Carr, D. (1979). The logic of knowing how and ability. *Mind, 88*(351), 394–409.

Cohen, P. R., & Levesque, H. J. (1990). Intention is choice with commitment. *Artificial Intelligence, 42*(2), 213–261.

Conradie, W., Goranko, V., & Vakarelov, D. (2006). Algorithmic correspondence and completeness in modal logic. I. The core algorithm SQEMA. *Logical Methods in Computer Science, 2*(1), 1–26.

Davidson, D. (1963). Actions, reasons, and causes. *The Journal of Philosophy, 60*(23), 685–700.

Davidson, D. (1980). *Essays on actions and events*. Oxford: Clarendon Press.

Decker, K. S. (1995). *Environment centered analysis and design of coordination mechanisms*. PhD Thesis, University of Massachusetts.

Duijf, H. (2015). Performing conditional strategies in strategic STIT theory. In M. Kaeshammer & P. Schulz (Eds.), *Proceedings of the ESSLLI 2015 Student Session* (pp. 13–24).

Duijf, H., & J. Broersen (2016). Representing strategies. In A. Lomuscio & M. Y. Vardi (Eds.), *Proceedings of the Fourth International Workshop on Strategic Reasoning*, Volume 218 of *Electronic Proceedings in Theoretical Computer Science* (pp. 15–26). Open Publishing Association.

Duijf, H., Broersen, J., Kuncová, A., & Ramírez Abarca, A. I. (2021). Doing without action types. *The Review of Symbolic Logic, 14*(2), 380–410.

Duijf, H., Broersen, J., & Meyer, J.-J. C. (2019). Conflicting intentions: Rectifying the consistency requirements. *Philosophical Studies, 176*(4), 1097–1118.

Elgesem, D. (1993). *Action theory and modal logic*. PhD Thesis, University of Oslo.

Epstein, B. (2015). *The ant trap: Rebuilding the foundations of the social sciences*. New York: Oxford University Press.

Fagin, R., Moses, Y., Vardi, M. Y., & Halpern, J. Y. (2003). *Reasoning about knowledge*. Cambridge: MIT Press.

Fantl, J. (2008). Knowing-how and knowing-that. *Philosophy Compass, 3*(3), 451–470.

Feinberg, J. (1970). *Doing and deserving: Essays in the theory of responsibility*. Princeton: Princeton University Press.

Fikes, R. E., & N. J. Nilsson (1971). STRIPS: A new approach to the application of theorem proving to problem solving. *Artificial Intelligence, 2*(3), 189–208.

Fischer, J. M., & M. Ravizza (1998). *Responsibility and control: A theory of moral responsibility*. Cambridge: Cambridge University Press.

Fodor, J. A. (1968). The appeal to tacit knowledge in psychological explanation. *The Journal of Philosophy, 65*(20), 627–640.

Gauthier, D. (1975). Coordination. *Dialogue, 14*(2), 195–221.

Ghallab, M., Nau, D., & Traverso, P. (2004). *Automated planning: Theory and practice*. Amsterdam: Elsevier.

Ginet, C. (2000). The epistemic requirements for moral responsibility. *Philosophical Perspectives, 14*, 267–277.

Glick, E. (2011). Two methodologies for evaluating intellectualism. *Philosophy and Phenomenological Research, 83*(2), 398–434.

Goldman, A. I. (1971). The individuation of action. *The Journal of Philosophy, 68*(21), 761–774.

Hawke, P. (2017). The logic of joint ability in two-player tacit games. *The Review of Symbolic Logic, 10*(3), 481–508.

Herzig, A., & F. Schwarzentruber (2008). Properties of logics of individual and group agency. In C. Areces & R. Goldblatt (Eds.), *The Seventh Conference on Advances in Modal Logic* (pp. 133–149). College Publications.

Herzig, A., & N. Troquard (2006). Knowing how to play: Uniform choices in logics of agency. In P. Stone & G. Weiss (Eds.), *Proceedings of the Fifth International Conference on Autonomous Agents and Multiagent Systems* (pp. 209–216). ACM.

van der Hoek, W., & M. Wooldridge (2003). Cooperation, knowledge, and time: Alternating-time temporal epistemic logic and its applications. *Studia Logica, 75*(1), 125–157.

Horling, B., Lesser, V., Vincent, R., Wagner, T., Raja, A., Zhang, S., Decker, K., & Garvey, A. (1999). The TAEMS white paper. Unpublished manuscript.

Horty, J. F. (2019). Epistemic oughts in stit semantics. *Ergo, 6*(20191108), 71–120.

Horty, J. F., & N. Belnap (1995). The deliberative stit: A study of action, omission, ability, and obligation. *Journal of Philosophical Logic, 24*(6), 583–644.

Horty, J. F., & Pacuit, E. (2017). Action types in stit semantics. *The Review of Symbolic Logic, 10*(4), 617–637.

Jamroga, W., & Ågotnes, T. (2007). Constructive knowledge: What agents can achieve under imperfect information. *Journal of Applied Non-Classical Logics, 17*(4).

Jamroga, W., & van der Hoek, W. (2004). Agents that know how to play. *Fundamenta Informaticae, 63*(2-3), 185–220.

Jennings, N. R. (2000). On agent-based software engineering. *Artificial Intelligence, 117*(2), 277–296.
Kolodny, N., & MacFarlane, J. (2010). Ifs and oughts. *The Journal of Philosophy, 107*(3), 115–143.
Kuncová, A., Broersen, J., Duijf, H., & Ramírez Abarca, A. I. (manuscript). Ability and knowledge: Stit theory and transition systems. Unpublished manuscript.
Lewis, D. K. (1969). *Convention: A philosophical study*. Cambridge: Harvard University Press.
Lismont, L. (1993). La connaissance commune en logique modale. *Mathematical Logic Quarterly, 39*(1), 115–130.
Lorini, E., Longin, D., & Mayor, E. (2014). A logical analysis of responsibility attribution: Emotions, individuals and collectives. *Journal of Logic and Computation, 24*(6), 1313–1339.
Markoff, J. (2011). Computer wins on 'Jeopardy!': Trivial, it's not. *The New York Times*.
McNamara, P. (2019). Toward a systematization of logics for monadic and dyadic agency & ability, revisited. *Filosofiska Notiser, 6*(1), 157–188.
Metz, C. (2016). Google's AI wins fifth and final game against Go genius Lee Sedol. *WIRED*.
Metz, C. (2017). A mystery AI just crushed the best human players at poker. *WIRED*.
Meyer, J.-J. C., & van der Hoek, W. (1995). *Epistemic logic for AI and computer science*. New York: Cambridge University Press.
Pacuit, E., & Roy, O. (2017). Epistemic foundations of game theory. In E. N. Zalta (Ed.), *The stanford encyclopedia of philosophy* (Summer 2017 ed.).
Parfit, D. (1988). What we together do. Unpublished manuscript.
Payette, G. (2014). Decidability of an xstit logic. *Studia Logica, 102*(3), 577–607.
Ramírez Abarca, A. I., & Broersen, J. (2019a). A logic of objective and subjective oughts. In F. Calimeri, N. Leone, & M. Manna (Eds.), *Logics in artificial Intelligence*. Lecture notes in computer science (pp. 629–641). Cham: Springer International Publishing.
Ramírez Abarca, A. I., & Broersen, J. (2019b). A logic of objective and subjective oughts (full paper with proofs). https://arxiv.org/abs/1903.10577. Unpublished manuscript.
Rao, A. S., & Georgeff, M. P. (1991). Modeling rational agents within a BDI-architecture. In J. Allen, R. Fikes, & E. Sandewall (Eds.), *Proceedings of the Second International Conference on Principles of Knowledge Representation and Reasoning* (Vol. 91, pp. 473–484). Morgan Kaufmann.
Regan, D. (1980). *Utilitarianism and co-operation*. New York: Oxford University Press.
Russell, S., & Norvig, P. (1995). *Artificial intelligence: A modern approach*. Englewood Cliffs: Prentice Hall.
Ryle, G. (1949). *The concept of mind*. London: Hutchinson.
Schelling, T. C. (1960). *The strategy of conflict*. Cambridge: Harvard University Press.
Schobbens, P.-Y. (2004). Alternating-time logic with imperfect recall. In W. van der Hoek, A. Lomuscio, E. de Vink, & M. Wooldridge (Eds.), *Logic and communication in multi-agent systems* (Vol. 85, pp. 82–93). Elsevier.
Searle, J. (1990). Collective intentions and actions. In P. R. Cohen, J. Morgan, & M. E. Pollack (Eds.), *Intentions in communication* (pp. 401–415). Cambridge: MIT Press.
Shoham, Y. (1993). Agent-oriented programming. *Artificial Intelligence, 60*(1), 51–92.
Stanley, J. (2011). *Know how*. Oxford: Oxford University Press.
Stanley, J., & Williamson, T. (2001). Knowing how. *The Journal of Philosophy, 98*(8), 411–444.
Sugden, R. (1993). Thinking as a team: Towards an explanation of nonselfish behavior. *Social Philosophy and Policy, 10*(1), 69–89.
Sugden, R. (1995). A theory of focal points. *The Economic Journal, 105*(430), 533–550.
Sugden, R. (2003). The logic of team reasoning. *Philosophical Explorations, 6*(3), 165–181.
Tamminga, A., & Duijf, H. (2017). Collective obligations, group plans and individual actions. *Economics & Philosophy, 33*(2), 187–214.
Vranas, P. B. M. (2007). I ought, therefore I can. *Philosophical Studies, 136*(2), 167–216.
Wang, Y. (2018). A logic of goal-directed knowing how. *Synthese, 195*(10), 4419–4439.
Wikipedia Contributors (2017). Automated planning and scheduling. https://en.wikipedia.org/w/index.php?title=Automated_planning_and_scheduling
Wilson, G. M. (1989). *The intentionality of human action*. Stanford: Stanford University Press.

Wooldridge, M. (1997). Agent-based software engineering. *IEE Proceedings Software Engineering, 144*(1), 26–37.
Wooldridge, M., & Jennings, N. R. (1995). Intelligent agents: Theory and practice. *The Knowledge Engineering Review, 10*(2), 115–152.
Xu, M. (2015). Combinations of stit with ought and know. *Journal of Philosophical Logic, 44*(6), 851–877.
Yu, E. (2001). Agent orientation as a modelling paradigm. *Wirtschaftsinformatik, 43*(2), 123–132.
Zimmerman, M. J. (1997). Moral responsibility and ignorance. *Ethics, 107*(3), 410–426.
Zimmerman, M. J. (2008). *Living with uncertainty: The moral significance of ignorance*. Cambridge: Cambridge University Press.

Chapter 5
Joint Action, Participatory Intentions, and Team Reasoning

> *Call this way of conceiving of action a participatory intention: an intention to do my part of a collective act, where my part is defined as the task I ought to perform if we are to be successful in realizing a shared goal. This conception of oneself as contributing to a collective, as manifested in one's deliberation and action, is what lies at the heart of collective action generally, from simple coordination to complex cooperation.*
>
> *Christopher Kutz (2000, p. 81)*

5.1 Introduction

Agents are often held responsible for harms that they intentionally brought about.[1] It is commonplace that such intentional wrongdoings and omissions yield a higher level of culpability (Dubber, 2002). The commonly accepted doctrine of "double effect" holds that there is a distinction between intending and foreseeing consequences, that is, between actions that are done knowingly and those that are done intentionally (Bratman, 1987; Duff, 1982). The idea that an agent's intentions play a role in our responsibility attributions can be made precise in several logically distinct ways. For instance, on one of these conceptions of intentional responsibility, an agent can be held morally responsible for something if (and only if) she did not

Parts of this chapter draw from (Duijf, 2018) and (Duijf, 2021). It is also influenced by published joint work with (Tamminga & Duijf, 2017) and with Jan Broersen and John-Jules Meyer (Duijf et al., 2019).

[1] For example, Mele and Sverdlik (1996, p. 274) write: "In *prototypical* cases (and paradigms in that sense) of actions for which their agents are morally responsible, the agents intentionally perform the actions at issue, but they also *intend* to perform them, or at least intend to try to perform them."

© The Author(s), under exclusive license to Springer Nature Switzerland AG 2022

H. Duijf, *The Logic of Responsibility Voids*, Synthese Library 456,
https://doi.org/10.1007/978-3-030-92655-7_5

intend to avoid it. In any case, the central presupposition of this chapter is that we need to inspect agents' intentions in order to determine who can be held responsible for what.

To investigate the possibility and scope of responsibility gaps, we need to explore the relation between collective and individual blameworthiness. From the perspective of intentional responsibility systems, I hence propose to study the connection, if any, between collective and individual intentionality. When a group of agents has come together to strive for a collective or joint goal, they must act in such a way that their joint action promotes the realization of their collective goal. What kind of personal objective should the members of a group adopt to guarantee that they together promote the realization of their collective goal? What is the relation between a group's collective intention and its members' individual intentions?

To address these questions, I will study various types of intentions that a group member could plausibly adopt when the group collectively aims to achieve a collective goal. Let us call such individual intentions *we-intentions*, as they relate to the group's collective intention. I will characterize and investigate three types of we-intentions: so-called *pro-group*, *team-directed*, and *participatory intentions*.[2] Although the details of these three types of we-intentions are important, they need not worry us at present. One of this chapter's vital contributions is to systematically explain the intricate differences between these we-intentions using logical machinery (Sect. 5.4).

One may think that the group will jointly select an optimal group action regardless of the type of we-intention that its members adopt. I will show that this is, however, not the case. The adoption of, for example, pro-group intentions may produce different group acts from the adoption of participatory intentions. It is therefore important to investigate for each type of we-intention the class of games for which it guarantees successful cooperation. My central results will show that participatory intentions *surpass* both team-directed and pro-group intentions in guaranteeing successful cooperation (Sect. 5.6, visualized in Fig. 5.1). That is, in *any* scenario if either team-directed or pro-group intentions guarantee that a best joint action is performed, then so do participatory intentions. So when a group of agents strives to achieve some joint goal, its members should adopt participatory intentions, rather than team-directed or pro-group intentions.

The chapter is set out as follows. In Sect. 5.2, I will provide a background by discussing team reasoning and prominent philosophical accounts of collective intentionality to highlight and clarify the aim of this chapter. In Sect. 5.3, I will then extend traditional game forms with intentions and introduce a modal logic of agency and intentionality, which is interpreted on these game forms. In Sect. 5.4, the modal-logical machinery is used to accurately characterize the three types of we-intentions—pro-group, team-directed, and participatory intentions. In addition,

[2] Although 'pro-group' and 'team-directed' are hardly distinguishable in plain English, it will become clear in Sect. 5.2 that my terminology tracks the distinction between so-called 'pro-group I-mode reasoning' and 'team-directed reasoning'.

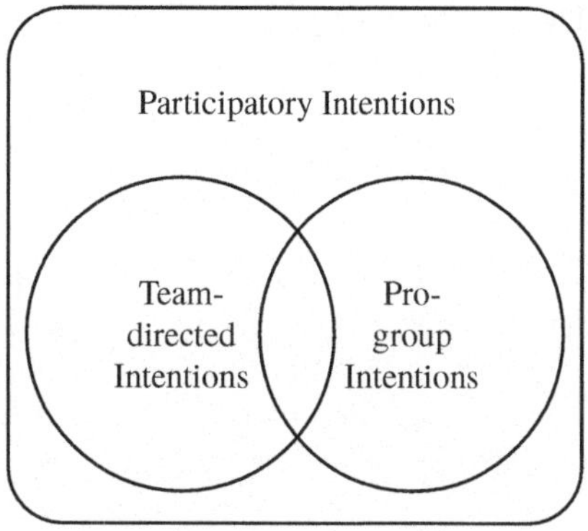

Fig. 5.1 Cooperating successfully: each area depicts the class of games for which the respective intention type guarantees successful cooperation

I will show that team-directed intentions yield the same action recommendations as team reasoning. In Sect. 5.5, I will explore the implications of my work for the work on fairness and cooperation in economics and sociology—this material is optional for the main argument of the chapter. In Sect. 5.6, I will investigate the classes of games for which the three types of we-intentions guarantee successful cooperation. In the concluding section, I will discuss the relation between collective and individual responsibility from the perspective of intentional responsibility systems and my theory of participatory intentions.

5.2 Team Reasoning and Collective Intentionality

The philosophical debate on collective intentionality has recently been enriched by the economics literature on team reasoning. On the one hand, philosophical accounts typically rely on members to form a *personal intention* of sorts.[3] On the other hand, the economic literature on team reasoning claims to yield a better understanding of collective intentionality (Gold & Sugden, 2007; Hakli et al., 2010). Instead of relying on members' personal intentions, the latter approach appeals to the *reasoning process* leading up to the formation of the intention and argues that this focus is needed to grasp collective intentionality. In short, philosophers focus on the intentions of the members, while economists focus on their reasoning process. Although these accounts seem to differ fundamentally, one of the goals of this chapter is to show that team reasoning yields the same action recommendations as one of the we-intentions, viz. team-directed intentions (Result 5.1). I will briefly present these accounts to clarify the scope and limits of my study with regard to

[3] Philosophical accounts of collective intentionality build on participatory intentions (Kutz, 2000), contributory intentions (discussed and rejected by Gilbert, 2009), intentions that we J (Bratman, 2014), and we-intentions (Searle, 1990; Tuomela, 2000, 2005).

Fig. 5.2 The Hi-Lo game

		Player 2: High	Player 2: Low
Player 1	High	2, 2	0, 0
	Low	0, 0	1, 1

team reasoning and to highlight the implications for the philosophical debate on collective intentionality.

5.2.1 Team Reasoning

The idea of team reasoning originates from ethical theories of utilitarianism. Hodgson (1967) used it to demonstrate that rule and act utilitarianism rely on different modes of reasoning. Regan (1980) later expanded on this argument in his theory of 'cooperative utilitarianism'. In the nineties Sugden (1991, 1993) has fruitfully introduced team reasoning to the field of game theory. The core idea of team reasoning is that a member of a group asks herself 'What should *we* do?' rather than 'What should *I* do?'. Team reasoning hence relies on a we-perspective. This means that a team reasoner first considers the group actions available to the group, assesses these group actions in terms of their consequences, finds the group action that best furthers their common or collective interests, and then chooses her component of that group action.[4]

To explain team reasoning in more detail and to contrast it with traditional rational choice theory, let us consider the Hi-Lo game depicted in Fig. 5.2. Team-reasoning theorists claim that traditional rational choice theory does not adequately address the Hi-Lo game. It seems that (*high*, *high*) is the only rational solution, but the players have no reason for preferring one action over the other if they are guided by traditional rational choice theory. Let us see why. It is evident that player 1 should choose *high* if she expects player 2 to choose *high* too. Likewise, she should choose *low* if she expects her opponent to choose *low*. In particular, according to expected utility theory, a player should choose *high* if and only if she judges the probability that her opponent chooses *high* to be greater than ⅓.[5] This means that

[4] Similar ideas have been proposed by Anderson (2001), Hurley (1989); and Gilbert (1989).

[5] The Principle of Indifference (often attributed to Keynes, 1921, Chap. 4) may be invoked to argue that player 1 should assign equal probability to player 2 choosing *high* and player 2 choosing *low*. As desired, this would then entail that that she should choose *high*. However, I seriously doubt that

what is rational for player 1 depends on what player 2 can be expected to choose. At best, this gives conditional recommendations. At worst, it gives her an indeterminate unconditional recommendation. Similar objections apply to dominance reasoning. In such cases game theorists typically invoke the assumption of common knowledge of rationality.

What can player 1 expect player 2 to do under the assumption of common knowledge of rationality? One may think that the Nash equilibrium concept captures this assumption.[6] An action profile is a Nash equilibrium if and only if no player can be better off by unilaterally changing her component action (see Definition 2.5). It is a state of equilibrium because no one has an incentive to deviate from performing her component individual action, given that everyone else performs their respective part. The Hi-Lo game, however, contains two (pure) Nash equilibria: (*high*, *high*) and (*low*, *low*).[7] As a response to this multiplicity, one may want to refine the Nash equilibria by appealing to the Pareto dominance of (*high*, *high*) over (*low*, *low*) in order to select the Nash equilibrium (*high*, *high*) as the only rational solution.[8] There are two problems with such a solution. First, what is the status of the Pareto principle in standard rational choice theory? Hollis and Sugden (1993, p. 13) argue that the Pareto principle "is a principle of rationality only to players who conceive of themselves as a team, but not for players who do not". It is therefore plausible that the rationalization of the Pareto principle requires a departure from the central assumption in rational choice theory that agency is only invested in individuals. Second, in any case, such a (Pareto-dominant) Nash equilibrium only captures a possible status-quo: *if* everyone expected the others to play their part in the Nash equilibrium, *then* they would have a reason to do the same. It hence gives only a conditional recommendation and triggers an infinite regress of reasons.[9] This inadequate response to the Hi-Lo game by traditional rational choice theory stands to be corrected, which is what team reasoning (as studied by Bacharach, Sugden, and Gold) has been designed for.

Bacharach (2006, Chap. 1) and Sugden (2000, Sects. 2, 3, 7 and 8) argue that traditional rational choice theory needs to be augmented with a collectivistic reasoning method to successfully address the Hi-Lo game. Team-reasoning theorists

---

the application of the Principle of Indifference can be justified in the Hi-Lo game as a principle of rationality. Simply stated, I think its application is only compatible with theories of *bounded* rationality (see also Bacharach, 2006, Sect. 1.6).

[6] In fact, the initial question prompted the field of epistemic game theory (see the textbook by Perea, 2012). Among others, such developments have led to a concept of rationalizability (Bernheim, 1984; Pearce, 1984), which is more general than the Nash equilibrium concept. In particular, epistemic game theorists have disproved the claim that common knowledge of rationality entails Nash equilibrium play.

[7] I will restrict my discussion to pure strategies. This restriction is harmless as mixed strategies do not succeed in addressing the present worries.

[8] Harsanyi and Selten (1988) argue for Pareto dominance as a principle of equilibrium selection.

[9] Hollis and Sugden (1993), Sugden (2000, pp. 179–182) and Bacharach (2006, pp. 35–68) provide more elaborate treatments of these objections to traditional rational choice theory.

appeal to the *reasoning process* by which an individual agent reasons about what to do. An individual agent engaged in team reasoning "works out the best feasible combination of actions for all the members of her team, then does her part in it" (Bacharach, 2006, p. 121). In the Hi-Lo game, this reasoning goes as follows: the row player first identifies (*high*, *high*) as the best combination of individual actions that they can perform and then decides to perform her part in that combination, i.e. *high*. Similar reasoning prescribes *high* for the column player. Team reasoning therefore entails that *high* is the only rational option, and selects (*high*, *high*) as the only rational outcome. Problem solved.[10]

To help clarify the scope and limits of my study, let me briefly discuss three questions that the literature on team reasoning needs to address. First, under which conditions should or will an individual agent team reason rather than reason individualistically? Bacharach's (2006) theory of team reasoning is constructed within his variable frame theory. On his view, "among the many different dimensions of the frame of a decision-maker is the 'unit of agency' dimension: the framing agent may think of herself as an individual doer or as part of some collective doer" (p. 137). Group identification is one of the key factors for determining whether an agent adopts the 'we-frame', which, according to Bacharach, may be prompted by psychological factors.[11] Robert Sugden (2003), in contrast, thinks that endorsing team reasoning may depend on an assurance that others will likewise endorse it. He writes: "team reasoning does not generate reasons for choice unless each member of a team has reason to believe that there is common reason to believe that each member of the team endorses and acts on team reasoning. This is a condition of assurance" (pp. 176–177). The details of this condition are spelled out in terms of a Lewisian analysis of reason to believe (for a useful summary, see Gold & Sugden, 2007, Sect. III.3). Although this does not settle the issue, my brief discussion shows that there are diverging views on what triggers team reasoning. For my current purposes, it suffices to assume that team reasoning is prompted in the context of collective intentional action.[12]

Second, what is the group's collective objective? Team reasoning is generally taken to presuppose a group preference (see Bacharach, 1999; Sugden, 2000). There are only a handful of proposals in the literature that specify what this group preference generally involves. Sugden (2010, 2011, 2015) seems to rely on a notion

[10] Bardsley et al. (2010) and Faillo et al. (2013) present ample experimental evidence that people generally agree that *high* is the right thing to do.

[11] Because it may be uncertain which individuals adopt a we-frame, it may be helpful to add that Bacharach (1999, Sect. 2) presents a model of 'unreliable team interactions', which is meant to capture this kind of uncertainty.

[12] Sugden (2003, p. 168) writes: "By 'team reasoning, narrowly defined' I mean a mode of reasoning, followed by one individual, which prescribes that he should perform his part of whichever profile is best for the team. This mode of reasoning may be embedded in a larger logic which specifies the conditions under which team reasoning, narrowly defined, should be used." My analysis is thus limited to 'team reasoning, narrowly defined'; I do not study the larger logic.

of mutual advantage or benefit.[13] Bacharach (2006, p. 59), on the other hand, hypothesizes that a team reasoner "ranks all act-profiles, using a Paretian criterion". There has been some discussion on the relation between the group preference and the individual preferences. For example, Gold (2012, p. 195) writes that Bacharach "allowed in principle that the group objective might be welfare decreasing for some members" and according to Sugden (2000, p. 176) "the preferences of a team are not necessarily reducible to, or capable of being constructed out of, the preferences that govern the choices that the members of the team make as individuals". In the context of collective intentional action, it seems plausible that the group's collective objective is given. Therefore I will assume that the collective objective is specified. My study is hence independent of any particular account of group preferences.

It is helpful to add that team reasoning, interpreted strictly, does not operate on the Hi-Lo game, as represented in Fig. 5.2, because the game only shows the individual preferences. Because team reasoning relies on group preferences, we need to make some assumption regarding these group preferences. It is nonetheless uncontroversial that the group prefers (*high*, *high*) over (*low*, *low*). Team reasoning thus yields a convincing argument for choosing *high* in the Hi-Lo game.[14]

There is a subtle difference between team reasoning and team-directed reasoning. To clarify team reasoning, Sugden (2000, p. 195) writes, for a given group $\mathcal{G}$: "Suppose the following two conditions are satisfied. First, each individual $i \in \mathcal{G}$ engages in team-directed reasoning with respect to $\mathcal{G}$ and [the team-directed preferences]. Second, each individual $i \in \mathcal{G}$ has full team confidence with respect to $\mathcal{G}$ and [the team-directed preferences]. Then ... the team engages in *team reasoning*." Moreover, in these circumstances, the team-directed preferences represent the group preferences. To explain the difference between team-directed and team reasoning, consider the following description by Sugden (2000, p. 195): "Team-directed reasoning is something that one individual can engage in, independently of any others. Similarly, team-directed preferences are preferences that can be held by any individual, independently of any others. In contrast, team reasoning, team preferences and team agency are properties of *a set of* individuals, and require a network of common beliefs." Since I will not study the network of common beliefs required for full team confidence, and because I study individual agents' independent reasoning, my study can be viewed as focusing on team-directed reasoning. However, because my study is cast against the background of collective intentional action, it seems plausible that the collective objective is given and that the condition of full team confidence is met. Hence, my discussions and results also pertain to team reasoning.

[13] Karpus and Radzvilas (2018) develop a detailed formal account of mutual advantage.

[14] In recent years, Sugden (2015, p.156) seems to embrace a theory of team reasoning that relies on notions of *mutual advantage* and *conventions*. For example, he writes: "If individuals are to cooperate effectively, they need to be ready to play their parts in mutually beneficial practices that seem to them to be—and perhaps really are—less than ideal." His new theory of team reasoning is, for instance, consistent with (*low*, *low*)-play in the Hi-Lo game. Nonetheless, I will stick to the original idea that team reasoning is designed to explain why *high* is uniquely rational.

Third, how can the theory of team reasoning be extended to apply to a greater variety of problems—not just the Hi-Lo game?[15] This is exactly my concern in this chapter. By studying the logical form of the we-intentions that may result from team reasoning, I will provide a framework for investigating a wide range of problems. Most importantly, my study will include cases where there is no unique best group action. That is, it includes scenarios in which the group preference does not determine a unique best combination of individual actions. I will show that team reasoning may be improved by taking the resulting we-intentions to be participatory intentions (Sect. 5.6).

5.2.2 Collective Intentionality and We-intentions

To introduce philosophical analyses of collective intentionality it is best to start with one of the most influential accounts. The conditions for a shared intentional activity to J are summarized by Michael Bratman as follows:

(i) we each intend that we J.
(ii) we each intend the following: that we J by way of the intentions of each that we J (and that the route from these intentions to our joint activity satisfies the connection condition).
(iii) we each intend the following: that we J by way of meshing sub-plans of each of our intentions in favour of our J-ing.
(vii) there is common knowledge among the participants of the conditions cited in this construction. (p. 60 Bratman, 2014, —amended notation)[16]

Many contemporary theorists disagree with some part of Bratman's analysis, but they largely remain faithful to its conceptual apparatus. Most importantly, a collective intention is typically viewed as an interlocking web of individual intentions.[17] There is much debate on how to view these individual intentions, which has prompted two opposing theories: either suggesting that these individual intentions

[15] Compare Bacharach (2006, p. 58—amended notation): "There are three requirements for a good theory of why people play *high* in Hi-Lo: (i) that it imply observed behaviour, that is, the almost universal choice of *high* in normal circumstances; (ii) that it do so intelligibly to us, which (to the extent that *high* intuitively and stably seems to us the only rational thing to do) involves displaying *high* as uniquely rational—that is, giving principles of rationality which are themselves persuasive, and showing they dictate doing *high*; and (iii) that it be part of a unified theory of a wide range of problems, not just Hi-Lo—for example, all problems of cooperation." My study mainly addresses the third requirement.

[16] Unfortunately I cannot do full justice to his elaborate theory, yet this characterization includes Bratman's most vital building blocks and highlights the gist of his approach.

[17] Compare, for example, Tuomela (2005, p. 330): "it can technically be said that a joint intention consists of the participants' we-intentions about the existence of which the participants have mutual belief".

are held in a particular *mode*, or suggesting that they have a particular *content*.[18] More specifically, mode-based accounts hold that the individual intentions underlying a collective intention are fundamentally different from standard individual intentions; content-based accounts deny this. Bratman's account is best interpreted as a content-based account since he notes that the difference between standard intentions to act and intentions that we *J* "is not between two fundamentally different attitudes, but between two different kinds of contents of the attitude of intending" (Bratman, 2014, p. 14).[19] The three types of we-intentions that will be introduced in this chapter—pro-group, team-directed, and participatory intentions—are best viewed as standard intentions that are distinguished by their content. Hence, my theory of we-intentions is best viewed as a content-based account.[20]

To explain the gist of mode-based accounts of collective intentionality and to discuss the implications of my central results, I focus on Tuomela's philosophical theory of sociality (Tuomela, 2000, 2005, 2006, 2007), which relies on the distinction between the I-mode and the we-mode: "The we-mode involves functioning as a group member and not as a private person while the I-mode is concerned only with functioning as a private person" (Tuomela, 2006, p. 49). Following Hakli et al. (2010, pp. 315–318), it is useful to divide the we-mode reasoning process up into three stages: the first results in the formation of "a group preference matrix", the second reaches "a joint intention to act", and in the third "the agents select their part-actions".[21] I focus solely on the third stage of the we-mode reasoning process.

My study is thus cast against the background of collective intentional action. For my purposes, the notions of *pro-group I-mode* and *we-mode* in decision making are essential.

> The pro-group I-mode is concerned with promoting the group's interests. (Hakli et al., 2010, p. 296)

[18] There is a third minority view which analyses collective intention and action by appealing to a plural subject. Gilbert (1990, p. 7), for instance, writes: "When a goal has a plural subject, each of a number of persons (two or more) has, in effect, offered his will to be part of a pool of wills which is dedicated, as one, to that goal."

[19] Kutz (2000, p. 74) concurs: "I will defend an account of collective action in which what makes a set of individual acts a case of jointly intentional action is the content of the intentions with which the individuals act."

[20] My use of the term 'participatory intentions' is inspired by Kutz (2000), although I do not study the relation between our notions. Kutz writes: "On the one hand, collective activity is an ineliminable part of the content of agents' participatory intentions. [...] On the other hand, participatory intentions are simply a special class of ordinary intentions, differentiated by their group-oriented content" (pp. 85–86). He thus has in mind a standard intention.

[21] Hakli et al. (2010, p. 318) extensively discuss these three stages and argue that the result of the first stage is common knowledge, but the latter two "can be performed by the individual agents autonomously as generally supposed in non-cooperative game theory". Because the latter two stages of we-mode reasoning do not require a network of beliefs, this means that they can be viewed as team-directed reasoning.

That is, a pro-group I-mode agent transforms her preferences and adopts the group's objectives as if they were her own personal objectives. Then she decides what to do by way of individualistic reasoning. In such a case, I will say that she forms a *pro-group intention*, meaning that she intends to further the group's objective.[22] Note that adopting a pro-group intention may require her to take the perspective of the group to determine the group's objective.[23]

In contrast, we-mode reasoning naturally relates to team reasoning:

> We-mode reasoning and Bacharach's team reasoning yield the same action recommendations in game-theoretic choice situations. (Hakli et al., 2010, p. 301)

That is, for my purposes, a we-mode reasoner and a team reasoner are the same. I will show that the results of team reasoning can be explained by so-called team-directed intentions, which are best viewed as standard intentions with a particular content (Result 5.1). The distinction between pro-group I-mode and we-mode can therefore be characterized in my content-based account as the distinction between pro-group intentions and team-directed intentions.[24] This means that an important part of the distinguished we-mode reasoning can be reduced to I-mode reasoning with a team-directed intention. This opposes Hakli et al. (2010, Thesis (5) on p. 307): "We-mode reasoning is not reducible to pro-group I-mode reasoning, i.e. it is not definable by or functionally constructable from I-mode reasoning."[25] Moreover, since I will argue that team-directed intentions can be improved to participatory intentions, an important part of we-mode reasoning can be improved by taking the resulting intentions to be participatory intentions (Sect. 5.6).

---

[22] Compare Bacharach's (1999, p. 128—notation adapted) notion of a "group benefactor": "Let us call a type of player who reasons individualistically but whose payoff function coincides with that of a team $\mathcal{G}$ a *benefactor* of $\mathcal{G}$." Hakli et al. (2010, p. 301) argue that "pro-group I-mode reasoning, in cases in which agents adopt the group preferences, and Bacharach's reasoning as a team benefactor yield the same action recommendations." So, a pro-group I-mode reasoner, a group benefactor, and a pro-group intention adopter yield the same action recommendations.

[23] Hakli et al. (2010, Section 3.2) describe the formation of group preferences by means of we-mode reasoning. It thus seems possible that a pro-group I-mode reasoner partially reasons in the we-mode, though not till the very end. To be more precise, a pro-group I-mode reasoner only follows the first stage of we-mode reasoning.

[24] When assuming the natural candidate for the group preference in the Hi-Lo game, the theory of team reasoning solves the Hi-Lo game by letting the agents adopt a particular reasoning method, my theory of team-directed intentions, instead, can be interpreted as solving the Hi-Lo game by letting the agents adopt a particular intention.

[25] These opposing results derive from the fact that Hakli et al. (2010) assume that I-mode reasoning is connected to equilibrium-based reasoning, whereas I assume that I-mode reasoning is connected to dominance reasoning.

5.3 Formal Preliminaries

5.3.1 Games and Intentions

A game form can be taken to represent an interdependent decision context involving a finite set N of individual agents where each agent has a finite set of available actions A_i. (See Definition 2.1 and Sect. 2.2 for a more detailed introduction to the theory of games and further notational conventions.) To study various types of we-intentions, these game forms need to be supplemented with intentions. Though philosophers have studied various guises of intentions, I will restrict my attention to future-directed intentions as studied in the planning theory of intentions advanced by Bratman (1987).[26] There are two different types of future-directed intentions: one can intend to perform a certain action, or one can intend to realize a certain state of affairs. I will focus primarily on intentions to realize a certain state of affairs. Because I assume that an action profile fully determines the future state of the world, (the content of) an intention can be modelled by a set of action profiles.[27] Intuitively, an agent's intention is modelled by $J \subseteq A$ if she intends to realize the aspects that all outcomes of the action profiles in J have in common. For simplicity's sake, I will restrict to agents having just a single intention. So the intention of an—individual or collective—agent $\mathcal{G}$ is modelled by a set of action profiles $Int_{\mathcal{G}} \subseteq A$ and, furthermore I propose to say that the agent intends to $Int_{\mathcal{G}}$. To model that rational intentions are feasible, I require that $Int_{\mathcal{G}} \neq \emptyset$.

Definition 5.1 (Games with Intentions) A *game with intentions* S is a tuple $\langle N, (A_i), (Int_{\mathcal{G}})\rangle$, involving a game form $\langle N, (A_i)\rangle$ and intentions $Int_{\mathcal{G}} \in A$ ($Int_{\mathcal{G}} \neq \emptyset$), one for each group of agents $\mathcal{G}$. To picture these intentions, I often use utilities ($u_{\mathcal{G}}$) where

$$u_{\mathcal{G}}(a) = \begin{cases} 1, \text{ if } a \in Int_{\mathcal{G}} \\ 0, \text{ otherwise.}^{28} \end{cases}$$

A *game model with intentions* is a game with intentions supplemented with a valuation $V : \mathcal{P} \to 2^A$ (see also Sect. 2.4).

---

[26] These future-directed intentions (such as my intention to submit this paper by the end of the month) have been distinguished from intentions in action (such as my typing with the intention to finish this introduction) and intentional acts (such as my typing these words intentionally) (see Anscombe, 1963).

[27] As discussed in Sect. 2.4, game forms correspond to *deterministic* stit models. In this regard, the framework is very similar to that of van Hees and Roy (2008). Alternatively, if one wants to retain indeterminism, an agent called 'nature' can be added to model the indeterminacy. That is, once every agent has made her choice, the exact outcome is determined by nature's move.

[28] Although my conceptual analysis involves intentions, a decision theorist can view my formal analysis as being restricted to only binary utility functions.

Intentions provide a "*filter of admissibility* for options" (Bratman, 1987, p. 33). Although Bratman does not use this term in any decision-theoretic sense, I accept the intuition that an agent intending to J is required to avoid inadmissible actions, i.e. avoid dominated actions. (See Sect. 2.2 for a more elaborate discussion of this dominance principle.) Admissibility captures the idea that an agent takes all actions of the other agents into consideration; none is entirely ruled out. Avoiding inadmissible actions is more restrictive than avoiding *strictly* dominated actions. I thus take 'providing a filter of admissibility' to mean that an agent's intention requires her to choose an admissible action, that is, one that is not dominated.[29]

In traditional rational choice theory it is common to derive this dominance ordering from exogenously given utilities (see Sect. 2.2). However, I am interested in the dominance orderings resulting from the endogenously adopted intentions. I therefore submit that a dominance ordering is relative to a certain intention. A group action $a_{\mathcal{G}}$ is admissible with respect to an intention to J if and only if no other group action promotes the realization of J, regardless of what the group's non-members do, better than $a_{\mathcal{G}}$ does. So I require that an agent intending to J should also promote J, that is, should perform an action that is admissible with respect to J.

Since I only consider intentions to realize a state of affairs, the adopted dominance ordering is relative to the realization of some state of affairs, instead of maximizing payoffs, as is usually the case in traditional rational choice theory.[30] Moreover, note that altering the state of affairs impacts the resulting dominance ordering. In decision-theoretic terms, an agent may want to optimize her own happiness, but she could instead aim at optimizing their collective, perhaps average or minimum, happiness; pursuing these different states of affairs may result in different dominance orderings. Still, the principle by which the dominance ordering results from a certain state of affairs is uniform.

The principle guiding the dominance orderings combines the sure-thing principle and reasoning by cases. More specifically, a group action $a_{\mathcal{G}}$ simply dominates $a'_{\mathcal{G}}$ with respect to a given intention if and only if $a_{\mathcal{G}}$ promotes realizing that intention at least as well as $a'_{\mathcal{G}}$, regardless of what the group's non-members do (see Sect. 2.2 and Definitions 2.7 and 3.2).

Definition 5.2 (Dominance) Let $S = \langle N, (A_i) \rangle$ be a game form, let $\mathcal{G} \subseteq N$ be a group of agents, and let $J \subseteq A$ represent a state of affairs. Let $a_{\mathcal{G}}$ and $a'_{\mathcal{G}}$ be group

[29] Note that I do not employ iterated admissibility, i.e. iterated deletion of dominated actions (see the discussion in Kohlberg & Mertens (1986, Section 2.7) and the discussion of epistemic characterizations of iterated admissibility in Brandenburger et al. (2008, Section 2.6)). One of the main reasons for refraining from doing so is that iterated admissibility is subject to some paradoxes: for instance, it is well known that the order in which dominated strategies are eliminated can affect the outcome of the process. Furthermore, I believe the core results (Results 5.1 through 5.4) of this chapter are sustained if iterated admissibility is taken to entail that inadmissible actions are avoided.

[30] However, note that, despite the absence of beliefs and degrees of beliefs, these are intimately related as I interchangeably model the intentions by using a set of possible worlds and a utility function (see Definition 5.1).

actions available to $\mathcal{G}$. Then $a_{\mathcal{G}}$*simply dominates* $a'_{\mathcal{G}}$ *with respect to* J, notation $a_{\mathcal{G}} \succeq_J a'_{\mathcal{G}}$, is defined by:

$a_{\mathcal{G}} \succeq_S a'_{\mathcal{G}}$ iff for all $a''_{-\mathcal{G}} \in A_{-\mathcal{G}}$ it holds that $(a'_{\mathcal{G}}, a''_{-\mathcal{G}}) \in J$ implies $(a_{\mathcal{G}}, a''_{-\mathcal{G}}) \in J$.

Weak dominance is defined in terms of simple dominance: $a_{\mathcal{G}} \succ_J a'_{\mathcal{G}}$ if and only if $a_{\mathcal{G}} \succeq_J a'_{\mathcal{G}}$ and $a'_{\mathcal{G}} \not\succeq_S a_{\mathcal{G}}$.

The set of *admissible group actions with respect to* J that are available to a group $\mathcal{G}$ in a game form S are defined in terms of the dominance ordering on $A_{\mathcal{G}}$. A group action $a_{\mathcal{G}}$ in $A_{\mathcal{G}}$ is admissible if and only if it is not weakly dominated by any group action in $A_{\mathcal{G}}$:

Definition 5.3 (Admissible Actions) Let $S = \langle N, (A_i)\rangle$ be a game form, let $\mathcal{G} \subseteq N$ be a group of agents, and let $J \subseteq A$ represent a state of affairs. Then the set of $\mathcal{G}$'s *admissible actions in* S *with respect to* J, denoted by $\mathit{Admissible}_S(\mathcal{G}, J)$, is given by

$\mathit{Admissible}_S(\mathcal{G}, J) = \{a_{\mathcal{G}} \in A_{\mathcal{G}} \mid \text{there is no } a'_{\mathcal{G}} \in A_{\mathcal{G}} \text{ such that } a'_{\mathcal{G}} \succ_J a_{\mathcal{G}}\}$.

When we represent the content of an intention by a binary utility function rather than a set of possible worlds, this definition translates to: $a_{\mathcal{G}} \succeq_J a'_{\mathcal{G}}$ if and only if for all $a''_{-\mathcal{G}} \in A_{-\mathcal{G}}$ we have $u_J(a'_{\mathcal{G}}, a''_{-\mathcal{G}}) \geq u_J(a_{\mathcal{G}}, a''_{-\mathcal{G}})$ (where $u_J(a) = 1$ if $a \in J$ and 0 otherwise). This highlights a straightforward connection to the standard simple dominance ordering, which is studied in traditional rational choice theory.

Note that this definition implies that for every group of agents and any collective intention there is at least one admissible group action with respect to that collective intention (because A is assumed to be finite).

To illustrate the dominance ordering and admissibility, consider game S_2 in Fig. 5.3. First, observe that there is no connection between personal and group intentions in this particular example. Second, regarding the dominance ordering, since agent i's intention is not realized at (a'_i, a'_j), we can see that for agent i only actions a_i and a''_i are admissible with respect to her intention. For agent j, action a''_j is dominated by a_j with respect to her intention, while a_j and a'_j are incomparable and, hence, both admissible. That is, $a_j \succ_{Int_j} a''_j$, $a_j \not\succeq_{Int_j} a'_j$, and $a'_j \not\succeq_{Int_j} a_j$. For the group $\mathcal{G}$, consisting of agents i and j, the admissible group actions with respect to its collective intention are (a_i, a_j), (a'_i, a_j), and (a_i, a''_j). Since we accept the intuition that an agent intending to J should avoid inadmissible actions, this means that agent i can choose a_i and agent j can choose a'_j, with regard to their respective individual intention. It follows that the individual intentions allow (a_i, a'_j), which is

Fig. 5.3 Game model S_2, where the intentions are represented by a triple of utilities representing i's, j's, and $\{i, j\}$'s intention

		Agent j		
		a_j	a'_j	a''_j
Agent i	a_i	1,1,1	1,0,0	0,1,1
	a'_i	1,1,1	0,0,0	0,0,0
	a''_i	1,0,0	1,1,0	0,0,0

inadmissible with respect to the collective intention. The individual intentions hence do not guarantee that a best *group action* is performed, which is not a surprise in this example because of our first observation.

5.3.2 Modal Logic of Agency and Intentionality

In this section I will introduce a modal-logical language, which supplements the traditional stit language with two operators. (See Sect. 2.3 for a more detailed introduction to the stit theory of agency and further notational conventions.) Let me briefly give intuitive readings of these operators before considering the respective formal semantics and providing a more detailed conceptual discussion. The language includes the central operators of the stit theory of agency, viz. $[\mathcal{G}\ \mathsf{stit}]\varphi$ and $\Box\varphi$, and adds two operators: $[\mathcal{G}\ \mathsf{int}]\varphi$ expresses that 'group $\mathcal{G}$ intends to φ' and $[\mathcal{G}\ \mathsf{prom}]\varphi$ expresses that 'group $\mathcal{G}$ promotes φ regardless of what the others do'.

Definition 5.4 (Syntax) The formal language $\mathfrak{L}_{istit}$ is as follows:

$$\varphi := q \mid \neg\varphi \mid \varphi \wedge \varphi \mid \Box\varphi \mid [\mathcal{G}\ \mathsf{stit}]\varphi \mid [\mathcal{G}\ \mathsf{int}]\varphi \mid [\mathcal{G}\ \mathsf{prom}]\varphi,$$

where q ranges over a given countable set of propositions $\mathcal{P}$ and $\mathcal{G}$ ranges over subsets of a given finite set of agents N.

The game models with intentions and the dominance ordering, presented in the previous section, are used to provide formal semantics for this logical language:

Definition 5.5 (Semantics) Let $S = \langle N, (A_i), (Int_{\mathcal{G}}), V\rangle$ be a game model with intentions and let $\varphi \in \mathfrak{L}_{istit}$. Then the truth of φ at a profile a in S, notation: $S, a \models \varphi$, is given by the following (suppressing the standard propositional clauses):

$S, a \models \Box\varphi$	iff	every $b \in A$ satisfies $S, b \models \varphi$;
$S, a \models [\mathcal{G}\ \mathsf{stit}]\varphi$	iff	every $b \in A$ with $b_{\mathcal{G}} = a_{\mathcal{G}}$ satisfies $S, b \models \varphi$;
$S, a \models [\mathcal{G}\ \mathsf{prom}]\varphi$	iff	$a_{\mathcal{G}}$ is admissible with respect to $\{b \mid S, b \models \varphi\}$;[31]
$S, a \models [\mathcal{G}\ \mathsf{int}]\varphi$	iff	we have $Int_{\mathcal{G}} = \{b \mid S, b \models \varphi\}$.[32]

[31] A technical remark: the semantics for the $[\mathcal{G}\ \mathsf{prom}]$ operator could also have been given by neighbourhood semantics, where the neighbourhoods for a group $\mathcal{G}$ of a profile a would be given by the collection $\{M \subseteq A \mid a_{\mathcal{G}}$ is admissible with respect to $M\}$.

[32] Note the equality sign, which means that we employ neighbourhood semantics. If we had employed the standard possible-worlds semantics, it would have read '$Int_{\mathcal{G}}$ consists only of φ-worlds', meaning $Int_{\mathcal{G}} \subseteq \{a \in A \mid a$ satisfies $\varphi\}$. Konolige and Pollack (1993) were the first to model intentions using neighbourhood semantics instead of the standard possible-worlds semantics.

The first two clauses implement the ideas from stit theory regarding the semantics of statements of the form 'it is historically settled that φ' (formalized by $\Box\varphi$) and 'group $\mathcal{G}$ sees to it that φ' (formalized by $[\mathcal{G}\ \mathsf{stit}]\varphi$), respectively. It may be useful to add that the stit modality $[\mathcal{G}\ \mathsf{stit}]\varphi$ can be interpreted, relative to a profile a, as 'group $\mathcal{G}$ guarantees that φ holds regardless of what the others do'. Indeed, the truth condition of $S, a \models [\mathcal{G}\ \mathsf{stit}]\varphi$ is equivalent to requiring that for every $b_{-\mathcal{G}} \in A_{-\mathcal{G}}$ we have $S, (a_{\mathcal{G}}, b_{-\mathcal{G}}) \models \varphi$. In other words, in playing $a_{\mathcal{G}}$ group $\mathcal{G}$ is α-effective for φ. This reveals that the group has enough control to ensure φ.

The dual stit modality $\langle \mathcal{G}\ \mathsf{stit}\rangle\varphi$ expresses that 'group $\mathcal{G}$ allows for φ', that is, group $\mathcal{G}$'s action does not rule out φ. At a profile $a \in A$, this means that there is a combination of actions of the other agents $b_{-\mathcal{G}} \in A_{-\mathcal{G}}$ such that $S, (a_{\mathcal{G}}, b_{-\mathcal{G}}) \models \varphi$. Or, equivalently, group action $a_{\mathcal{G}}$ is compatible with φ.

The new modality $[\mathcal{G}\ \mathsf{prom}]\varphi$ expresses that group $\mathcal{G}$ performs a best group action with respect to realizing φ, where 'best' is equated with 'admissible'. The underlying intuition is that there may be multiple best actions, each of which is admissible. So, this operator expresses that group $\mathcal{G}$ avoids actions that are inadmissible with respect to φ. This operator hence refers to admissibility, as introduced in Definition 5.3.[33] The intuition that an agent intending to φ is required to avoid actions that are inadmissible with respect to φ thus means that an agent intending to φ is required to promote φ.[34]

One may ask whether the $[\mathcal{G}\ \mathsf{prom}]$-operator can be reduced to an $\mathfrak{L}_{stit}$-formula.[35] In general, this is impossible (Lemma D.1). This means that extending the standard stit logic with the $[\mathcal{G}\ \mathsf{prom}]$-operator increases the expressivity of the logic. However, for a given game model S, if there is a group action $a_{\mathcal{G}} \in A_{\mathcal{G}}$ that is $\preceq_{\varphi}$-maximal in $A_{\mathcal{G}}$, then the $[\mathcal{G}\ \mathsf{prom}]$-operator can be reduced to an $\mathfrak{L}_{stit}$-formula, viz. $[\mathcal{G}\ \mathsf{prom}]\varphi$ is equivalent to $[\mathcal{G}\ \mathsf{stit}](\langle -\mathcal{G}\ \mathsf{stit}\rangle\varphi \rightarrow \varphi)$ in such models (Lemma D.2), which is equivalent to $[\mathcal{G}\ \mathsf{stit}](\neg\varphi \rightarrow [-\mathcal{G}\ \mathsf{stit}]\neg\varphi)$. The latter formula expresses that group $\mathcal{G}$ guarantees that if φ does not hold, then the other agents guarantee that φ does not hold regardless of what group $\mathcal{G}$ does. Since these details need not distract us at the moment, I refer the interested reader to Appendix D.

The semantics of the intention operator emphasize that we only consider intentions to realize a certain state of affairs, which is represented by a set of action profiles. The truth condition for $[\mathcal{G}\ \mathsf{int}]\varphi$ employs neighbourhood semantics and thus induces the reading that the group's intention is represented by φ. These neighbourhood semantics are usually employed to avoid problems concerning logical omniscience, that is, to avoid intentions being closed under logical implica-

---

[33] A similar operator has been used by Broersen (2011) to model attempts. Whereas he uses maximizing expected utility, I adopted admissibility as the underlying decision principle. Although there might be some connections to attempts, here I do not want to argue that the $[\mathcal{G}\ \mathsf{prom}]$-operator adequately models attempts.

[34] In a game with intentions S, one could formalize this requirement by the schema $[i\ \mathsf{int}]\varphi \rightarrow [i\ \mathsf{prom}]\varphi$.

[35] Recall that $\mathfrak{L}_{stit}$ only contains the operators $\Box\varphi$ and $[\mathcal{G}\ \mathsf{stit}]\varphi$ (Definition 2.13).

tions.[36] More specifically, these semantics are typically used to avoid the side-effect problem.[37] My motivation is different: it is generally impossible for an agent to perform an action that is both admissible with regard to her intention and admissible with regard to all its logical consequences.[38]

Since my aim is to contribute to a conceptual analysis of collective agency and team reasoning, a complete logical investigation is well beyond my current ambition.[39] Still, it is useful for my current purposes to examine some logical properties of the new $[\mathcal{G}\ \mathsf{prom}]$-operator:

Proposition 5.1 *Let φ be an $\mathfrak{L}_{istit}$-formula and let $\mathcal{G}$ be a group of agents, possibly a singleton. Then*

1. $\models \Diamond[\mathcal{G}\ \mathsf{prom}]\varphi$, *one is always able to promote φ,*
2. $\not\models [\mathcal{G}\ \mathsf{prom}]\varphi \to [\mathcal{G}\ \mathsf{stit}]\varphi$, *promoting φ does not entail ensuring φ,*
3. $\models [\mathcal{G}\ \mathsf{stit}]\varphi \to [\mathcal{G}\ \mathsf{prom}]\varphi$, *guaranteeing φ entails promoting φ,*
4. $\models [\mathcal{G}\ \mathsf{prom}]\varphi \wedge \Diamond\varphi \to \langle \mathcal{G}\ \mathsf{stit}\rangle\varphi$, *promoting φ while φ is possible entails allowing φ,*
5. $\models [\mathcal{G}\ \mathsf{prom}]\varphi \wedge \Diamond[\mathcal{G}\ \mathsf{stit}]\varphi \to [\mathcal{G}\ \mathsf{stit}]\varphi$, *promoting φ while being able to ensure φ entails guaranteeing φ,*
6. $\models \Diamond[\mathcal{G}\ \mathsf{stit}]\varphi \to ([\mathcal{G}\ \mathsf{prom}]\varphi \leftrightarrow [\mathcal{G}\ \mathsf{stit}]\varphi)$, *if one is able to guarantee φ, then promoting φ is equivalent to ensuring φ.*

Item **1** establishes that one is always able to promote φ, irrespective of its logical form. The fact that this includes infeasible properties, in particular logical inconsistencies, may seem unsatisfactory; however, for infeasible φ it does not matter what one does, because one's choice of action does not change the fact that φ will not be realized. Items **2** and **3** show that guaranteeing φ is logically stronger than promoting φ. Item **4** expresses that if φ is feasible, promoting φ entails that one performs an action that is compatible with φ. Or, equivalently, if one performs an action that is incompatible with φ, then one is surely not promoting φ. Items **5** and **6** show that, although promoting φ is logically weaker than guaranteeing φ, if one is able to ensure φ, then promoting φ is equivalent to guaranteeing φ. This shows that one is definitely devoted to realizing φ if one promotes φ.

Because my primary interest is in how intentions constrain the choice of strategy of the respective agents, I refrain from a logical analysis of the intention operator. Nonetheless, including these intention operators allows us to represent those cases

[36] More formally, there exist φ and ψ such that $\models \varphi \to \psi$ while $\not\models [i\ \mathsf{int}]\varphi \to [i\ \mathsf{int}]\psi$.

[37] This is why Konolige and Pollack (1993, p. 178) decide to model intentions using neighbourhood semantics.

[38] To see this, reconsider the game model S_2 in Fig. 5.3. We have already noticed that only a_i and a_i'' are admissible with respect to Int_i. However, both fail to be admissible with respect to $Int_i \cup \{(a_i', a_j'), (a_i', a_j'')\}$.

[39] For those who are interested in completing this logical investigation, it may be helpful to recall the correspondence results (Sect. 2.4) and the completeness result for epistemic stit theory (Sect. 4.2).

where agents have certain intentions and it paves the way for representing different intentional responsibility systems (see Sect. 5.7 and Footnotes 59 and 65). Instead of pursuing a logical analysis, I will investigate the outcomes that certain individual intentions guarantee. To do so, I rely on the intuition that an agent intending to φ is required to avoid actions that are inadmissible with respect to φ. That is, an agent intending to φ is required to promote φ. Individual intentions therefore guarantee that individual agents choose actions that are admissible with regard to their respective intentions. To generalize, a set of individual intentions guarantee a certain property ψ only if it is the case that whenever the individual agents choose actions that are admissible with respect to their intentions, then ψ holds. It is natural to interpret this as a conditional: if agent i were to intend φ, and therefore perform an individual action that is admissible with respect to φ, then ψ will hold. That is, whenever the agent promotes φ then ψ will hold.

Definition 5.6 Let S be a game model with intentions, let $a \in A$ be a profile, let φ and ψ be formulas in $\mathfrak{L}_{istit}$, and let i be an individual agent. Then we say that, in S, agent i's intention to φ guarantees ψ if and only if $S, a \vDash \Box([i \text{ prom}]\varphi \rightarrow \psi)$.[40]

More generally, let $\mathcal{G}$ be a group of agents and let ψ and φ_i be formulas in $\mathfrak{L}_{istit}$, one for each $i \in \mathcal{G}$. Then we say that, in S, the collection of individual intentions represented by $(\varphi_i)_{i\in\mathcal{G}}$ guarantees ψ if and only if $S, a \vDash \Box(\bigwedge_{i\in\mathcal{G}}[i \text{ prom}]\varphi_i \rightarrow \psi)$.

The latter can be semantically interpreted as follows: let $P \subseteq A$ and J_i represent a state of affairs, one for each $i \in \mathcal{G}$. Then we say that, in S, the individual intentions $\{J_i\}_{i\in\mathcal{G}}$ guarantee that P holds if and only if for every $b \in A$, if for every $i \in \mathcal{G}$ it is the case that b_i is admissible with respect to J_i, then property P holds at b, that is, $b \in P$.

The focus, later in the chapter, is going to be on whether certain we-intentions guarantee that a best group action is performed.

5.4 Three Types of We-intentions

Which individual attitudes are warranted in the context of a collective intention? This section serves three purposes. First, in the following, the logical language is used to formalize and study so-called pro-group intentions, team-directed intentions, and participatory intentions. The running example to illustrate these types of we-intentions is displayed in Fig. 5.4. Second, in Sect. 5.4.2 I will show that team reasoning and team-directed intentions yield the same action recommendations (Result 5.1). Finally, at the end of Sect. 5.4.3 I will show, using the running example, that these three types of we-intentions yield different action recommendations.

[40] Note that this does not preclude the possibility that $S, a \nvDash [i \text{ int}]\varphi$.

Agent k: a_k

Agent i \ Agent j	a_j	a'_j	a''_j
a_i	φ 1	φ 1	0
a'_i	φ 1	0	0
a''_i	0	0	φ 1

Agent k: a'_k

Agent i \ Agent j	a_j	a'_j	a''_j
a_i	φ 1	φ 1	0
a'_i	φ 1	0	0
a''_i	0	0	0

Fig. 5.4 Game model S_4: a three-player game, where $\{i, j\} = \mathcal{G}$ collectively intends to φ, showing only the collective intention of $\mathcal{G}$

I henceforth presuppose that group $\mathcal{G}$ collectively intends to φ and investigate what team reasoning and the we-intention types amount to. Just as an individual agent's intention requires her to perform an individual action that is admissible with respect to that individual intention, a group's collective intention requires the group to perform a group action that is admissible with respect to its collective intention. Or, equivalently, the group's collective intention provides a filter of admissibility for the available group actions in which the admissible group actions are best. The group should therefore perform a group action that promotes the realization of what is collectively intended.

5.4.1 *Pro-group Intentions*

A member i of $\mathcal{G}$ could adopt the collective goal as her own, instead of furthering her personal goals, and pursue it to the best of her abilities. In this case, I propose to say that agent i's intention is *pro-group*. The agent's pro-group intention ignores the contributions others can make and simply requires the agent to do her best to realize the collective intention regardless of what others do. The pro-group intention of the agent is represented by φ. Various game-theoretic enterprises try to explain cooperative behaviour by transforming the preferences of the group members (see Sect. 5.5); the same intuition underlies this first we-intention type:

Definition 5.8 (Pro-group Intentions) Suppose group $\mathcal{G}$ collectively intends to φ. Let $i \in \mathcal{G}$ be a member of the group $\mathcal{G}$. Agent i's intention is *pro-group* iff she

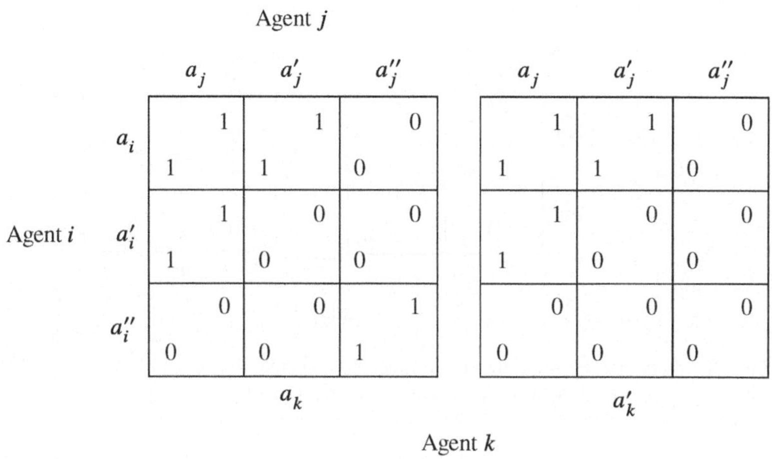

Fig. 5.5 The pro-group intentions of individual agents i and j in game model S_4

intends to promote the group's objective, in other words, if and only if $[i \ \mathsf{int}]\varphi$ obtains.[41]

In game model with intentions S_4 of Fig. 5.4, observe that the pro-group intentions of individual agents i and j are represented by φ, as depicted in Fig. 5.5. Let us consider which individual actions are admissible with respect to these pro-group intentions. We have $a_i \succ_\varphi a'_i$, because for instance $S_4, (a'_i, a'_j, a_k) \nvDash \varphi$ and $S_4, (a_i, a'_j, a_k) \vDash \varphi$. And, because $S_4, (a''_i, a'_j, a_k) \nvDash \varphi$, we also have $a''_i \not\succeq_\varphi a_i$. Likewise, by comparing (a_i, a''_j, a_k) and (a''_i, a''_j, a_k), we derive that $a_i \not\succeq_\varphi a''_i$. Hence, for agent i, only a_i and a''_i are admissible with respect to her pro-group intention. By symmetry, for agent j, only a_j and a''_j are admissible with respect to her pro-group intention.

5.4.2 *Team-Directed Intentions*

Discontent with preference transformations, Bacharach, Sugden, and Gold argue, on various occasions, that team reasoning is more appropriate for explaining and predicting cooperative behaviour. Instead, they propose an *agency* transformation. When engaging in team reasoning, a member of a group first identifies a best combination of individual actions that the group members can perform and then decides to perform the individual action that is her part of that combination.

[41] In a game with intentions S, the requirement that group members adopt pro-group intentions could be formalized by the schema $[\mathcal{G} \ \mathsf{int}]\varphi \rightarrow [i \ \mathsf{int}]\varphi$.

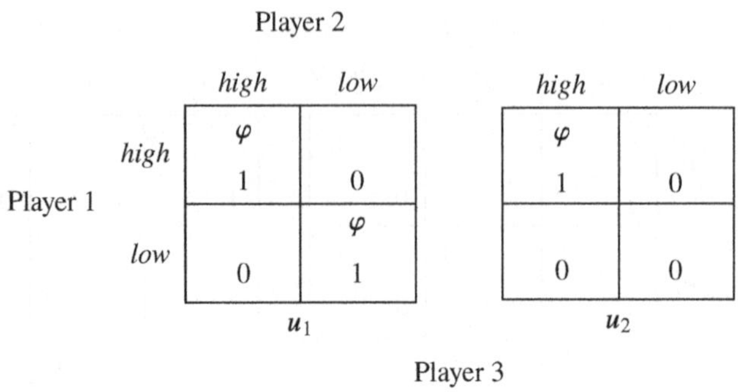

Fig. 5.6 The alternative Hi-Lo game S_3: a three-player game, where {player 1, player 2} $= \mathcal{G}$ collectively intends to φ, showing only the collective intention of $\mathcal{G}$

To illustrate the benefit of team reasoning in games with intentions, consider the *alternative Hi-Lo game* depicted in Fig. 5.6. Note that, for group $\mathcal{G}$ consisting of player 1 and 2, in the context of group $\mathcal{G}$'s collective intention to φ, the best group action is (*high*, *high*), because it is the only group action that ensures φ. An agent engaged in team reasoning therefore first identifies (*high*, *high*) as the unique best group action and then decides to perform her part in that combination, therefore recommending *high* to both player 1 and player 2. So, in this game, team reasoning by players 1 and 2 ensures that group $\mathcal{G}$ performs a best group action, that is, a group action that is admissible with respect to its collective intention.

To show that team reasoning yields the same action recommendations as a certain we-intention, I introduce *team-directed intentions*, which are standard individual intentions with a certain type of content. An agent adopting a team-directed intention transforms her preferences and adopts as her personal objective performing an individual action that is compatible with a best group action. This may require her to put herself in the shoes of the group agent to determine the best group actions. Then she takes as her personal objective performing an individual action that is compatible with a best group action and decides what to do by way of individualistic reasoning. The realization of her objective hence does not depend on the actions of other agents: any action profile in which she performs an individual action that is compatible with a best group action realizes the team-directed intention. To find the best group actions, she applies the dominance principle at the level of the group. Then, she decides what to do by determining the individual actions that are admissible with respect to her team-directed intention, which are exactly those individual actions that are compatible with a best group action.

Theorem 5.1 (Team-Directed Intentions) *Suppose group $\mathcal{G}$ collectively intends to φ. Let $i \in \mathcal{G}$ be a member of the group $\mathcal{G}$. Individual agent i's intention is* team-

Agent j

a_k:

Agent i	a_j	a'_j	a''_j
a_i	1 (top), 1 (bottom)	1 (top), 1 (bottom)	0 (top), 1 (bottom)
a'_i	1 (top), 1 (bottom)	1 (top), 1 (bottom)	0 (top), 1 (bottom)
a''_i	1 (top), 0 (bottom)	1 (top), 0 (bottom)	0 (top), 0 (bottom)

a'_k:

Agent i	a_j	a'_j	a''_j
a_i	1 (top), 1 (bottom)	1 (top), 1 (bottom)	0 (top), 1 (bottom)
a'_i	1 (top), 1 (bottom)	1 (top), 1 (bottom)	0 (top), 1 (bottom)
a''_i	1 (top), 0 (bottom)	1 (top), 0 (bottom)	0 (top), 0 (bottom)

Agent k

Fig. 5.7 The team-directed intentions of individual agents i and j in the game model S_4

directed *if she intends to act in a way that is compatible with a best group action, in other words, if and only if* $[i \text{ int}]\langle i \text{ stit}\rangle[\mathcal{G} \text{ prom}]\varphi$ *obtains.*[42]

It may be helpful to note that team-directed intentions differ from pro-group intentions. After all, if the group faces uncertainty then the collective goal could be realized although the individual agent ensures that the group does not perform a best group action. For example, in the alternative Hi-Lo game, the collective goal is realized in (*low*, *low*, u_1) even though player 1 rules out that a best group action, viz. (*high*, *high*), is realized if she chooses *low*. So in (*low*, *low*, u_1) the pro-group intention is realized while the team-directed intention is not.

To get some feeling for the recommendations yielded by team-directed intentions, let us reconsider S_4 of Fig. 5.4. The members team-directed intentions are depicted by Fig. 5.7. Let me explain why. First, note that, for the group $\mathcal{G}$ consisting of agents i and j, (a_i, a_j), (a'_i, a_j), and (a_i, a'_j) are the only group actions that are admissible with respect to φ. Indeed, since these are the only group actions that ensure that φ is realized, these are the best group actions (see, for instance, Proposition 5.1 item **6**). So, for agent i, for example, any profile in which she performs a_i or a'_i will realize her team-directed intention. It then follows that only a_i and a'_i are admissible with respect to agent i's team-directed intention. By symmetry, only a_j and a'_j are admissible with respect to agent j's team-directed intention.

An individual agent performs an action that is admissible with respect to her team-directed intention if and only if she performs an individual action that is her component of a best combination of actions that the members can perform

[42] In a game with intentions S, the requirement that group members adopt team-directed intentions could be formalized by the schema $[\mathcal{G} \text{ int}]\varphi \rightarrow [i \text{ int}]\langle i \text{ stit}\rangle[\mathcal{G} \text{ prom}]\varphi$.

(Observation D.1). Although team-reasoning theorists typically presuppose that there is a *unique* best group action, I follow Bacharach (1999, p. 120—adapted notation): "I shall say that agent i team reasons (for $\mathcal{G}$) when she first computes a best profile $a^*_{\mathcal{G}}$ (in terms of $u_{\mathcal{G}}$), next computes a^*_i, and lastly decides to do a^*_i because this is the component under her control of a best profile." It is unsurprising that individual actions resulting from team reasoning coincide with individual actions admissible with respect to the team-directed intention. (All claims are proved in Appendix D.)

Result 5.1 Let S be a game model with intentions. Suppose group $\mathcal{G}$ collectively intends to φ. Let $a \in A$. Then team reasoning admits the individual action a_i if and only if $S, a \models \langle i\ \mathsf{stit}\rangle[\mathcal{G}\ \mathsf{prom}]\varphi$, which is, in turn, equivalent to saying that the individual action a_i is admitted by agent i's team-directed intention.

This result shows that the outcomes of team reasoning can be equally well explained by team-directed intentions. Or, equivalently, it shows that an important part of we-mode reasoning can be reduced to I-mode reasoning with a team-directed intention. So, the effects of the agency transformation in team reasoning can be mirrored by the preference transformation in team-directed intentions.

In particular, this means that team-directed intentions provide the same action recommendations as team reasoning in the alternative Hi-Lo game S_3 of Fig. 5.6. Note that (*high*, *high*) is the only group action of $\mathcal{G}$ that ensures φ regardless of what player 3 does. Therefore, for example, player 1's team-directed intention is only realized in profiles where her component is *high*. Hence, Fig. 5.8 depicts the team-directed intentions of players 1 and 2.

This connection shows that we need not focus on the *mental processes* by which collective intentions are formed, because it suffices to study the *mental states* of

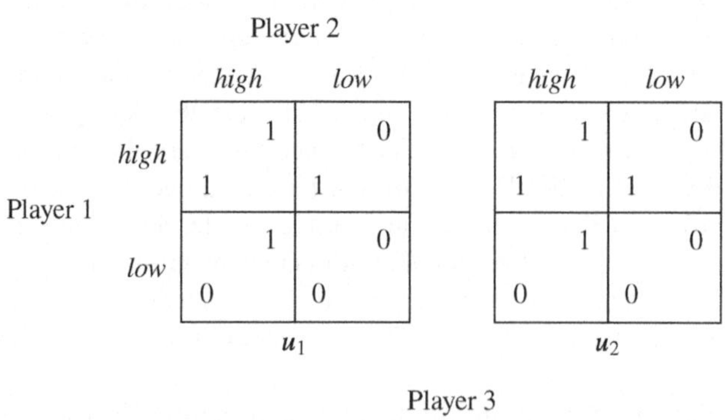

Fig. 5.8 The team-directed intentions of players 1 and 2 in the alternative Hi-Lo game S_3

the members.[43] The result therefore complements the analysis by Gold and Sugden (2007), who argue that team reasoning leads to collective intentions:

> Team reasoning results in the formation of intentions. ...references to the group are noneliminable parts of the reasoning process that led to the formation of the intention. Thus, it is natural to regard the intentions that result from team reasoning as collective intentions. (Gold & Sugden, 2007, p. 126)

If all of this is correct, then the connection between team-directed intentions and team reasoning, established by the result, reveals that it is equally natural to suppose that team-directed *intentions* are essential for collective intentions. In line with the philosophical literature, this purports a relation between personal and collective intentionality.

5.4.3 Participatory Intentions

Let us proceed with participatory intentions. Observing that team reasoning corresponds to we-intentions of the form $[i \ \mathsf{int}]\langle i \ \mathsf{stit}\rangle[\mathcal{G} \ \mathsf{prom}]\varphi$ invites a natural objection. This objection originates from the oddity of using two consecutive modalities to express (the content of) the team-directed intention. Team-directed intentions merely require the members to perform an individual action that is *compatible* with a best group action. This is a very weak demand. Therefore, I put forward a third we-intention type: *participatory intentions*, which require an individual agent to *promote* the realization of a best group action. That is, she adopts as her objective that a best group action is performed and then decides what to do by way of individualistic reasoning.

Definition 5.9 (Participatory Intentions) Suppose group $\mathcal{G}$ collectively intends to φ. Let $i \in \mathcal{G}$ be a member of the group $\mathcal{G}$. Agent i's intention is *participatory* if she intends that the group promotes the group's objective, regardless of what others do, in other words, if and only if $[i \ \mathsf{int}][\mathcal{G} \ \mathsf{prom}]\varphi$ obtains.[44]

Note the following minor, yet crucial, difference: pro-group intentions are such that the individual agent adopts the *group's objectives* as her own, whereas a participatory intention is such that she adopts as her personal objective that a *best group action is performed*. This reveals that participatory intentions can be viewed as a preference transformation. This preference transformation is not the result of the aggregation of individual preferences, but crucially relies on group notions.

---

[43] Compare Hakli et al. (2010, p. 299): "We study processes of we-reasoning concentrating on the difference between we-mode reasoning and pro-group I-mode reasoning. The difference is not in the aims of the agents because in both cases the agents aim at the benefit of the group. Rather, the difference is in the reasoning process: It is individualistic in the I-mode case."

[44] In a game with intentions S, the requirement that group members adopt participatory intentions could be formalized by the schema $[\mathcal{G} \ \mathsf{int}]\varphi \rightarrow [i \ \mathsf{int}][\mathcal{G} \ \mathsf{prom}]\varphi$.

After all, an agent forming such a participatory intention is required to answer the question ‘What should *we* do?’ before being able to answer the question ‘What should *I* do (with respect to my participatory intention)?’. The appeal to an agency transformation in the team-reasoning literature is thus taken up by participatory intentions. However, in contrast to altering the reasoning process, a participatory intention alters the preferences.

It may be helpful to note that participatory intentions differ from team-directed intentions. After all, an individual agent may perform an individual action that is compatible with a best group action even though no best group action is performed. For example, in the alternative Hi-Lo game, at (*high*, *low*, u_1) the best group action, viz. (*high*, *high*), is not performed despite the fact that player 1 performs an individual action that is compatible with the best group action. So in (*high*, *low*, u_1) player 1’s team-directed intention is realized while her participatory intention is not.

To illustrate the action recommendations yielded by participatory intentions, let us reconsider S_4 of Fig. 5.4. Again, note that (a_i, a_j), (a_i', a_j), and (a_i, a_j') are the only group actions that are admissible with respect to φ for the group $\mathcal{G}$ consisting of agents i and j. This means that Fig. 5.9 accurately represents the members’ participatory intentions. It follows that the individual action a_j'' is incompatible with a best group action, and that a_j dominates a_j'. Therefore, only a_j is admissible with respect to agent j’s participatory intention. By symmetry, only a_i is admissible with respect to agent i’s participatory intention. Lastly, one can easily verify that Fig. 5.10 presents the participatory intentions in the alternative Hi-Lo game, and show that only *high* is admissible with respect to the participatory intentions.

In this section, I have introduced and discussed three we-intention types, but why bother? The discussions of game model with intentions S_4 illustrate that these three we-intention types yield different action recommendations. If agent i adopted

Agent k: a_k

Agent i \ Agent j	a_j	a_j'	a_j''
a_i	1, 1	1, 1	0, 0
a_i'	1, 1	0, 0	0, 0
a_i''	0, 0	0, 0	0, 0

Agent k: a_k'

Agent i \ Agent j	a_j	a_j'	a_j''
a_i	1, 1	1, 1	0, 0
a_i'	1, 1	0, 0	0, 0
a_i''	0, 0	0, 0	0, 0

Fig. 5.9 The participatory intentions of i and j in the game model S_4

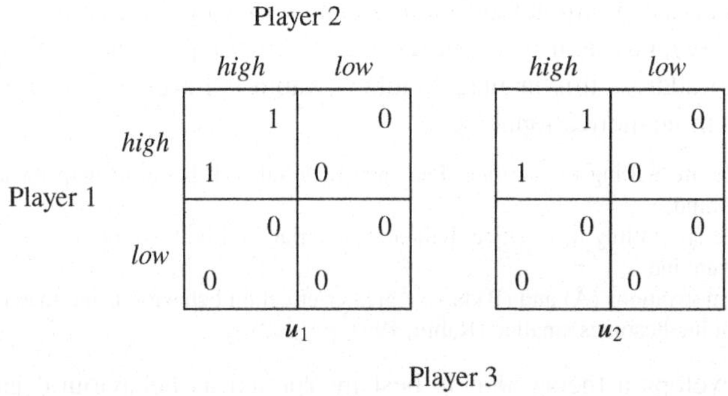

Fig. 5.10 The participatory intentions of players 1 and 2 in the alternative Hi-Lo game S_3

the pro-group intention, then individual actions a_i and a_i'' would be admissible. If instead she adopted the team-directed intention, then individual actions a_i and a_i' would be admissible. Finally, only individual action a_i would be admissible if she adopted the participatory intention. This shows that there is a significant difference between these three we-intention types.

5.5 Related Research on Fairness and Cooperation

At this point it may be useful to explain in some detail how these we-intentions relate to the existing literature on fairness and cooperation in economics and sociology.[45] More specifically, it might be helpful to explicate why these we-intentions can be viewed as an *extension* of preference transformation theories. This is important because the team-reasoning literature has made two mutually reinforcing claims regarding preference transformations:

1. It is claimed that team reasoning cannot be captured by a preference transformation. Rather, team reasoning is best viewed as an *agency transformation*.
2. It is claimed that preference transformations cannot explain why anyone should play *high* in the Hi-Lo game, nor can they explain why most people actually choose *high*.

This failure points to a serious drawback of preference transformation theories, one that the team-reasoning account of cooperation aims to overcome. To explain, and eventually *discount*, these two claims, it is helpful to start by discussing some prominent preference transformation theories.

It is well known that standard, egoistic, rational choice theory is unable to explain some trivial examples of human decision-making. For instance, the traditional the-

[45] This section draws from my (Duijf, 2021), which contains more details.

ory of self-interested rational individuals cannot explain, at least not satisfactorily, why people vote, pay their taxes, or sacrifice their own prospects in favour of those of a peer. To address this lacuna, Matthew Rabin believes we need a model that incorporates three motivational facts:

(A) People are willing to sacrifice their own material well-being to help those who are being kind.
(B) People are willing to sacrifice their own material well-being to punish those who are being unkind.
(C) Both motivations (A) and (B) have a greater effect on behavior as the material cost of sacrificing becomes smaller. (Rabin, 1993, p. 1282)

Rabin develops a theory that is best interpreted as behavioural game theory, which is the field of game theory that aims to provide a theory that explains human behaviour and experimental findings rather than a theory that provides normative guidance for agents that face interdependent decision problems. Preference transformation theories study *what* motivates people and propose that people are not exclusively pursuing their material self-interest, but also care about fairness, equality, inequity, and other social considerations. Such theories are typically thought of as methods to convert a so-called material game into a psychological game by transforming the utilities.

Let me give two examples. First, the socio-psychological literature on *social value orientations* (SVO) (Deutsch, 1949; Murphy & Ackermann, 2014; Van Lange, 1999) uses linear payoff transformations to represent different SVO types. For instance, in the simple two-player case involving agents i and j, agent i is said to have the *cooperative* value orientation if her transformed utility is given by the sum of their individual payoffs. Second, Rabin's theory of fairness postulates that the expected transformed utility for an individual agent will depend on three factors: "(i) his strategy, (ii) his beliefs about the other player's strategy choice, and (iii) his beliefs about the other player's beliefs about his strategy" (Rabin, 1993, p. 1286). The details need not worry us at present, but it may be helpful to note that his theory relies on so-called kindness functions to model this transition. These and similar models have been used to fruitfully explain various empirical findings in economics (Bolton & Ockenfels, 2000; Fehr & Schmidt, 1999) and in social psychology and sociology (Deutsch, 1949; Murphy & Ackermann, 2014; Van Lange, 1999).[46]

What is the relation between we-intentions and preference transformation theories? It is important to note that preference transformation theories use rationality principles from orthodox rational choice theory to derive the predicted or observed behaviour in experimental settings. That is, these theories *only* change the utilities; a decision-maker then aims to maximize expected transformed utility. If we assume that these preference transformation theories accurately model the group utility, then

[46] To illustrate the popularity of this methodological strategy, note that Bicchieri (2006, p. 3) studies social norms as a type of preference transformation: "social norms, as I shall argue, *transform* mixed-motive games into coordination ones. This transformation, however, hinges on each individual expecting enough other people to follow the norm, too. If this expectation is violated, an individual will revert to playing the original game and to behaving 'selfishly.'"

a preference transformation theory is best interpreted using pro-group intentions: the members of the group adopt the transformed preference as their own and then reason individualistically.[47] Accordingly, a preference transformation theory may be implemented in my theory of we-intentions to yield predicted or observed behaviour in experimental settings.

What about team-directed intentions? The theory of team reasoning, in contrast to preference transformation theories, revises the rationality principles of traditional rational choice theory by adopting a new reasoning method. Since the action recommendations yielded by team-directed intentions align with those resulting from team reasoning, there is no behavioural difference between my theory of team-directed intentions and the theory of team reasoning. This means that any experimental evidence for team reasoning will also be experimental evidence for my theory of team-directed intentions. To distinguish between these theories we thus need to go beyond the behavioural realm and include mental constructs.

Are team-directed intentions theoretically and psychologically plausible? The preference transformation associated with team-directed intentions is certainly very unorthodox and it might not cohere with other mental constructs in an agent's psychological economy. For example, the transformed preference suggests that an individual agent prefers any outcome in which she herself acts compatibly with a joint act that promotes the realization of the group's objective over any outcome in which she acts differently. Such properties are not standardly included in the outcomes of a game. For instance, in his seminal contribution to decision theory, Savage (1954) models actions as functions from states to outcomes. So standard preferences on outcomes cannot encompass this preference transformation. Following Dietrich and List (2016), we may say that the preference transformation corresponding to team-directed intentions is based on "context-related" properties.[48] If non-outcome-based preferences are accepted, then team-directed intentions are theoretically defensible.

The team-directed intentions are remarkable in that the corresponding transformed preference only depends on the agent's own act. The team-directed intention is realized if and only if the agent performs an action that is compatible with a best group action. This may not be psychologically plausible: it would imply that both (*high*, *high*) and (*high*, *low*) best satisfy player 1's preferences (see Fig. 5.2). Things are different for participatory intentions: their satisfaction not only depends on an agent's own act but also on what others do. In the Hi-Lo game, an agent who adopts the participatory intention can be taken to prefer an outcome in which everybody plays her part in (*high*, *high*) over any outcome in which someone deviates from playing her part. For these reasons, one could argue that participatory intentions

[47] Strictly speaking, my theory relies on the admissibility principle rather than expected utility theory. Nonetheless, both are principles from orthodox rational choice theory.

[48] Dietrich and List (2016, p. 177) write that "the motivationally salient properties may go beyond 'intrinsic' properties of the options and include 'context-related' properties. Examples are whether an option conforms to a context-specific social norm (e.g. is it polite?), whether it is above average quality among the available options, or whether the choice menu offers luxury options".

are psychologically more credible, despite the fact that participatory intentions and team-directed intentions yield the same behavioural predictions in the Hi-Lo game.

Can preference transformation theories explain why anyone actually chooses *high* in the Hi-Lo game? In (Duijf, 2021), I provide three general impossibility theorems which show that three prominent preference transformation theories cannot explain the choice of *high* in the Hi-Lo game: The theories of fairness (Rabin, 1993), inequity aversion (Fehr & Schmidt, 1999), and social value orientations (Deutsch, 1949; Murphy & Ackermann, 2014; Van Lange, 1999) all fail in this regard. Nonetheless, in (Duijf, 2021) I take inspiration from my theory of participatory intentions to identify a class of preference transformation theories that successfully explains why people choose *high* in the Hi-Lo game and why people choose to *cooperate* in the prisoner's dilemma. I call these *participatory* preference transformations because they incorporate two stylized ideas:

(∗) People might be willing to sacrifice their own material well-being to do their part in a collective act, where their part is defined as the individual action they ought to perform if the group is to be successful in realizing a shared goal.

(∗∗) Motivation (∗) has greater effect on behavior as the material cost of sacrificing becomes smaller.

In this brief exposition I have shown how we-intentions relate to preference transformation theories and team reasoning. I have argued that the two claims of team-reasoning theorists cannot be upheld, at least not without turning to a discussion of mental constructs rather than rational play. After all, the preference transformation corresponding to team-directed intentions can fully account for the behaviour predicted and observed by team reasoning. Nonetheless, team-directed intentions may not be psychologically plausible. I pointed out that participatory intentions correct some of the conceptual flaws in team-directed intentions and therefore seem to be the better candidate for future research.

5.6 Participatory Intentions Prevail

The three we-intention types—pro-group, team-directed, and participatory intentions (Sect. 5.4)—have been introduced to predict and explain cooperative behaviour and incentives. In this section I will focus on their *effectiveness* with regard to guaranteeing that a best group action is performed. If these intention types have anything to say about cooperation they should certainly advance best group actions across a wide range of games.[49] I thus investigate the classes of games for which these we-intention types guarantee that a best group action is performed. The results

[49] Bacharach (2006, p. 58—adapted notation) writes: "There are three requirements for a good theory of why people play *high* in Hi-Lo: [. . .] (iii) that it be part of a unified theory of a wide range of problems, not just Hi-Lo–for example, all problems of cooperation."

Fig. 5.11 Game model S_5, where the group $\{i, j\} = \mathcal{G}$ collectively intends to φ, showing only the collective intention of $\mathcal{G}$

Agent *i* \ Agent *j*		*L*	*R*
	U	φ 1	φ 1
	D	φ 1	0

of this section are collected in Fig. 5.1 on page 117. As the title of this section already reveals, I will prove that the theory of participatory intentions, in contrast with team-directed intentions or pro-group intentions, is the *prevalent* account of cooperation.

5.6.1 A Stand-off

It may be thought that even though team-directed intentions and pro-group intentions yield different action recommendations, they nonetheless yield the same cooperative outcomes. In this section, I show that the alternative Hi-Lo game illustrates that this is false. Since team reasoning succeeds in selecting a best group action in this particular game whereas pro-group intentions fail to do so, it might then be thought that team-directed intentions surpass pro-group intentions with regard to guaranteeing successful cooperation in *all* scenarios. I show that this is also false. This means that team reasoning is on an unsatisfactory par with pro-group intentions.

The alternative Hi-Lo game S_3 of Fig. 5.6 on page 134 presents a scenario in which team-directed intentions ensure successful cooperation. Pro-group intentions do not fare well in that example: since neither individual action dominates the other with respect to the group's objective, both are admissible. Pro-group intentions hence fail to dismiss all inferior group actions, for instance (*high*, *low*). I take this to reveal that there are games in which pro-group intentions fail to explain the obvious collective incentives, whereas team reasoning succeeds in doing so.

There are, however, games revealing the opposite. In game model S_5 of Fig. 5.11, team-directed intentions do not have much to offer: since group $\mathcal{G}$'s actions (U, L), (U, R), and (D, L) ensure φ, they are the best group actions in the context of the collective intention to φ.[50] So any individual action is compatible with a best group action. In particular, team-directed intentions admit D and R for agents i and j respectively, and hence do not dismiss (D, R). Pro-group intentions do not suffer from this flaw: they recommend U over D and L over R for agents i and j,

[50] Note that this game resembles the many-hands problem discussed in Sect. 2.2, Fig. 2.2.

respectively. So, whereas team-directed intentions risk performing an inferior group action, namely (D, R), pro-group intentions guarantee that a best group action is performed, namely (U, L). This illustrates that there is a game in which team reasoning fails to select a best group action whereas pro-group intentions succeed in doing so.

I agree with Bacharach (2006, p. 60, Sect. 8.3) that a theory should only be determinate when our intuitions are. We should hence not presuppose the determinacy of reason.[51] The team reasoning literature has, however, predominantly focused on cases where there is a *unique* best group action.[52] I wish to avoid this restriction and introduce a more general theory of cooperation. When dropping the uniqueness assumption, the above discussion reveals that team reasoning does not surpass pro-group intentions.

My discussion seems to contradict the result of Bacharach (1999, Theorem 2), which is interpreted as showing that "team reasoning differs from, and is more powerful than, adopting the group's objective and then reasoning in the standard individualistic way" (p. 144).[53] Our results are, however, mutually consistent. The difference between my approach and Bacharach's is the employed individualistic reasoning method: I adopt the admissibility requirement, which states that individuals reason in such a way as to avoid dominated actions; Bacharach relies on equilibrium reasoning, which states that individuals determine an "individualistic best reply" (p. 127).

To summarize, I argued that the class of games for which team-directed intentions guarantee that a best group action is performed is not a proper superset of the corresponding class for pro-group intentions, nor vice versa. So it is unclear which of these theories offers the best account of cooperation. This results in a stalemate with regard to the range of problems for which they guarantee successful cooperation.

Result 5.2 Team-directed intentions and pro-group intentions are on a par with regard to guaranteeing successful cooperation.

[51] In contrast, Harsanyi and Selten (1988, p. 13) write: "Clearly a theory telling us no more than that the outcome can be any one of these equilibrium points will not give us much useful information. We need a theory selecting one equilibrium point as the solution of the game."

[52] As mentioned before, Bacharach (1999, p. 120—adapted notation) is a notable exception: "I shall say that agent i team reasons (for $\mathcal{G}$) when she first computes a best profile a^* (in terms of $u_{\mathcal{G}}$), next computes a_i^*, and lastly decides to do a_i^* because this is the component under her control of a best profile." Also see the helpful discussion on cases where there are multiple best group actions by Karpus and Radzvilas (2018, Sect. 4.7).

[53] Hakli et al. (2010, Thesis (3), p. 306) agree with Bacharach and write: "The we-mode tends to create more collective order than the pro-group I-mode: It can decrease the amount of equilibria but it cannot increase them."

5.6.2 Overcoming the Deadlock

Given the stand-off between team-directed and pro-group intentions, it is natural and important to enquire whether this deadlock can be overcome. In this section, I thus investigate two issues: do participatory intentions guarantee that a best group action is performed when team-directed intentions do so? And when pro-group intentions do so? The answer to both questions turns out to be affirmative. This means that the theory of participatory intentions is the prevalent account of cooperation. That is, if a group of individuals comes together to strive for some collective or joint goal, the best they can do is to each adopt the participatory intention (and act accordingly), rather than adopting a team-directed or pro-group intention.

Let us start with participatory intentions and team-directed intentions. It seems uncontroversial to claim that whenever an individual agent decides to perform an individual action that is incompatible with any best group action, then she is certainly not promoting the realization of a best group action. It indeed follows logically that

$\models [i\ \mathsf{prom}][\mathcal{G}\ \mathsf{prom}]\varphi \rightarrow [i\ \mathsf{prom}]\langle i\ \mathsf{stit}\rangle[\mathcal{G}\ \mathsf{prom}]\varphi$ (Observation D.2).

Participatory intentions hence refine team-directed intentions' action recommendations.

Do participatory intentions guarantee that a best group action is performed if team-directed intentions do? Suppose a scenario is given in which team-directed intentions guarantee ψ. Since participatory intentions refine the action recommendations yielded by team-directed intentions, this means that participatory intentions will also guarantee ψ. This immediately implies that whenever team-directed intentions guarantee that a best group action is performed, then so do participatory intentions. In particular, this shows that participatory intentions guarantee that a best group action is performed in scenarios in which there is a unique best group action, since team-directed intentions are effective in those scenarios.

Let us briefly pause here. One of the main justifications for team reasoning is that it advances cooperative behaviour in Hi-Lo games. Whether the cooperative incentives in the Hi-Lo game actually lead to team reasoning is not at issue. Team reasoning sets out to address what makes (*high*, *high*) the only rational option. As such, the theory of participatory intentions is on an equal footing. After all, the action recommendations resulting from team reasoning coincide with those resulting from participatory intentions in the Hi-Lo game. This justification for the team-reasoning account of cooperation therefore transfers to the theory of participatory intentions.

Result 5.3 (below) can be viewed as generalizing and strengthening this justification for the theory of participatory intentions. On a positive note, my result establishes that whenever team reasoning is successful in picking out a best group action, then so are participatory intentions. On a negative note, there are scenarios in which team reasoning fails in this respect, whereas participatory intentions succeed.[54] Hence:

Result 5.3 Participatory intentions surpass team-directed intentions with regard to guaranteeing successful cooperation.

Let us now turn to participatory intentions and pro-group intentions. The standoff between team reasoning and pro-group intentions originates from game S_5 in Fig. 5.11. So let us investigate how participatory intentions fare in that scenario. Recall that, for group $\mathcal{G}$, group actions (U, L), (U, R), and (D, L) are the best group actions in the context of the collective intention to φ. Since these coincide with the φ-worlds, the results of pro-group intentions and participatory intentions coincide in this game. That is, the action recommendations yielded by these we-intention types are identical in this scenario. In particular, this shows that participatory intentions champion the objection posed to team reasoning.

Can we come up with a different objection against participatory intentions, in favour of pro-group intentions? That is, does a scenario exist in which participatory intentions fail to guarantee that a best group action is performed whereas pro-group intentions succeed in doing so? It is tempting to think that the action recommendations yielded by participatory intentions refine those of pro-group intentions. This is, however, *not* the case.[55] Still, the answer to the questions is negative: the following result shows that participatory intentions also surpass pro-group intentions with regard to guaranteeing successful cooperation.[56]

Result 5.4 Participatory intentions surpass pro-group intentions with regard to guaranteeing successful cooperation.

This result emphasizes that the theory of participatory intentions surpasses team reasoning *and* pro-group intentions in selecting cooperatively rational solutions. Indeed, in *any* scenario in which pro-group intentions guarantee successful cooperation, participatory intentions do so too. So, to cooperate successfully, it is generally better if all members take up the participatory intention.

Considered together, the results of this section purport that the theory of participatory intentions, in contrast with team reasoning or pro-group intentions, is the prevalent account of cooperation. Since team reasoning does not surpass pro-group intentions in some scenarios, this provides ample justification for the theory of participatory intentions beyond the team-reasoning account of cooperation.

---

[54] The discussion below shows that the game in Fig. 5.11 is a case in point.

[55] To see this, imagine if we slightly change game S_4 in Fig. 5.4: drop φ at (a_i, a'_j, a'_k) and thus remove (a_i, a'_j, a'_k) from $Int_{\mathcal{G}}$. One can check that if agent i adopted the pro-group intention, only a_i and a''_i would be admissible. In contrast, if agent i adopted the participatory intention, only a_i and a'_i would be admissible. This example hence proves the point.

[56] Because the action recommendations of participatory intentions do not refine those of pro-group intentions, the proof that participatory intentions surpass pro-group intentions is more complicated than that of Result 5.3.

After all, whereas team reasoning surpasses pro-group intentions with regard to guaranteeing successful cooperation only in *some* scenarios, participatory intentions surpass both in *all* scenarios. The theory of participatory intentions therefore best explains and predicts cooperation.

Alternatively, since my analysis focused solely on the third stage of we-mode reasoning,[57] one could view my study as attempting to understand the logical form of the we-intentions resulting from team reasoning. The logical machinery helps to address this question more precisely than has been done before. I revised the theory by showing that we-mode reasoning at the third stage may be improved by taking these resulting we-intentions to be participatory intentions rather than team-directed intentions.

5.7 Discussion: Intentional Responsibility Systems

What are the conditions for the existence of responsibility voids and gaps from the perspective of intentional responsibility systems? Suppose some morally undesirable state of affairs ψ results from the interaction of several individuals. According to an intentional responsibility system, we need to inspect the agents' intentions in order to determine who can be held responsible. Let me mention some logically distinct intentional responsibility systems (this is not meant to be an exhaustive list):

- An agent is morally responsible for ψ if (and only if) she intended ψ;
- An agent is morally responsible for ψ if (and only if) her intentions did not exclude ψ (in other words, her intentions were compatible with ψ);
- An agent is morally responsible for ψ if (and only if) she did not intend to realize the opposite $\neg\psi$.

Notice that these intention-based requirements for responsibility attribution are decreasing in strength: for example, whenever an agent intends ψ, then her intentions are compatible with ψ; and whenever an agent's intention is compatible with ψ, then she did not intend $\neg\psi$.[58] So, what does this entail for the conditions under which responsibility voids can arise? The strongest requirement lets individuals off the hook most frequently and is, therefore, most susceptible to the existence of such voids.[59] Accordingly, the weakest intentional responsibility system has the best prospect of circumventing the problem of responsibility voids.

---

[57] These three stages have been discussed in Sect. 5.2.2 (see Hakli et al., 2010, Sect. 4).

[58] At least, these implications hold under the common assumption that one's intentions are mutually consistent—for an argument against this common assumption, see my joint work (Duijf et al., 2019).

[59] One could formalize the strongest and the weakest intentional responsibility system using the intention operator: agent i is responsible for ψ according to the strongest intentional responsibility system if and only if $[i \ \mathsf{int}]\psi$; and agent i is responsible for ψ according to the weakest intentional responsibility system if and only if $\neg[i \ \mathsf{int}]\neg\psi$.

Let us briefly investigate the conditions under which such voids can arise for the weakest intentional responsibility system. So, can ψ result from the interaction of several individuals, each of whom intended to realize the opposite $\neg\psi$? Let us assume that agents perform actions that are admissible with respect to their intention. Then, this question is structurally similar to the one addressed in Chap. 3: whereas the present discussion focuses on the realization of ψ or $\neg\psi$, the work in that chapter relies on (binary) deontic ideality functions, which can be taken to reflect an ordering of action profiles as good or bad. The discussion and conclusion of that chapter can therefore be transferred: responsibility voids cannot arise unless communication is restricted or agreement is problematic.

What is the relation between collective blameworthiness and individual intentional action? As noted before, I take it that collective blameworthiness entails that the group failed to fulfil its obligation. If we construe the group's collective obligation as performing a group act that promotes deontic ideality, then this means that they failed to perform a deontically optimal group act. As noted in Chap. 3, the fulfilment of a collective obligation is neither sufficient nor necessary for the fulfilment of individual obligations (Sect. 3.2). If a group is able to communicate and agree upon a group plan in order to fulfil its collective obligation, it should adopt a *good plan*, which consists only of deontically optimal group acts and is interchangeable (Sect. 3.4). If a good plan has been adopted, the group's failure to fulfil its collective obligation *logically entails* that at least one member failed to fulfil her member obligation, and, moreover, it entails that at least one member failed to fulfil her individual obligation in the updated decision context.

My discussion of intentionality and several we-intentions sheds some additional light on this case. Agreement-based joint action is one of the paradigm cases of collective intention (see Sect. 3.3). If a group plan has been adopted, then we may say that the group collectively intends to carry out the plan. Consider team-directed intentions and recall that an individual agent is required to promote the realization of her individual intention. In these circumstances, if an agent adopts the team-directed intention, then she is committed to performing an individual action that is her component of one of the group actions in the plan. Accordingly, an agent acts in a way that is faithful to the team-directed intention *if and only if* she fulfils her member obligation. In combination with the aforementioned insights from Chap. 3, it follows that, if the group adopted a good plan, failing to fulfil its collective obligation *logically entails* that at least one of its members failed to act according to her team-directed intention.[60]

I showed that participatory intentions refine the action recommendations of team-directed intentions, that is, an agent acts according to the participatory intention only if she acts in a way that is faithful to the team-directed intention. Hence, when a

[60] Notice that there are two cases where a member may fail to act according to her team-directed intention: (a) the member's intention was simply not team-directed; or (b) the member's intention was team-directed, yet for some reason she failed to perform an action that is admissible with respect to her intention.

group regulates its joint action by adopting a group plan, an agent acts according to the participatory intention *only if* she fulfils her member obligation. Or, conversely, if an agent fails to fulfil her member obligation then she does not act in a way that is faithful to the participatory intention.[61] In sum, this means that, if the group adopted a good plan, failing to fulfil its collective obligation *logically entails* that at least one of its members failed to act according to her participatory intention.

Be that as it may, in cases where the group cannot communicate or agree upon a good plan to fulfil its collective obligation, the relation between fulfilling its collective obligation and fulfilling a member obligation may be obscured. Consequently, in such cases, the aforementioned connection between collective blameworthiness and individual intentional action—in particular, participatory intentions— may be unclear.

Nonetheless, I think it is important to note that participatory intentions enhance member obligations, with respect to successfully fulfilling the group's collective obligation. Recall that participatory intentions refine the action recommendations of team-directed intentions. I argued that an agent fulfils her member obligation if and only if she acts according to the team-directed intention. If it is impossible for the group to adopt a good plan, the group may fail to fulfil its collective obligation even though each member acts according to her team-directed intention. However, participatory intentions surpass team-directed intentions in selecting cooperatively rational outcomes (Result 5.3). After all, in some scenarios, participatory intentions guarantee that the collective obligation is fulfilled whereas team-directed intentions fail to do so. Accordingly, in some cases, acting according to participatory intentions may guarantee successfully fulfilling a collective obligation, whereas fulfilling member obligations fails to do so.

What is the relation between collective and individual blameworthiness from the perspective of intentional responsibility systems? I assume that collective blameworthiness supports the claim that not fulfilling an obligation is a necessary condition for being blameworthy. Let me consider the weakest and strongest intentional responsibility systems. On the weakest conception, an agent can be held responsible for a given outcome if and only if she did not intend to avoid it. On the strongest conception, an agent can be held responsible for a given outcome if and only if she intended to realize it. Accordingly, each demonstrates a particular type of failure that may ground the group's collective blameworthiness: (i) *absence of the intention*: the group did not collectively intend to fulfil its collective obligation; and (ii) *intentional omission*: the group collectively intentionally refrained from fulfilling its collective obligation.

The first type of failure is the absence of an intention: the group might be collectively blameworthy for *not collectively intending* to fulfil its collective obligation. In this chapter, I only argued for one particular direction of the relation between collective and individual intentions, viz. a group collectively intends to φ only if each member adopts the corresponding participatory intention. The other

[61] The entailments mentioned so far even hold for group plans that fail to be interchangeable.

direction of the relation, however, also seems plausible. Christopher Kutz, for instance, writes:

> So long as the members of a group overlap in the conception of the collective end to which they intentionally contribute, they act collectively, or jointly intentionally. I call this the minimalist conception of joint action. (Kutz, 2000, p. 90)

Overlapping intentions form the basis for Kutz's analysis of collective intentional action. That is, Kutz argues, whenever a set of individuals all adopt the participatory intention, then they act jointly intentionally. Or, conversely, a group does not act collectively intentionally *only if* some of its members did not intentionally participate. If this is correct, then we can conclude that if a group is collectively blameworthy for not collectively intending to fulfil its collective obligation, then at least some members did not intend to participate in jointly fulfilling its collective obligation. The absence of a member's participatory intention could prompt individual blameworthiness. Hence, prima facie, collective blameworthiness implies individual blameworthiness.

There may be cases where the absence of a member's participatory intention does not yield individual blameworthiness. However, one might want to argue that, in certain cases, it would constitute culpable recklessness on the part of the member. That is, following Dubber (2002) on the mode of acting recklessly, one might argue that a law-abiding member would have intentionally participated in jointly fulfilling a collective obligation. The study of the scope and application of this suggestion has to be left for future research.

The second type of failure consists in the group *intentionally failing to fulfil its collective obligation*. In that case, my theory of participatory intentions entails that each member intentionally participates. That is, every member intended to participate in this collective failure. It seems plausible that intentional participation in collective intentional omissions implies individual blameworthiness. As a result, ceteris paribus, collective blameworthiness entails individual blameworthiness.

Christopher Kutz has used the Complicity Principle to argue that intentional participation can ground individual blameworthiness:

> The Complicity Principle assumes a different view of collective action. Intuitively, marginally effective participants in a collective harm are accountable for the victims' suffering, not because of the individual differences they make, but because their intentional participation in a collective endeavor directly links them to the consequences of that endeavor. The notion of participation rather than causation is at the heart of both complicity and collective action. (Kutz, 2000, p. 138)[62]

[62] Tracy Isaacs (2011, p. 102) does not build on participatory *intentions*; rather, she writes: "The action of an individual may warrant descriptions that invoke collective content. In some situations, this collective content may, as in the individual case, make reference to act descriptions that guide us to moral judgments. ... An individual act of murder, performed as a part of a larger initiative of genocide, has a distinct moral character that it would lack outside the genocidal context because in genocide it is performed with the aim of destroying a group."

Intentionally participating in a collective endeavour may therefore induce *inclusive authorship* for the consequences brought about by that collective endeavour.[63] It is important to contrast this sense of authorship with a mere causal sense of co-authorship.[64] Following Kutz, it could be argued that each member can be held responsible for her intentional participation in a collective harm. Therefore, every member would be *complicit* in the group's harmful group act.[65] The study of the application and extent of these considerations of inclusive authorship are beyond the scope of the current chapter. Nonetheless, these arguments highlight how my theory could be used to relate collective blameworthiness to members' individual blameworthiness.

I end with a summary of my findings on the possibility and scope of the problem of responsibility voids and gaps. Intentional responsibility systems are vulnerable to responsibility voids and gaps only in certain circumstances:

- If communication is unrestricted and agreement is unproblematic, then the group should adopt a good plan and responsibility voids cannot arise unless members are exempted from acting in a way that is faithful to their participatory intention.
- The weakest intentional responsibility system substantiates the claim that collective blameworthiness *entails* that at least some members did not intend to participate in jointly fulfilling the collective obligation. Hence, responsibility gaps cannot arise unless members who refrained from intentionally participating in jointly fulfilling the collective obligation are excused.
- The strongest intentional responsibility system substantiates the claim that collective blameworthiness *entails* that every member intentionally participated in the collective wrongdoing. Therefore, responsibility gaps cannot arise unless members who intentionally participated in collective wrongdoing are excused.

[63] Compare Tomasello (2016, p. 107): "claims of inclusive authorship are licensed by the fact that each member's acts are explained by the overlapping goal of realizing the group's plans".

[64] Braham and van Hees (2012) base their account of moral responsibility on a purely causal sense of co-authorship. Their account includes a condition of "Causal Relevancy Condition", which "is necessary because we cannot say that an outcome bears the stamp of 'authorship' of a person if the person played no causal role in bringing it about" (Braham & van Hees, 2012, pp. 605–606). In Sect. 4.7 I highlighted how causal co-authorship may be used to ground individual responsibility by concluding that, from the perspective of my theory of collective know-how, collective blameworthiness entails "that at least one member knowingly risked that she is causally responsible for the group's failure to fulfil its subjective collective obligation".

[65] The intentional responsibility system that is based on intentional participation and complicity could be formalized as follows. Suppose group $\mathcal{G}$ collectively fulfils its collective obligation if and only if $\mathcal{G}$ sees to it that $p_{\checkmark}$. By symmetry, $\mathcal{G}$ fails to fulfil its collective obligation if and only if $\neg[\mathcal{G}\ \mathsf{stit}]p_{\checkmark}$ obtains. Then, the complicity principle states that a member i of $\mathcal{G}$ is complicit if and only if $[i\ \mathsf{int}]\neg[\mathcal{G}\ \mathsf{stit}]p_{\checkmark}$ holds.

Appendix D: Joint Action, Participatory Intentions, and Team Reasoning

D.1 Modal Logic of Agency and Intentionality

Lemma D.1 *Let $p \in \mathcal{P}$, and let $\mathcal{G}$ be a group of agents. Then* $[\mathcal{G}\ \mathsf{prom}]p$ *cannot be characterized by a formula ψ in $\mathfrak{L}_{stit}$. The incorporation of the* $[\mathcal{G}\ \mathsf{prom}]$*-operator in $\mathfrak{L}_{istit}$ entails that it is a proper extension of $\mathfrak{L}_{stit}$.*

Proof In modal logic, the standard technique for proving non-characterizability is to use bisimulations. It therefore seems better to use standard modal-logical models, viz. stit models, rather than game models to prove this result. Given the correspondence between game models and stit models, the result transfers to game models (see Sects. 2.3.2–2.4).

To prove this lemma, I focus on $[i\ \mathsf{prom}]p$ and use the two stit models $\mathcal{M}_1$ and $\mathcal{M}_2$ depicted in Figs. 5.12 and 5.13. The bisimulation $Z \subseteq Ind_1 \times Ind_2$ is given by the following: for any m_1/h_1 in $\mathcal{M}_1$ and any m_2/h_2 in $\mathcal{M}_2$ it holds that

$Z(m_1/h_1, m_2/h_2)$ iff exactly the same propositions hold at m_1/h_1 and m_2/h_2.

It is now routine to check that Z is indeed a bisimulation (with respect to the language $\mathfrak{L}_{stit}$). Let us prove one property:

(∗) $Z(m_1/h_1, m_2/h_2)$ and $m_1/h_1 \in Act_i(m_1/h)$ implies that there is a $m_2/h' \in Ind_2$ such that $m_2/h_2 \in Act_i(m_2/h')$ and $Z(m_1/h, m_2/h')$.

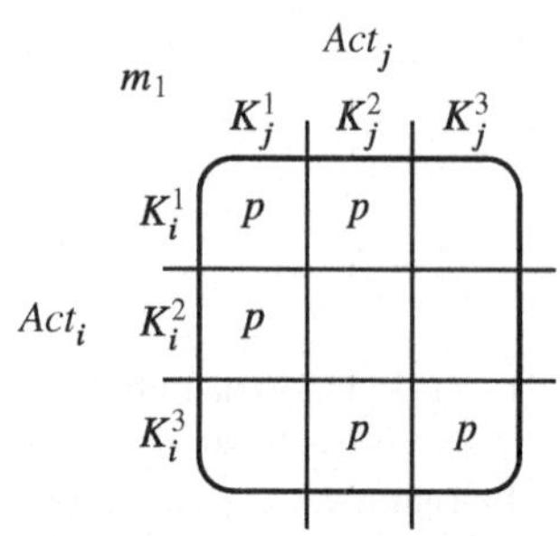

Fig. 5.12 The initial model $\mathcal{M}_1$

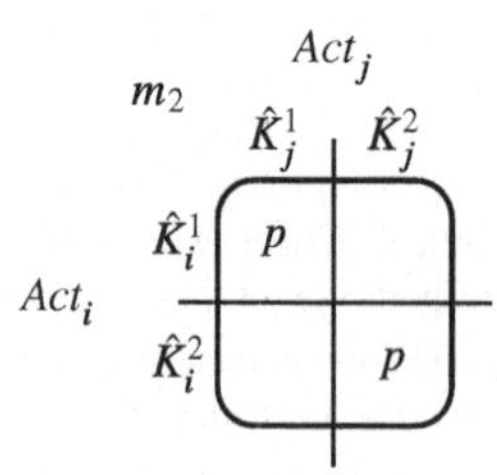

Fig. 5.13 The constructed model $\mathcal{M}_2$

Since, in both $\mathcal{M}_1$ and $\mathcal{M}_2$, every row contains both a p-world and a $\neg p$-world. This property immediately follows.

Finally, I argue by contradiction to prove the lemma. Suppose that $\psi \in \mathfrak{L}_{stit}$ characterizes $[i\ \mathsf{prom}]p$. Note that $[i\ \mathsf{prom}]p$ holds in any world in $\mathcal{M}_2$. Hence, by assumption, ψ holds at any world in $\mathcal{M}_2$. Take any $m_1/h \in K_i^2 \cap K_j^2$. Remark that $\mathcal{M}_1, m_1/h \models \psi$ since Z is a bisimulation (with respect to $\mathfrak{L}_{stit}$). However, note that $[i\ \mathsf{prom}]p$ does not hold at $\mathcal{M}_1, m_1/h$. Contradiction. We conclude that $[i\ \mathsf{prom}]p$ cannot be characterized by an $\mathfrak{L}_{stit}$-formula. □

Lemma D.2 *Let S be a game model, let $\mathcal{G}$ be a group of agents, and let $\varphi \in \mathfrak{L}_{istit}$. Then the following are equivalent:*

1. *there is an $a_{\mathcal{G}} \in A_{\mathcal{G}}$ such that for every $b_{\mathcal{G}} \in A_{\mathcal{G}}$ it holds that $a_{\mathcal{G}} \succeq_\varphi b_{\mathcal{G}}$ (i.e. $A_{\mathcal{G}}$ has a $\succeq_\varphi$-maximal element);*
2. *in S, $[\mathcal{G}\ \mathsf{prom}]\varphi$ is characterized by $[\mathcal{G}\ \mathsf{stit}](\langle -\mathcal{G}\ \mathsf{stit}\rangle\varphi \to \varphi)$.*

Proof Note that the following are equivalent: (i) $S, a \models [\mathcal{G}\ \mathsf{stit}](\langle -\mathcal{G}\ \mathsf{stit}\rangle\varphi \to \varphi)$, (ii) for every $c_{-\mathcal{G}}$ it holds that if $S, (a_{\mathcal{G}}, c_{-\mathcal{G}}) \models \langle -\mathcal{G}\ \mathsf{stit}\rangle\varphi$ then $S, (a_{\mathcal{G}}, c_{-\mathcal{G}}) \models \varphi$, (iii) for every $c_{-\mathcal{G}}$ it holds that if there is a $d_{\mathcal{G}} \in A_{\mathcal{G}}$ such that $S, (d_{\mathcal{G}}, c_{-\mathcal{G}}) \models \varphi$ then $S, (a_{\mathcal{G}}, c_{-\mathcal{G}}) \models \varphi$. It follows that if $S, a \models [\mathcal{G}\ \mathsf{stit}](\langle -\mathcal{G}\ \mathsf{stit}\rangle\varphi \to \varphi)$ then for every $b_{\mathcal{G}} \in A_{\mathcal{G}}$ it holds that $a_{\mathcal{G}} \succeq_\varphi b_{\mathcal{G}}$. The converse is also easy to see. Suppose that $a_{\mathcal{G}}$ is such that for every $b_{\mathcal{G}} \in A_{\mathcal{G}}$ it holds that $a_{\mathcal{G}} \succeq_\varphi b_{\mathcal{G}}$. If $c_{-\mathcal{G}}$ and $d_{\mathcal{G}}$ satisfy $S, (d_{\mathcal{G}}, c_{-\mathcal{G}}) \models \varphi$, then $S, (a_{\mathcal{G}}, c_{-\mathcal{G}}) \models \varphi$ holds because $a_{\mathcal{G}} \succeq_\varphi d_{\mathcal{G}}$.

(1. ⇒ 2.) Assume 1. Since there is a $\succeq_\varphi$-maximal element in $A_{\mathcal{G}}$, it is the case that, for every $a \in A$, $S, a \models [\mathcal{G}\ \mathsf{prom}]\varphi$ holds if and only if for every $b_{\mathcal{G}} \in A_{\mathcal{G}}$ it holds that $a_{\mathcal{G}} \succeq_\varphi b_{\mathcal{G}}$. (This equivalence does not hold if there is no maximal element.) Hence, $S, a \models [\mathcal{G}\ \mathsf{prom}]\varphi$ if and only if $S, a \models [\mathcal{G}\ \mathsf{stit}](\langle -\mathcal{G}\ \mathsf{stit}\rangle\varphi \to \varphi)$.

(2. ⇒ 1.) Assume 2. First note that there is an admissible group action, say $a_{\mathcal{G}}$. Then $S, a \models [\mathcal{G}\ \mathsf{prom}]\varphi$ and, by assumption, $S, a \models [\mathcal{G}\ \mathsf{stit}](\langle -\mathcal{G}\ \mathsf{stit}\rangle\varphi \to \varphi)$. Our initial observation entails that $a_{\mathcal{G}}$ is a $\succeq_\varphi$-maximal element in $A_{\mathcal{G}}$. □

Proposition 5.1 *Let φ be an $\mathfrak{L}_{istit}$-formula and let $\mathcal{G}$ be a group of agents, possibly a singleton. Then*

1. *$\models \Diamond[\mathcal{G}\ \mathsf{prom}]\varphi$, one is always able to promote φ,*
2. *$\not\models [\mathcal{G}\ \mathsf{prom}]\varphi \to [\mathcal{G}\ \mathsf{stit}]\varphi$, promoting φ does not entail ensuring φ,*
3. *$\models [\mathcal{G}\ \mathsf{stit}]\varphi \to [\mathcal{G}\ \mathsf{prom}]\varphi$, guaranteeing φ entails promoting φ,*
4. *$\models [\mathcal{G}\ \mathsf{prom}]\varphi \wedge \Diamond\varphi \to \langle \mathcal{G}\ \mathsf{stit}\rangle\varphi$, promoting φ while φ is possible entails allowing φ,*
5. *$\models [\mathcal{G}\ \mathsf{prom}]\varphi \wedge \Diamond[\mathcal{G}\ \mathsf{stit}]\varphi \to [\mathcal{G}\ \mathsf{stit}]\varphi$, promoting φ while being able to ensure φ entails guaranteeing φ,*
6. *$\models \Diamond[\mathcal{G}\ \mathsf{stit}]\varphi \to ([\mathcal{G}\ \mathsf{prom}]\varphi \leftrightarrow [\mathcal{G}\ \mathsf{stit}]\varphi)$, if one is able to guarantee φ, then promoting φ is equivalent to ensuring φ.*

Proof Let $S = \langle N, (A_i), (Int_{\mathcal{G}}), V\rangle$ be any game model.

1. Follows from the fact that we only consider finite game forms (see Lemma B.1 in Appendix B).

2. The previous item shows that if this were a validity, then $\models \Diamond[i \text{ stit}]\varphi$ would follow. In other words, one is always able to ensure φ, no matter its logical form. This is, however, not always the case.
3. Suppose $S, a \models [\mathcal{G} \text{ stit}]\varphi$. Then for any $c_{-\mathcal{G}} \in A_{-\mathcal{G}}$ we have $S, (a_{\mathcal{G}}, c_{-\mathcal{G}}) \models \varphi$. Hence, for any $b \in A$ and any $c_{-\mathcal{G}} \in A_{-\mathcal{G}}$ it holds that $S, (b_{\mathcal{G}}, c_{-\mathcal{G}}) \models \varphi$ implies $S, (a_{\mathcal{G}}, c_{-\mathcal{G}}) \models \varphi$. In other words, $a_{\mathcal{G}} \succeq_\varphi b_{\mathcal{G}}$, so $a_{\mathcal{G}}$ is admissible with respect to φ.
4. Suppose $S, a \models [\mathcal{G} \text{ prom}]\varphi \wedge \Diamond\varphi$. Then there is a profile, say b, such that $S, b \models \varphi$. We argue by contradiction that $S, a \models \langle \mathcal{G} \text{ stit}\rangle\varphi$: suppose $S, a \not\models \langle \mathcal{G} \text{ stit}\rangle\varphi$. Then for any $c_{-\mathcal{G}} \in A_{-\mathcal{G}}$ it is the case that $S, (a_{\mathcal{G}}, c_{-\mathcal{G}}) \not\models \varphi$. Hence, for any $c_{-\mathcal{G}} \in A_{-\mathcal{G}}$ it holds that $S, (a_{\mathcal{G}}, c_{-\mathcal{G}}) \models \varphi$ implies $S, (b_{\mathcal{G}}, c_{-\mathcal{G}}) \models \varphi$, vacuously, i.e. $b_{\mathcal{G}} \succeq_\varphi a_{\mathcal{G}}$. Moreover, since $S, b \models \varphi$, $b_{\mathcal{G}} \not\preceq_\varphi a_{\mathcal{G}}$ and therefore $b_{\mathcal{G}} \succ_\varphi a_{\mathcal{G}}$. This shows that $a_{\mathcal{G}}$ is not admissible with respect to φ, which contradicts with our assumption that $S, a \models [\mathcal{G} \text{ prom}]\varphi$.
5. We argue by contradiction. Suppose $S, a \models [\mathcal{G} \text{ prom}]\varphi$ and $S, b \models [\mathcal{G} \text{ stit}]\varphi$, yet $S, a \not\models [\mathcal{G} \text{ stit}]\varphi$. Recall from the proof of item 3 that $S, b \models [\mathcal{G} \text{ stit}]\varphi$ entails that $b_{\mathcal{G}}$ simply dominates every group action. In particular, $a_{\mathcal{G}} \preceq_\varphi b_{\mathcal{G}}$. The assumption that $S, a \not\models [\mathcal{G} \text{ stit}]\varphi$ entails that there is a $c_{-\mathcal{G}} \in A_{-\mathcal{G}}$ satisfying $S, (a_{\mathcal{G}}, c_{-\mathcal{G}}) \models \neg\varphi$. In particular, $S, (b_{\mathcal{G}}, c_{-\mathcal{G}}) \models \varphi$ implies that $S, (a_{\mathcal{G}}, c_{-\mathcal{G}}) \models \varphi$ does not hold. Hence $a_{\mathcal{G}} \prec_\varphi b_{\mathcal{G}}$ holds, which contradicts the assumption that $S, a \models [\mathcal{G} \text{ prom}]\varphi$ holds.
6. This follows immediately from the previous item and item 3. □

D.2 We-intentions

Observation D.1 Let S be a game model, let $a \in A$ be a profile, let $\mathcal{G}$ be a group of agents, let $i \in \mathcal{G}$, and let $\varphi \in \mathfrak{L}_{istit}$. Then the following are equivalent:

1. At a, agent i performs an individual action that is admissible with respect to her team-directed intention. In other words, a_i is admissible with respect to $\langle i \text{ stit}\rangle[\mathcal{G} \text{ prom}]\varphi$ or, equivalently, $S, a \models [i \text{ prom}]\langle i \text{ stit}\rangle[\mathcal{G} \text{ prom}]\varphi$ holds.
2. At a, agent i performs an individual action that is her component in an admissible group action. In other words, there is a $b_{\mathcal{G}} \in Admissibles_S(\mathcal{G}, \varphi)$ such that $a_i = b_i$ or, equivalently, $S, a \models \langle i \text{ stit}\rangle[\mathcal{G} \text{ prom}]\varphi$.

Proof Note that $\models \langle i \text{ stit}\rangle\chi \leftrightarrow [i \text{ stit}]\langle i \text{ stit}\rangle\chi$, since $[i \text{ stit}]$ is an S5-operator. Given item **1** of Proposition 5.1, it holds that $\models \Diamond[\mathcal{G} \text{ prom}]\varphi$. Since $\models \Diamond\chi \rightarrow \Diamond\langle i \text{ stit}\rangle\chi$ holds, item **6** of Proposition 5.1 entails that $\models [i \text{ prom}]\langle i \text{ stit}\rangle[\mathcal{G} \text{ prom}]\varphi \leftrightarrow \langle i \text{ stit}\rangle[\mathcal{G} \text{ prom}]\varphi$ holds, as desired. □

Result 5.1 Let S be a game model with intentions. Suppose group $\mathcal{G}$ collectively intends to φ. Let $a \in A$. Then team reasoning admits the individual action a_i if and only if $S, a \models \langle i \text{ stit}\rangle[\mathcal{G} \text{ prom}]\varphi$, which is, in turn, equivalent to saying that the individual action a_i is admitted by agent i's team-directed intention.

Proof First note that for any profile $a \in A$ it holds that $S, a \vDash [i \ \mathsf{prom}]\langle i \ \mathsf{stit}\rangle [\mathcal{G} \ \mathsf{prom}]\varphi$ if and only if $S, a \vDash \langle i \ \mathsf{stit}\rangle[\mathcal{G} \ \mathsf{prom}]\varphi$ (by Observation D.1).

Second, recall that team reasoning implies that individual agent i first identifies a best combination that the group members can perform, say $a'_{\mathcal{G}}$, and then decides to perform the individual action that is her part in that combination, which is a'_i. Hence, in the context of a collective intention to φ, for any $a \in A$, the following are equivalent: (1) team reasoning admits a_i, (2) there is an $a'_{\mathcal{G}-i} \in A_{\mathcal{G}-i}$ such that $(a_i, a'_{\mathcal{G}-i})$ is a best group action that the group members can perform, (3) there is a $a'_{-i} \in A_{-i}$ such that $S, (a_i, a'_{-i}) \vDash [\mathcal{G} \ \mathsf{prom}]\varphi$, and finally (4) $S, a \vDash \langle i \ \mathsf{stit}\rangle[\mathcal{G} \ \mathsf{prom}]\varphi$. □

Observation D.2 Let $\mathcal{G}$ be a group of agents, let $i \in \mathcal{G}$, and let $\varphi \in \mathfrak{L}_{istit}$. Then

$$\vDash [i \ \mathsf{prom}][\mathcal{G} \ \mathsf{prom}]\varphi \rightarrow [i \ \mathsf{prom}]\langle i \ \mathsf{stit}\rangle[\mathcal{G} \ \mathsf{prom}]\varphi$$

Proof Observation D.1 shows that $\langle i \ \mathsf{stit}\rangle[\mathcal{G} \ \mathsf{prom}]\varphi$ entails $[i \ \mathsf{prom}]\langle i \ \mathsf{stit}\rangle [\mathcal{G} \ \mathsf{prom}]\varphi$. Items **1** and **4** of Proposition 5.1 immediately show that the former is entailed by $[i \ \mathsf{prom}][\mathcal{G} \ \mathsf{prom}]\varphi$. Hence, the statement follows by transitivity of the implication. □

Result 5.4 Participatory intentions surpass pro-group intentions with regard to guaranteeing successful cooperation.

To prove this result, I rely on the following lemma:

Lemma D.3 *Let S be a game model. Let $a \in A$ satisfy $S, a \nvDash [i \ \mathsf{prom}]\varphi$ and $S, a \vDash \bigwedge_{j\in\mathcal{G}}[j \ \mathsf{prom}][\mathcal{G} \ \mathsf{prom}]\varphi$. Then there is a profile $b \in A$ satisfying:*

1. $S, (b_i, a_{-i}) \vDash [i \ \mathsf{prom}]\varphi$
2. $b_i \preceq_{[\mathcal{G} \ \mathsf{prom}]\varphi} a_i$
3. $S, (b_i, a_{-i}) \vDash \bigwedge_{j\in\mathcal{G}}[j \ \mathsf{prom}][\mathcal{G} \ \mathsf{prom}]\varphi$

Proof Assume all the mentioned assumptions. Since $S, a \nvDash [i \ \mathsf{prom}]\varphi$, there is a $b \in A$ satisfying $b_i \succ_\varphi a_i$ and $S, b \vDash [i \ \mathsf{prom}]\varphi$. Hence, for any $c_{-i} \in A_{-i}$ it holds that $S, (a_i, c_{-i}) \vDash \varphi$ implies $S, (b_i, c_{-i}) \vDash \varphi$. This entails that for any $c_{-i} \in A_{-i}$, $(b_i, c_{\mathcal{G}-i}) \succeq_\varphi (a_i, c_{\mathcal{G}-i})$ holds. Hence, for any $c_{-i} \in A_{-i}$ it holds that $S, (a_i, c_{-i}) \vDash [\mathcal{G} \ \mathsf{prom}]\varphi$ implies $S, (b_i, c_{-i}) \vDash [\mathcal{G} \ \mathsf{prom}]\varphi$. In other words, $b_i \succeq_{[\mathcal{G} \ \mathsf{prom}]\varphi} a_i$ holds. Since $S, a \vDash [i \ \mathsf{prom}][\mathcal{G} \ \mathsf{prom}]\varphi$, this entails that $b_i \preceq_{[\mathcal{G} \ \mathsf{prom}]\varphi} a_i$ and $S, (b_i, a_{-i}) \vDash [i \ \mathsf{prom}][\mathcal{G} \ \mathsf{prom}]\varphi$ hold. To prove the third item, we need to show that for every $j \in \mathcal{G} - i$, $S, (b_i, a_{-i}) \vDash [j \ \mathsf{prom}][\mathcal{G} \ \mathsf{prom}]\varphi$ holds. This follows immediately from the fact that the j-th component in (b_i, a_{-i}) equals that in a and the assumption that $S, a \vDash \bigwedge_{j\in\mathcal{G}}[j \ \mathsf{prom}][\mathcal{G} \ \mathsf{prom}]\varphi$. □

Proof of Result 5.4 Let $S = \langle N, (A_i), (Int_{\mathcal{G}}), V\rangle$ be a game model. Suppose $\mathcal{G}$ collectively intends to φ, and suppose that pro-group intentions guarantee that a best group action is performed. Let $a \in A$ satisfy $S, a \vDash \bigwedge_{i\in\mathcal{G}}[i \ \mathsf{prom}][\mathcal{G} \ \mathsf{prom}]\varphi$. Using the previous lemma, we can show, by induction on the size of $\mathcal{F} := \{j \in \mathcal{G} \mid S, a \nvDash [j \ \mathsf{prom}]\varphi\}$, that there is a $b \in A$ satisfying (1) $S, (b_{\mathcal{F}}, a_{-\mathcal{F}}) \vDash$

$\bigwedge_{j \in \mathcal{G}}[j \text{ prom}]\varphi$ and (2) $b_j \preceq_{[\mathcal{G} \text{ prom}]\varphi} a_j$ for every $j \in \mathcal{G}$. In light of the assumption that pro-group intentions guarantee that a best group action is performed, (1) implies $S, (b_{\mathcal{F}}, a_{-\mathcal{F}}) \models [\mathcal{G} \text{ prom}]\varphi$. Using (2), this can be shown, by induction on the size of $\mathcal{F}$, to imply $S, a \models [\mathcal{G} \text{ prom}]\varphi$. This shows that participatory intentions guarantee that a best group action is performed. □

References

Anderson, E. (2001). Unstrapping the straitjacket of 'preference': A comment on Amartya Sen's contributions to philosophy and economics. *Economics & Philosophy, 17*(1), 21–38.

Anscombe, G. E. M. (1963). *Intention*. Cambridge: Harvard University Press.

Bacharach, M. (1999). Interactive team reasoning: A contribution to the theory of co-operation. *Research in Economics, 53*(2), 117–147.

Bacharach, M. (2006). *Beyond individual choice: Teams and frames in game theory*, N. Gold & R. Sugden (Eds.). Princeton: Princeton University Press.

Bardsley, N., Mehta, J., Starmer, C., & Sugden, R. (2010). Explaining focal points: Cognitive hierarchy theory versus team reasoning. *The Economic Journal, 120*(543), 40–79.

Bernheim, B. D. (1984). Rationalizable strategic behavior. *Econometrica, 52*(4), 1007–1028.

Bicchieri, C. (2006). *The grammar of society*. Cambridge: Cambridge University Press.

Bolton, G. E., & A. Ockenfels (2000). ERC: A theory of equity, reciprocity, and competition. *The American Economic Review, 90*(1), 166–193.

Braham, M., & van Hees, M. (2012). An anatomy of moral responsibility. *Mind, 121*(483), 601–634.

Brandenburger, A., Friedenberg, A., & Keisler, H. J. (2008). Admissibility in games. *Econometrica, 76*(2), 307–352.

Bratman, M. E. (1987). *Intention, plans, and practical reason*. Cambridge: Harvard University Press.

Bratman, M. E. (2014). *Shared agency: A planning theory of acting together*. Oxford: Oxford University Press.

Broersen, J. (2011). Modeling attempt and action failure in probabilistic stit logic. In T. Walsh (Ed.), *Proceedings of the Twenty-Second International Joint Conference on Artificial Intelligence* (pp. 792–797). AAAI Press.

Deutsch, M. (1949). A theory of co-operation and competition. *Human Relations, 2*(2), 129–152.

Dietrich, F., & C. List (2016). Reason-based choice and context-dependence: An explanatory framework. *Economics & Philosophy, 32*(02), 175–229.

Dubber, M. D. (2002). *Criminal law: Model penal code*. New York: Foundation Press.

Duff, A. (1982). Intention, responsibility and double effect. *The Philosophical Quarterly, 32*(126), 1–16.

Duijf, H. (2018). Beyond team-directed reasoning: Participatory intentions contribute to a theory of collective agency. *Logique et Analyse, 61*(243), 269–298.

Duijf, H. (2021). Cooperation, fairness, and team reasoning. *Economics & Philosophy, 37*(3), 413–440.

Duijf, H., Broersen, J., & Meyer, J.-J. C. (2019). Conflicting intentions: Rectifying the consistency requirements. *Philosophical Studies, 176*(4), 1097–1118.

Faillo, M., Smerilli, A., & Sugden, R. (2013). The roles of level-k and team reasoning in solving coordination games. Cognitive and Experimental Economics Laboratory Working Paper 6-13.

Fehr, E., & Schmidt, K. M. (1999). A theory of fairness, competition, and cooperation. *The Quarterly Journal of Economics, 114*(3), 817–868.

Gilbert, M. (1989). *On social facts*. London: Routledge.

Gilbert, M. (1990). Walking together: A paradigmatic social phenomenon. *Midwest Studies in Philosophy, 15*(1), 1–14.

Gilbert, M. (2009). Shared intention and personal intentions. *Philosophical Studies, 144*(1), 167–187.

Gold, N. (2012). Team reasoning, framing and cooperation. In S. Okasha & K. Binmore (Eds.), *Evolution and rationality: decisions, co-operation and strategic behaviour* (pp. 185–212). Cambridge: Cambridge University Press.

Gold, N., & Sugden, R. (2007). Collective intentions and team agency. *The Journal of Philosophy, 104*(3), 109–137.

Hakli, R., Miller, K., & Tuomela, R. (2010). Two kinds of we-reasoning. *Economics & Philosophy, 26*(3), 291–320.

Harsanyi, J. C., & Selten, R. (1988). *A general theory of equilibrium selection in games*. Cambridge: MIT Press.

Hodgson, D. H. (1967). *Consequences of utilitarianism*. Oxford: Clarendon Press.

Hollis, M., & Sugden, R. (1993). Rationality in action. *Mind, 102*(405), 1–35.

Hurley, S. L. (1989). *Natural reasons*. New York: Oxford University Press.

Isaacs, T. (2011). *Moral responsibility in collective contexts*. New York: Oxford University Press.

Karpus, J., & Radzvilas, M. (2018). Team reasoning and a measure of mutual advantage in games. *Economics & Philosophy, 34*(1), 1–30.

Keynes, J. M. (1921). *A treatise on probability*. London: Macmillan.

Kohlberg, E., & Mertens, J.-F. (1986). On the strategic stability of equilibria. *Econometrica, 54*(5), 1003–1037.

Konolige, K., & Pollack, M. E. (1993). A representationalist theory of intention. In R. Bajcsy (Ed.), *Proceedings of the Thirteenth International Joint Conference on Artifical Intelligence* (Vol. 1, pp. 390–395).

Kutz, C. (2000). *Complicity: Ethics and law for a collective age*. Cambridge: Cambridge University Press.

Mele, A., & Sverdlik, S. (1996). Intention, intentional action, and moral responsibility. *Philosophical Studies, 82*, 165–287.

Murphy, R. O., & Ackermann, K. A. (2014). Social value orientation: Theoretical and measurement issues in the study of social preferences. *Personality and Social Psychology Review, 18*(1), 13–41.

Pearce, D. G. (1984). Rationalizable strategic behavior and the problem of perfection. *Econometrica, 52*(4), 1029–1050.

Perea, A. (2012). *Epistemic game theory*. Cambridge: Cambridge University Press.

Rabin, M. (1993). Incorporating fairness into game theory and economics. *The American Economic Review, 83*(5), 1281–1302.

Regan, D. (1980). *Utilitarianism and co-operation*. New York: Oxford University Press.

Savage, L. J. (1954). *The foundations of statistics*. New York: John Wiley & Sons.

Searle, J. (1990). Collective intentions and actions. In P. R. Cohen, J. Morgan, & M. E. Pollack (Eds.), *Intentions in communication* (pp. 401–415). Cambridge: MIT Press.

Sugden, R. (1991). Rational choice: A survey of contributions from economics and philosophy. *The Economic Journal, 101*(407), 751–785.

Sugden, R. (1993). Thinking as a team: Towards an explanation of nonselfish behavior. *Social Philosophy and Policy, 10*(1), 69–89.

Sugden, R. (2000). Team preferences. *Economics & Philosophy, 16*(2), 175–204.

Sugden, R. (2003). The logic of team reasoning. *Philosophical Explorations, 6*(3), 165–181.

Sugden, R. (2010). Opportunity as mutual advantage. *Economics & Philosophy, 26*(1), 47–68.

Sugden, R. (2011). Mutual advantage, conventions and team reasoning. *International Review of Economics, 58*(1), 9–20.

Sugden, R. (2015). Team reasoning and intentional cooperation for mutual benefit. *Journal of Social Ontology, 1*(1), 143–166.

Tamminga, A., & Duijf, H. (2017). Collective obligations, group plans and individual actions. *Economics & Philosophy, 33*(2), 187–214.

Tomasello, M. (2016). *A natural history of human morality*. Cambridge: Harvard University Press.
Tuomela, R. (2000). Collective and joint intention. *Mind & Society, 1*(2), 39–69.
Tuomela, R. (2005). We-intentions revisited. *Philosophical Studies, 125*(3), 327–369.
Tuomela, R. (2006). Joint intention, we-mode and I-mode. *Midwest Studies in Philosophy, 30*(1), 35–58.
Tuomela, R. (2007). *The philosophy of sociality*. New York: Oxford University Press.
van Hees, M., & Roy, O. (2008). Intentions and plans in decision and game theory. In B. Verbeek (Ed.), *Reasons and intentions* (pp. 207–226). Aldershot: Ashgate.
Van Lange, P. A. M. (1999). The pursuit of joint outcomes and equality in outcomes: An integrative model of social value orientation. *Journal of Personality and Social Psychology, 77*(2), 337–349.

Chapter 6
Practical Reasoning and Cooperation

> *Let group agents be freed from the burden of being held responsible, and the door will open to abuses: there will be cases where no one is held responsible for actions that are manifestly matters of agential responsibility.*
>
> *Philip Pettit (2007, p. 196–197)*

6.1 Introduction

Many ethical theorists believe that reasons play a fundamental role for analyzing various normative concepts.[1] What one should do, according to this strand of literature, is determined by the reasons bearing on the actions available to you. Although these theorists typically conceive of reasons as being in competition and as representing trade-offs, I will adopt a more decision-theoretic way of conceiving reasons.[2] In this chapter, I will sketch a reasoning-based framework of responsibility based on so-called practical-reasoning schemas. Roughly stated, to assess whether an individual is responsible for a certain outcome, I will propose to investigate the practical reasoning that has led to her decision.

This chapter is largely based on my (Duijf, 2018b).

[1] This idea is often traced back to Ross' (1930) analysis of prima facie duties and it has been further developed by others (see, for instance Baier, 1958; Chisholm, 1964; Dancy, 2004; Parfit, 2011; Raz, 1975; Scanlon, 1998; Schroeder, 2007). To illustrate, Scanlon (1998, p. 271) writes: "If an action is blameworthy, then the agent has either failed to take account of or knowingly acted contrary to a reason that should, according to any principles that no one could reasonably reject, have counted against his action."

[2] Horty (2012, p. 3) introduces an alternative framework based on default logic to represent reasons and develops "a precise, concrete theory of the way in which reasons interact to support their outcomes".

© The Author(s), under exclusive license to Springer Nature Switzerland AG 2022

H. Duijf, *The Logic of Responsibility Voids*, Synthese Library 456,
https://doi.org/10.1007/978-3-030-92655-7_6

Based on my reasoning-based framework of moral responsibility for outcomes, I will assess the possibility and scope of the problem of responsibility voids and gaps. Inspired by the team-reasoning account of cooperation (Bacharach, 2006), I will adopt a new take on the problem of responsibility voids and gaps, and propose to use the distinction between cooperation and competition to assess the moral responsibility of individuals in collective action contexts. Team-reasoning theorists rely on different modes of *reasoning* to contrast cooperation and competition. Simply stated, an individual agent faces a competitive decision problem if and only if she reasons individualistically; she faces a cooperative decision problem if and only if she team reasons. To address typical collective action problems, I will show that the team-reasoning paradigm needs to be refined to what I will call *participatory reasoning*. The details of these reasoning methods need not worry us at present as they will be explicated in the following sections.

Although this chapter will analyse both responsibility gaps and voids, I will largely focus on the problem of responsibility gaps and enquire whether cases exist in which a group is collectively morally responsible for some outcome although no member can be held morally responsible for it. The question of the members' individual moral responsibility will depend on the facts of the particular case. The practical-reasoning schemas can be used to show *which* facts matter. In particular, these schemas will help to explicate the facts that must obtain for responsibility voids or gaps to exist.

The chapter is set out as follows. I will provide a sketch of a reasoning-based framework of moral responsibility using practical-reasoning schemas in Sect. 6.2. In Sect. 6.3, I will discuss the team-reasoning account of cooperation using practical-reasoning schemas, and argue that team reasoning needs to be refined to participatory reasoning in order to address collective action problems. In Sect. 6.4, I will analyse responsibility gaps and argue for two main claims: competitive decision problems are free from responsibility gaps; cooperative decision problems potentially host such gaps, but the conditions for the existence of such gaps differ depending on the type of uncertainty. In Sect. 6.5, I will analyse responsibility voids and characterize the conditions that must be met if such voids are to exist. I will conclude with a brief discussion of the implications for corporate responsibility and democratic decision-making.

6.2 Reasoning-Based Moral Responsibility

Let me start with sketching an outline of a reasoning-based framework for moral responsibility. For simplicity's sake, I will focus on blameworthiness for outcomes rather than praiseworthiness. Although I think it is useful and important to further develop this reasoning-based framework, for my present purposes this sketch will suffice to highlight its main features and, roughly, its application. In the next sections, I will apply the reasoning-based distinction between cooperation

(I1) I must choose either A or B (I2) If I choose A the outcome will be O1 (I3) If I choose B the outcome will be O2 (I4) I prefer O1 over O2
(I∘) I prefer choosing A over choosing B (I•) I should choose A

Fig. 6.1 Individual-reasoning schema: (I•) states the conclusion; (I∘) states an intermediate conclusion; and (I1)–(I4) state the premises

and competition (Sect. 6.3) to collective action problems, and to the problem of responsibility gaps and voids.

Following Gold and Sugden (2007), various forms of practical reasoning can be characterized by *schemas* of practical reasoning.[3] Such schemas illustrate how premises describing the decision context and describing what the agent seeks to achieve should be used to decide which action should be taken. In logic, a valid rule of inference illustrates how premises should be used to derive conclusions. Analogously, the fundamental idea is that a practical-reasoning schema infers conclusions about what the agent ought to do from premises which include propositions about what the agent is seeking to achieve. For instance, when reasoning individualistically, the agent first considers the individual actions available to her, assesses these individual actions in terms of their consequences, and then finds the individual action that best furthers her interests.

Figure 6.1 depicts a reasoning schema that characterizes individually instrumental reasoning.[4] The first premise (I1) expresses the available or eligible individual actions. The two premises (I2) and (I3) state that the available individual actions are evaluated on the basis of their possible consequences. Premise (I4) describes what the agent seeks to achieve in terms of a preference over outcomes. The individual-reasoning schema emphasizes that the personal preferences over outcomes (I4) are lifted to preferences over the available individual actions (I∘): since I prefer O1 over O2, I prefer choosing A over choosing B. Finally, this lifted preference delivers the conclusion of practical reasoning: because I must choose one of them, this entails that I should choose A (I•).

It may be helpful to note that this reasoning schema can be straightforwardly adopted in decision contexts that involve risk, that is, in cases where "each action leads to one of a set of possible outcomes, each outcome occurring with a known

[3] To be explicit, Gold and Sugden (2007) present and discuss schemes for individual reasoning, collective reasoning, and several schemes for team reasoning. The participatory-reasoning schema (see Sect. 6.3) is my novel addition to this range of practical-reasoning schemes.

[4] The 'I' is added to indicate that the statement occurs in the individual-reasoning schema. Similarly, for instance, a 'C' will be added to statements that occur in the collective-reasoning schema (see Fig. 6.2).

probability" (Luce & Raiffa, 1957, p. 13). To see this, imagine an individual agent playing a game of chess against a sophisticated computer. For simplicity's sake, let us imagine that she seeks to win the game. To decide on her next move, the individual agent has to consider the individual actions available to her. Plausibly, only individual actions that abide by the rules of chess are admissible for consideration. She then needs to assess the expected consequences of her eligible individual actions. Say she expects that choosing ♙**e4** has a 75% chance of leading to victory, whereas choosing ♛**d6** only has a 30% chance of doing so. Consequently, assuming she endorses something like expected utility maximization, she prefers choosing ♙**e4** over choosing ♛**d6** because it has the best chance of leading to victory. Finally, this will lead her to conclude that she should choose ♙**e4**.

We can see that the individual-reasoning schema can certainly fail to deliver a determinate solution.[5] That is, if individual reasoning delivers $\mathcal{A}$ as the set of recommended individual actions, then, on the one hand, one may think that each individual action $A \in \mathcal{A}$ is permitted, or admitted, by individual reasoning. On the other hand, one may think that the individual agent is required to choose one of the individual actions in $\mathcal{A}$.[6]

Since individual instrumental reasoning seems to naturally cohere with consequentialist moral reasoning, one may ask whether it can be generalized to incorporate deontological moral reasoning. This issue cannot be settled here, but I wish to add two comments. First, Portmore (2007, p. 39) gives a recipe for consequentializing non-consequentialist theories: "Take whatever considerations that the non-consequentialist theory holds to be relevant to determining the deontic status of an action and insist that those considerations are relevant to determining the proper ranking of outcomes." For example, if a deontological theory holds that it is wrong for an agent to violate someone's rights even for the sake of minimizing rights violations overall, then the corresponding consequentialist theory needs to hold that any outcome where the agent violates someone's rights ranks lower than any outcome where the agent doesn't do so, even if the agent's violation would prevent others from committing more rights violations. This suggests that if deontological theories are consequentializable then deontological moral reasoning can be incorporated by amending the preferences accordingly. Second, Dietrich and List (2017, p. 458) provide a reason-based decision-theoretic framework that can represent virtually any moral theory by way of a so-called 'reasons structure', "which encodes the theory's answer to the two-part question of which properties matter and how they do so". A moral theory's associated reasons structure can readily be plugged into the individual-reasoning schema.[7] Instead of assessing the

[5] The example of the chess-player could be amended to prove this point: if the agent expects that two individual actions, say ♙**e4** and ♖**g6**, have the same chance of leading to victory, then individualistic reasoning would yield the recommendation to choose either of these.

[6] I consider this indeterminacy an asset of the individual-reasoning schema. I agree with Bacharach (2006, p. 60, Sect. 8.3) that a theory should only be determinate when our intuitions are.

[7] Unfortunately, I can only hint at how this could be done as a detailed explication would lead me too far astray.

available options in terms of their consequences (as in (I2) and (I3)), they would be assessed in terms of their properties. These associated sets of properties are then compared using the reason structure's weighing relation, or defeat relation, rather than using a preference relation (as in (I4)). In this way, the amended individual-reasoning schema seems to be able to accommodate virtually any moral theory.

How can these reasoning schemas be used to analyse moral responsibility? Reasoning schemas highlight that there may be different reasons for holding an individual agent responsible for a certain outcome. As mentioned before, I will focus on moral blameworthiness for outcomes. The intuitive idea is that moral blameworthiness requires or relies on bad intentions or culpable ignorance, or at least on moral faultiness.

To illustrate how the individual-reasoning schema may help develop a reasoning-based framework of responsibility for outcomes, let us consider a case of committee decision-making. A hiring committee consists of three members, Marie, Malcolm, and Myra, and it has to make a choice about which of three candidates, Alice, Bill, and Charlie, is to join the company board. Committee decisions are made by majority, and with Marie, the chairperson, breaking ties. The committee members vote for Alice, Bill, and Charlie, respectively. The result is that Alice wins. Let us suppose that Alice turns out to be a bad candidate for the company board.

Is Malcolm blameworthy for the outcome that Alice wins? I provide three complementing analyses of this scenario; each emphasizes a particular type of concern and each is associated with some premises of the individual-reasoning schema.[8] First, Malcolm's preferences may have been such that it was irrelevant for him whether Alice wins. It may, for instance, have been the case that he randomly decided on his vote. In this case, Alice's winning played no role in his practical reasoning. It seems implausible to say that Malcolm is morally blameworthy for the result that Alice wins if it played no role in his practical reasoning. To assess Malcolm's responsibility in more detail, we need to ask whether it was reasonable for him to be indifferent about Alice's winning. He would be morally blameworthy for Alice's winning only if it was unreasonable for him to be so indifferent.[9] If it was unreasonable, then this would illustrate a moral failure in premise (I4) of the individual-reasoning schema, which describes what Malcolm seeks to achieve.

Second, Malcolm's preferences may have been such that he sought to let Alice lose. In such a case, Alice's losing played a vital role in his practical reasoning. How could voting for Bill have been permitted by individual reasoning? For example, he could have voted as he did if he expected that Myra would also vote for Bill. In that case, he would expect that his vote would yield Bill's winning. However, his expectation regarding Myra's vote was wrong, leading to Alice's winning. This

[8] Two of these concerns roughly correspond to what Braham and van Hees (2011) call "normative voids" and "epistemic voids". My first concern has no counterpart in their theory.

[9] Indeed, whether Malcolm actually made a *causal* contribution to Alice's winning is irrelevant. It is only important that it played a role in his practical reasoning. Causality, however, is relevant when he assesses the available individual actions in terms of their consequences.

illustrates a moral failure in premise (I2) or (I3) of the individual-reasoning schema, which describes Malcolm's expectation regarding the consequences of voting for Bill. So we may say that Malcolm is morally blameworthy for Alice's winning: his false expectation led to Alice's winning. To assess Malcolm's responsibility in more detail, we need to ask whether it was reasonable for him to expect that Myra would vote for Bill. Simply stated, he could be exculpated for Alice's winning if his expectations were reasonable.

Third, Malcolm may have considered only a subset of the viable options. For instance, he may have thought that casting a vote for Charlie was not an eligible option for him. In this case, Malcolm basically only considered voting for Bill or Alice, then reasoned so as to minimize the expectation that Alice wins, and finally decided to vote for Bill. It then seems plausible to say that Malcolm is not morally blameworthy for Alice's winning. To refine the assessment of moral responsibility, we may ask whether it was reasonable for him to think that voting for Charlie was not an eligible option. Simply stated, he would be morally blameworthy for Alice's winning if he should have known that voting for Charlie was, in fact, an eligible option. The blameworthiness would correspond to a moral failure in premise (I1) of the individual-reasoning schema, which states the eligible individual actions.[10]

6.3 Cooperation

To characterize competition and cooperation I will rely on the team-reasoning account of cooperation (Bacharach, 2006; Gold & Sugden, 2007; Sugden, 2000). (See Sect. 5.2.1 for an introduction to team reasoning.) The core idea of team reasoning is that an individual asks herself 'What should *we* do?' rather than 'What should *I* do?'. Contrary to the discussion of team reasoning in Sect. 5.2.1, my current analysis focuses on the fact that the team-reasoning account of cooperation appeals to the *reasoning method* by which an individual agent reasons about what to do. Following Gold and Sugden (2007), I will use practical-reasoning schemas to operationalize different reasoning methods.

Before moving to team reasoning, note that the individual-reasoning schema can be straightforwardly amended for groups: the collective-reasoning schema in Fig. 6.2 illustrates that the preferences over outcomes are lifted to the available group actions and the schema highlights that it may fail to deliver a determinate

[10] It should be clear from the above discussion that my view includes the possibility that the committee members try to 'manipulate' the collective outcome by voting untruthfully. This may contradict one's intuitions. However, for the assessment of moral responsibility it is wholly unclear why truthful votes should take moral priority in interdependent decision problems. I do not wish to claim that every form of strategic decision-making is morally acceptable—only some forms may be. I refer the interested reader to the paper by Dowding and Van Hees (2008) titled "In praise of manipulation".

(C1) We must choose (A,A), (A,B), (B,A), or (B,B)
(C2) If we choose (A,A) the outcome will be O1
(C3) If we choose (A,B) the outcome will be O2
(C4) If we choose (B,A) the outcome will be O3
(C5) If we choose (B,B) the outcome will be O4
(C6) O1 and O2 best satisfy our collective preferences

(C∘) Choosing (A,A) and choosing (A,B) best satisfy our collective preferences
(C•) We should choose (A,A) or choose (A,B)

Fig. 6.2 Collective-reasoning schema: (C•) states the conclusion; (C∘) states an intermediate conclusion; and (C1)–(C6) denote the premises

(C1) We must choose (A,A), (A,B), (B,A), or (B,B)
(C2) If we choose (A,A) the outcome will be O1
(C3) If we choose (A,B) the outcome will be O2
(C4) If we choose (B,A) the outcome will be O3
(C5) If we choose (B,B) the outcome will be O4
(T6) (A,A) *uniquely* maximizes our collective preferences

(T•) Each of us should choose her component of (A,A)

Fig. 6.3 Team-reasoning schema: (C1)–(C5) and (T6) state the premises, and (T•) states the conclusion

solution.[11] The only difference with the individual-reasoning schema is the level of agency: in the individual-reasoning schema, individual preferences over outcomes are lifted to preferences over individual actions; in the collective-reasoning schema collective preferences over outcomes (C6) are lifted to preferences over group actions (C∘). Given the symmetry, the collective-reasoning schema is valid if and only if the individual-reasoning schema is.[12]

It is helpful to emphasize that collective reasoning relies on group preferences. In line with the team-reasoning literature (see Bacharach, 1999; Sugden, 2000), I will assume that group preferences are given. As such, my study is independent of any specific account of group preferences.

Proponents of team reasoning have adopted the reasoning schema depicted in Fig. 6.3 for group members adopting a we-perspective. However, it is problematic

[11] In line with game-theoretical conventions, I use '(A,B)' to denote the strategy profile where the first player chooses A and the second player chooses B.

[12] Gold and Sugden (2007, p. 123—terminology adapted) write: "We assert that [the individual-reasoning schema and the collective-reasoning schema] are both forms of valid instrumental reasoning and that they are valid for agents, defined as those entities that use these modes of reasoning (individual agents in one case, group agents in the other)."

		Player 2: *high*	Player 2: *low*
Player 1	*X*	3, 3	1, 0
	Y	3, 3	1, 1
	low	0, 0	2, 2

Fig. 6.4 The ambiguous Hi-Lo game

that the team-reasoning schema can generally not be applied to typical collective action problems. To illustrate this defect and clarify the problem at this stage, consider the *ambiguous Hi-Lo game* depicted in Fig. 6.4. It seems that a satisfactory theory of cooperation should recommend *high* to player 2 and should recommend that player 1 chooses either *X* or *Y*, rather than *low*. Team reasoning, unfortunately, fails to deliver either of these recommendations because it relies on the premise that there is a *unique* best group action available, as stated in premise (T6).[13] In collective action problems, there are often multiple ways to successfully coordinate the individual actions of the group members. For example, in committee decision-making under the majority rule, it does not matter *who* votes for a particular option, it only matters that enough members vote accordingly. Similarly, in threshold public goods games, all strategy profiles in which sufficiently many individuals contribute is adequate. So team reasoning needs to be refined in order to apply it to collective action problems.

To overcome this defect in team reasoning, I aim to contribute to theories of cooperation by augmenting the team-reasoning paradigm to what I call *participatory reasoning*. Roughly stated, participatory reasoning consists of two stages. First, a participatory-reasoner considers the group actions available to them, assesses these group actions in terms of their consequences, and finds the group actions that best further their common or collective interest. Second, a participatory-reasoner then considers the individual actions available to her, assesses these individual actions in terms of whether they yield a best group action, and then chooses an individual action that promotes the realization of a best group action. Accordingly, a member who endorses participatory reasoning can be thought of as aiming to participate in a

[13] Gold and Sugden (2007, p. 125), for example, write: "[T]he schema yields conclusions only when a profile that is the unique maximizer of the team payoff function exists." In addition, Sugden (2000, p. 193) writes: "If two or more different combinations of strategies yield exactly the same utility for the team, this decision rule fails to determine what each individual should do."

(Stage 1: the collective level)

(C1) We must choose (A,A), (A,B), (B,A), or (B,B)
(C2) If we choose (A,A) the outcome will be O1
(C3) If we choose (A,B) the outcome will be O2
(C4) If we choose (B,A) the outcome will be O3
(C5) If we choose (B,B) the outcome will be O4
(C6) O1 and O2 best satisfy our collective preferences

(C∘) Choosing (A,A) and choosing (A,B) best satisfy our collective preferences
(C•) We should choose (A,A) or choose (A,B)

(Stage 2: the individual level for agent 1)

(I1) I must choose A or B
(P2) If I choose A the outcome will be that we choose (A,A) or that we choose (A,B)
(P3) If I choose B the outcome will be that we choose (B,A) or that we choose (B,B)
(C•) We should choose (A,A) or choose (A,B)

(P∘) Choosing A best promotes the realization of a best group act
(P•) I should choose A

Fig. 6.5 Participatory-reasoning schema: (P•) states the conclusion; (P∘), (C∘), and (C•) state intermediate conclusions; and the others state the premises

best group action.[14] If there are several best group actions, participatory reasoning can be viewed as yielding an individual action that maximizes the expectation of realizing a best group action. Figure 6.5 depicts the participatory-reasoning schema, which consists of two stages: the collective level and the individual level. That is, a participant first adopts the group perspective to answer the question 'What should *we* do?' and then asks herself 'What should *I* do?'.

Can the participatory-reasoning schema do without the problematic uniqueness assumption? At the first stage, the collective-reasoning schema is adopted, which could yield a set of group actions. In the ambiguous Hi-Lo game, at the first stage a participant concludes that we should choose (*X*, *high*) or (*Y*, *high*). At the second stage, player 1 considers the options available to her and assesses the associated consequences. Since she seeks to realize a best group action, and because choosing

[14] In Chap. 5, I study the relation between team reasoning and so-called participatory intentions. These participatory intentions naturally relate to the participatory-reasoning schema: for an individual agent, the adoption of "a participatory intention requires her to adopt as her personal objective that a *best group action is performed* " (Duijf, 2018a, p. 20–21).

X and choosing *Y* are both compatible with realizing a best group act whereas choosing *low* is not, participatory reasoning yields that she should either choose *X* or choose *Y*. This means that the participatory-reasoning schema can do without the problematic uniqueness assumption and can therefore be applied to a broader range of collective action problems.

Having refined team reasoning to participatory reasoning, let me end this section by addressing its main question: how do these practical-reasoning schemas relate to the distinction between competition and cooperation? To distinguish between the intentions that lie behind cooperative actions and the mutually consistent intentions that lie behind Nash equilibrium behaviour, Natalie Gold and Robert Sugden argue that

> collective intentions are the product of a distinctive mode of practical reasoning, team reasoning, in which agency is attributed to groups. (Gold & Sugden, 2007, p. 137)

Hence, whether a set of individual actions constitutes a collective intentional group action depends on the reasoning that led to the component individual actions. So what makes a set of individual actions a case of jointly intentional action is the form of reasoning endorsed by the members. Simply stated, if members endorse team reasoning, then the resulting pattern is a cooperative act, but if members endorse individual reasoning, then the resulting pattern is a mere aggregate of individual acts.

In cooperative settings, this means that the group members should endorse participatory reasoning rather than individual reasoning. Robert Sugden, for example, concurs:

> A cooperative morality enjoins each individual to do her part in achieving outcomes that are good for all. . . . [T]he individual does not ask whether her own actions, considered in isolation, yield preferred outcomes. (Sugden, 1993, p. 72)

This highlights that morality may even dictate which reasoning method is apt.[15] Roughly stated, competitive contexts are characterized by the fact that individualistic reasoning is apt, and cooperative decision contexts are characterized by the fact that participatory reasoning is apt. This distinction will ground my analysis of potential responsibility voids and gaps.

6.4 A Reasoning-Based Analysis of Responsibility Gaps

To distribute collective moral responsibility, my reasoning-based framework for moral responsibility highlights that it is useful to distinguish between two types of contexts: competitive and cooperative contexts. In other words, my framework

[15] For instance, Regan (1980, p. 11) develops a theory of cooperative utilitarianism, which "can be summed up in the statement that each agent ought to co-operate, with whoever else is co-operating, in the production of the best consequences possible given the behavior of non-co-operators".

Fig. 6.6 The discursive dilemma

	Research r	Service s	Teaching t	Tenure? $r \wedge s \wedge t$
M1	Yes	Yes	No	No
M2	No	Yes	Yes	No
M3	Yes	No	Yes	No
Group	Yes	Yes	Yes	→Yes / ↓No

distinguishes between endorsing individual or participatory reasoning. I will discuss these two cases in turn.

6.4.1 *Competitive Decision Contexts*

Do competitive decision contexts leave room for responsibility gaps? As argued before, competitive decision contexts are characterized by the fact that the involved agents, or at least some of them, endorse the individual-reasoning schema. Stated boldly, I will defend the claim that in a world of reasonable, rational individualists there is no gap between collective blameworthiness and the individual blameworthiness of its inhabitants. To be sure, there may be tragedy, but there is no gap between, on the one hand, collective responsibility and, on the other hand, members' responsibility.

Consider a prominent problem in the philosophical literature on collective decision-making: the *discursive dilemma*, which is also known as the doctrinal paradox in legal theory (Chapman, 1998; Kornhauser, 1992; the former introduced the term 'doctrinal paradox'). To illustrate the dilemma, suppose a committee of academics, consisting of M1, M2, and M3, is deciding on whether to award tenure to Mr Borderline. Imagine the university's tenure policy requires excellence in research, service, and teaching. Suppose the committee members are to decide on the tenure by first voting on each of these fields of competence, then aggregating their votes on each of these fields by majority, and finally deriving the collective decision on the tenure in line with the university's rules. If the members vote in accordance with Fig. 6.6, then it turns out that they collectively decide to award tenure even though they are unanimously opposed.

It could be that all committee members in the discursive dilemma reasoned individualistically and that the premises they endorsed were fully justified. Does this leave a responsibility gap with regard to the awarded tenure?[16] According to my reasoning-based framework, there are two, jointly exhaustive, cases to distinguish. First, they could be justified in endorsing individualistic reasoning.[17] This means that they reasonably faced a competitive problem. It is uncontroversial

[16] It is often argued that none of the committee members can be held responsible in the discursive dilemma (Copp, 2006; List & Pettit, 2011; Pettit, 2007).

[17] For my arguments it does not matter what grounds this justification.

that competitiveness undermines group cohesion and group agency. According to most theories of moral responsibility, this would imply that the group cannot be attributed moral responsibility.[18] Since this entails that the group is not *collectively* morally blameworthy for awarding tenure, it follows that there is no responsibility gap. The result may certainly be a grave tragedy, but not one in which there is some moral residue that should be distributed.

Second, members of the committee could be unjustified in endorsing individualistic reasoning. In this case, one could maintain that the group is collectively morally blameworthy for awarding tenure. For instance, the fact that the group forms a committee designed to decide on whether to award tenure may imply that the group is collectively morally blameworthy for the awarded tenure. On my reasoning-based framework of moral responsibility, this means that the committee members' individual blameworthiness should be traced through the adopted reasoning methods. However, collective intentional group acts require that the members reason participatorily rather than individualistically. Hence, the faultiness is the absence of a collective intentional act, whose absence is constituted by the fact that some members reason individualistically. Therefore any member who reasoned individualistically is an appropriate target of moral blame or sanction. That is, the group's collective moral responsibility for the awarded tenure is distributed to those members who reasoned individualistically.

In either case there is no responsibility gap: competitive decision contexts are free from responsibility gaps.

6.4.2 Cooperative Decision Contexts

Do cooperative decision contexts leave room for responsibility gaps? As discussed before, cooperative decision contexts are characterized by the fact that the involved individuals endorse the participatory-reasoning schema. For simplicity's sake, I assume that the decision context and the collective preferences are commonly known.[19] To discuss potential responsibility gaps it is helpful to distinguish between two different types of uncertainty that the members of the group may jointly face. This distinction is natural if we note that the participatory-reasoning method treats expectations regarding external factors and in-group coordination differently. This difference gives rise to two types of uncertainty:

---

[18] There are few exceptions; Chant (2015, Sects. 4–5) argues against this position and proposes the "*revised agency thesis*: If moral responsibility attaches to an entity, then that entity must be an agent or a collective constituted by agents".

[19] Relaxing these assumptions could reveal new ways in which responsibility gaps may obtain. In accordance with my discussion of moral responsibility using the individual-reasoning schema in Sect. 6.2, it may be helpful to say that these assumptions entail that I will only consider failures in premises (C2)–(C5), or (P2) or (P3), which describe the expected consequences of the available group acts and of the available individual acts, respectively.

Fig. 6.7 A two-player discursive dilemma, where the members need to decide to award tenure depending on the candidate's excellence in research

Bob (columns), Ann (rows)

high

Ann \ Bob	*Y*	*N*
Y	1	0
N	0	0

low

Ann \ Bob	*Y*	*N*
Y	0	0
N	0	1

Candidate's competence in research

- *External Uncertainty*. In the first stage of participatory reasoning, group preferences over outcomes are lifted to preferences over group actions using the agent's expectations regarding external factors. For example, these external factors may include what her opponents are doing, or it may concern physical properties of the world, such as whether it is currently raining.
- *Coordination Uncertainty*. In the second stage of participatory reasoning, preferences over individual actions are derived from the previously obtained best group actions and the agent's expectations regarding individuals inside the group.

Both of these types of uncertainty may leave room for responsibility gaps. However, the conditions for the existence of responsibility gaps differ.

6.4.2.1 External Uncertainty

To illustrate the characteristics of cooperative decision contexts that include external uncertainty it may be helpful to construct a simple game form. Imagine that two academics, Ann and Bob, form a committee that needs to decide on whether to award tenure to Mr Borderline. This time, they do so by only judging the candidate's excellence in research; say it is impossible for them to discuss this pre-vote or to adopt a premise-based decision procedure. The collective decision is based on unanimity, that is, the collective decision is *X* if and only if both of them voted for *X*. (This includes the possibility of collective indecision.)[20] This case is depicted in Fig. 6.7, where Ann and Bob need to vote *Y* or *N*, and the external factor is modelled as a third player. The group should coordinate on voting *Y* or on voting *N*, depending on whether the candidate is an excellent researcher. The best group action therefore depends on some external factor.

This case may uphold the possibility of a responsibility gap. Such gaps are possible if Ann and Bob have diverging beliefs regarding the candidate's excellence in research. Say Ann thinks it is likely that the candidate is an excellent researcher whereas Bob thinks the opposite. Therefore Ann will conclude, in the first stage of participatory reasoning, that they should coordinate on (*Y*, *Y*), whereas Bob will

[20] Although the story is similar to the discursive dilemma, it should be clear that the structure of the decision context is different.

conclude that they should coordinate on (*N*, *N*). Then, in the second stage, each will reach the opposite conclusion, thereby yielding (*Y*, *N*): collective indecision results. Let us suppose that the candidate is an excellent researcher, yet he is not hired because of Ann and Bob's collective indecision.

I will assume that the concept of collective moral responsibility makes sense in this case. Can any of the committee members be held responsible? The outcome results from the members' diverging expectations regarding an external factor, the research excellence of the candidate in this case. This expectation affects the first stage of participatory reasoning in the premises concerning the expected outcomes of the available group acts, viz. (C2)–(C5). One of the committee members must be wrong in his or her expectation, and hence, in the absence of a plausible excuse, the member who has the least accurate expectations is most blameworthy; under the given circumstances, this would be Bob. So there would be no responsibility gap.

However, if Bob has reasonable or justifiable expectations, then he would not be responsible for the collective outcome. His mistake would then be justifiable. The study of these cases is beyond the scope of the current chapter and a discussion of whether certain expectations are reasonable or justifiable has to be left for future work.

Let me briefly clarify how this discussion can be transferred to the original discursive dilemma (Fig. 6.6). Suppose the members award tenure in the way stated in the original formulation, but Mr Borderline is actually a poor candidate. This means that the candidate is poor in at least one of the fields of competence. Let's say that the candidate is poor in research. In that case, participatory reasoning helps to clarify that the failure is in the premises (C2)–(C5). For instance, M1 would falsely think that the candidate is excellent in research and that they should decide correspondingly. Accordingly, the committee members who voted for the candidate's excellence in research are most blameworthy; under the given circumstances, those are M1 and M3.

Although this brief discussion might not solve the responsibility distribution in cases of external uncertainty, it is important to note that the literature has largely neglected this type of uncertainty. Moreover, the literature on judgement aggregation (see List & Pettit, 2011, Chap. 2, for a useful overview) seems to largely focus on cases where the group jointly faces a decision problem under certainty. My discussion conveys the importance of cases of external uncertainty to debates on distributing responsibility.

6.4.2.2 Coordination Uncertainty

To illustrate the characteristics of cooperative decision contexts that include coordination uncertainty it may be helpful to provide an informal example, which I will

Fig. 6.8 The footballers' problem

		Devin *left*	Devin *right*
Clarice	*left*	1	0
Clarice	*right*	0	1

call the footballers' problem, and to construct the associated game form.[21] Suppose Clarice and Devin are two attackers of a football team. Clarice has the ball, but an opponent is approaching her. Devin, her team-mate, has more space, so she contemplates passing the ball to him. Let us suppose that there are two directions in which Devin could run, say, left and right. There are two corresponding points on the field, left and right, to which Clarice could pass the ball to be picked up by Devin. There is no time for communication, or for one player to wait and see what the other does: each must simultaneously choose left or right. Suppose that the move to the right puts Devin in an equally good position as the move to the left would. One could say that the probability that the pass will result in a goal if both choose right is the same as the probability if both choose left. If one chooses right and the other left, the probability is zero. Most importantly, this is a scenario in which the attackers must coordinate to solve the problem, there are two ways to solve the problem, and they are indifferent about which way they do it.[22] This game is depicted in Fig. 6.8, where Clarice and Devin need to choose *left* or *right* and they need to coordinate their actions to have the best chance of scoring a goal.[23] Let us suppose that they fail to coordinate and therefore fail to score a goal; as a result the team loses their match.

As noted before, I assume that collective moral responsibility makes sense in this case. That is, the team is collectively morally responsible for losing their match.[24]

[21] I have adapted the footballers' problem from Sugden (2000, pp. 179–180), who writes: "This problem is a simple model of a situation in which there is some objective (in this case, scoring a goal) which each of a set of individuals wants to achieve, and which can most effectively be achieved if those individuals coordinate their actions. Thus, we might say, it represents a situation in which social cooperation would be useful or valuable."

[22] This game can be interpreted as a coordination game (Lewis, 1969).

[23] One could say that Clarice and Devin have a shared intention to score a goal, which they can best realize by coordinating their individual actions. Bratman (1993, p. 99) writes: "Our shared intention performs at least three interrelated jobs: it helps coordinate our intentional actions; it helps coordinate our planning; and it can structure relevant bargaining." The footballers' problem shows that cooperation does not necessarily lead to successful coordination if communication is impossible.

[24] The following discussion hence assumes that the group of footballers is collectively morally responsible *even though* communication is hampered. It is unclear whether such a scenario is universally accommodated by prominent accounts of collective action and responsibility. On the one hand, Kutz (2000, p. 92) writes: "My claim that nonresponsive or independent action can be jointly intentional does depend upon a disputable thesis: agents need not believe beforehand that they will be likely to succeed in their aims for their actions to count as jointly intentional." On the

Now, let us study whether this case could host responsibility gaps, i.e. the absence of individual moral responsibility.

When endorsing participatory reasoning, the first stage will result in the conclusion that Clarice and Devin should coordinate on either (*left*, *left*) or (*right*, *right*). This underdetermination may result in a responsibility gap. Let us see how. Imagine that Clarice expects Devin to run *left*. At the second stage of participatory reasoning, she will think that her passing *left* is more likely to yield successful coordination, viz. (P2) and (P3). Consequently, she concludes that she should pass *left*. However, if Devin expects Clarice to pass *right*, he will, analogously, conclude that he should run *right*. Hence, the resulting group action will be (*left*, *right*), which is surely a suboptimal group act. In this case, it is impossible to point out who is at fault. Clarice may respond to Devin in two ways: 'Why did you not *foresee* that I would pass *left*?' or 'Why did you run *right*?', and hence, one blames the other for a wrong expectation or for a wrong choice. It is, however, unclear who is at fault: when Clarice blames Devin for not expecting her to pass *left*, Devin can react by blaming Clarice for not passing like he expected, that is, for failing to pass *right*.

Can any of the team members be held responsible? The outcome results from the members' diverging expectations regarding in-group coordination, whether to coordinate on the left or on the right side of the field in this case. Their expectation affects the second stage of participatory reasoning in the premises concerning the expected outcomes of the available individual acts, viz. (P2) and (P3). In the absence of a coordinating mechanism it is, however, impossible to say who has the least accurate expectation regarding coordination. A responsibility gap arises.

How can we circumvent such a responsibility gap? If communication is possible and agreement is unproblematic, then one way is to align the expectations of group members by letting them agree on a coordinating plan.[25] Raimo Tuomela writes:

> If agreement making is in question, there will also be a publicly existing social (or, if you like, quasi-moral) obligation to participate in joint action. This entailment of an obligation can be regarded as a conceptual truth about the notion of agreement. (Tuomela, 2005, p. 345)

If communication is impossible, an alternative way to address this responsibility gap is given by a theory of *salience*. In game theory, the most well-known discussion of salience is given by Thomas Schelling, who writes:

> Most situations provide some clue for coordinating behavior, some focal point for each person's expectation of what the other expects him to expect to be expected to do. (Schelling, 1960, p. 57)[26]

---

other hand, Gilbert (2000, Sect. 8.7—emphasis added) writes: "There is a group action if and only if the members of a certain population are jointly committed to pursuing a certain goal as a body, and in light of this joint commitment relevant members (perhaps not all) *successfully* act so as to *reach* the goal in question."

[25] In Chap. 3, I study how a group may regulate its group action by agreeing on a plan and characterize the conditions under which a group plan successfully coordinates the individual actions of the group members.

[26] Schelling (1960, p. 57) thinks that these focal points may not be found within a theory of games: "Finding the key, or rather finding a key—any key that is mutually recognized as the key becomes

A theory of salience may therefore highlight a particular strategy profile as salient. For example, in the footballers' problem it could be argued that in Sweden the salient focal point is that both people coordinate on the right point on the field, that is, to coordinate on (*right*, *right*). It may thus be reasonable to expect that both are aware of this focal point. This means that members who have opposing expectations, and therefore aim at coordinating on (*left*, *left*), could be held responsible. The existence of a salient focal point would avoid the type of responsibility gap just discussed.

Although agreements and focal points may circumvent this type of responsibility gap, it remains unclear whether they are available in *every* cooperative decision context that includes coordination uncertainty. When these mechanisms are unavailable, my discussion reveals that responsibility gaps potentially arise.

6.5 A Reasoning-Based Analysis of Responsibility Voids

To investigate the possibility and scope of responsibility voids, it is, once again, useful to distinguish between two types of contexts: competitive and cooperative contexts. Do cooperative decision contexts leave room for responsibility voids? According to my reasoning-based framework, cooperative contexts are characterized by the fact that the involved individuals endorse the participatory-reasoning schema. Therefore, the analysis of responsibility voids is analogous to the analysis of responsibility gaps in Sect. 6.4.2: under the simplifying assumption that the decision context and the collective preferences are commonly known, responsibility voids cannot arise unless false beliefs or expectations arising from external or coordination uncertainty are justified.

Do competitive decision contexts leave room for responsibility voids? As argued before, competitive decision contexts are characterized by the fact that the involved agents, or at least some of them, endorse the individual-reasoning schema. The individual-reasoning schema can be used to illustrate the different circumstances that could give rise to responsibility voids. For simplicity's sake, I assume that the agents commonly know the decision context.[27]

First, premise (I4) expresses what the individual agent seeks to achieve in terms of a preference over outcomes. Social dilemmas like the prisoner's dilemma demonstrate that cases exist where it is in everybody's personal interest to act in a certain way, yet each individual would be better off if they together acted differently

the key—may depend on imagination more than on logic; it may depend on analogy, precedent, accidental arrangement, symmetry, aesthetic or geometric configuration, casuistic reasoning, and who the parties are and what they know about each other."

[27] Relaxing this assumption could reveal new ways in which responsibility voids may obtain. In light of the individual-reasoning schema in Sect. 6.2, it may be helpful to say that this assumption entails that I will not consider failures in premise (I1), which describes the available or eligible acts.

(see Fig. 4.10). In such a dilemma, there is another course of action which would have resulted in an outcome that is preferred by every individual. Can any of the individuals be held responsible? To assess the moral responsibility of the individuals in more detail, we need to ask whether their preferences were reasonable. After all, a given individual would be blameworthy for the undesirable outcome if her preferences were unreasonable.

From this perspective, responsibility voids can arise if the individual *moral* preferences would give rise to a social dilemma. Can it be that morality permits that the individuals seek to achieve different ends? Such moral theories need to be agent-relative in the sense that agent-relative aims are morally permissible.[28] Moreover, these agent-relative aims need to be such that they could lead to social dilemmas. In any case, responsibility voids cannot arise because of faultiness in premise (I4) unless agent-relative moral preferences exist.

How can we circumvent such responsibility voids? Even if agent-relative moral preferences exist, they need not lead to social dilemmas. How could we design interactions so that they do not have the structure of a social dilemma? This depends on the agent-relative aims that could be morally significant. In the absence of a clear moral theory of agent-relative aims, it is hard to say anything definitive at this point. Nevertheless, one suggestion would be to take inspiration from work in social exchange theory. For example, Van Lange and Balliet (2015) mention six dimensions that affect people's motivations: the level of dependence, the mutuality of dependence, the basis of dependence, the covariation of interests, the temporal structure, and the availability of information. Let me briefly discuss three of these dimensions. First, people's motivations may align or conflict. Situations of conflicting interests, such as social dilemmas, induce the expression of cooperation versus conflict, and trust versus distrust. Hence, one way to avoid social dilemmas is to ensure that people's moral aims align. Second, the temporal dimension highlights that temporally extended situations can give rise to the expression of trust and loyalty. Although cooperating in the prisoner's dilemma might not best satisfy one's immediate goals, it may be better to cooperate in order to foster trust and loyalty by building a good reputation.[29] One solution might thus be to ensure that people are interdependent for many interactions. Lastly, people's motivations are partly influenced by their comfort or discomfort with dependence. Agents who can obtain outcomes irrespective of the actions of other agents are independent. Interactions with mutual dependence, where people are equally dependent on one another, tend

---

[28] After having described a moral theory he calls C, Parfit (1984, p. 27) remarks that "Since C gives to all agents common moral aims, I shall call C *agent-neutral*. Many moral theories do not take this form. These theories are *agent-relative*, giving to different agents, different aims." Agent-relativity should not be confused with ethical egoism, which assumes that an agent's moral reasons for performing a given action only refer to the extent to which that act would promote her own welfare.

[29] Axelrod (1984) analyses the tit-for-tat strategy and motivated it with the suggestion that people often cooperate because they foresee future rewards for cooperation and future costs or punishment for defection.

to feel safer and are more stable. One way to prevent moral social dilemmas might thus be to ensure that people are equally dependent.

Second, let me proceed with discussing faultiness in premises (I2) and (I3). These premises state that the available individual actions are evaluated on the basis of their expected consequences. It seems plausible that one could have false justified beliefs about the expected consequences of one's actions. The distinction between external and coordination uncertainty emphasizes that these false beliefs may concern external factors or the actions of other agents. In sum, responsibility voids cannot arise due to faultiness in premisses (I2) and (I3) unless false expectations or beliefs regarding external factors or the actions of other agents are morally justified.

How could we circumvent such responsibility voids? One way to diminish the risk of responsibility voids would be to reduce the uncertainty regarding external factors by making sure that all agents have access to the same body of evidence. In this way, it is less likely that agents can have morally justified false expectations regarding external factors. Another way to diminish the risk of responsibility voids would be to reduce the uncertainty regarding the actions of other agents. This could, for instance, be achieved by letting the agents perform their actions sequentially. In this way, agents could know the actions of the previous agents in the queue. Although these two solutions may help to prevent responsibility voids, these solutions might not always be implementable and they might have problems of their own. For example, how do you determine the order in which agents are to perform their individual actions?

6.6 Discussion: Reasoning-Based Responsibility System

I have discussed the outline of a reasoning-based framework for moral responsibility and highlighted its application in collective action problems. The existence of responsibility gaps depends on the nature of the decision context: competitive decision contexts are free of such gaps, whereas cooperative decision contexts may host such gaps. In the latter case, the conditions for the existence of these gaps rest on the type of uncertainty the group faces, that is, either external or coordination uncertainty. In a similar way, the conditions for the existence of responsibility voids also rest on the nature of the decision context: competitive decision contexts cannot give rise to responsibility voids unless agent-relative moral preferences exist or agents who have false beliefs regarding external factors or the actions of other agents are excused; and cooperative decision contexts cannot give rise to responsibility voids unless agents who have false beliefs regarding external factors or coordination are excused.

The common denominator in the conditions for the existence of responsibility gaps is that they include justified false beliefs or expectations. The assessment of the legitimacy of these beliefs is hence vital for the study of responsibility gaps. Let me briefly elaborate on cooperative decision contexts that include external uncertainty. I have argued that such cases may give rise to responsibility gaps only if at least one of the group members has a false belief regarding some external factor and, furthermore, this false belief is justified. Practically speaking, if this situation arises in a case study, then one needs to determine whether the group members' beliefs were justified *in that particular example*. For instance, in the discussion of the two-player discursive dilemma (Fig. 6.7), it is important to verify whether Bob's false beliefs relied on culpable ignorance or negligence, which may, for instance, depend on whether he carefully read and checked the candidate's CV.

In general, the importance of epistemic justification in collective action problems shows that theories of *expertise* and *disagreement* are relevant for the study of responsibility gaps in democratic institutions. After all, democratic institutions often rely on committee decision-making and expert opinions to deal with disagreement. I take it that an expert's judgement is generally justifiable. Hence, if the discursive dilemma is faced by experts, then it could be argued that each committee member's belief is justified, regardless of whether it is correct, which implies that a responsibility gap may result.

Responsibility gaps have recently been used to justify the need for corporate responsibility and agency, as opposed to individual responsibility and agency, in order to dissolve the deficit in the moral accounting books. In other words, corporate responsibility is needed to address cases where no individual can be held responsible yet "there is moral or rational fault that must be assigned somewhere" (Copp, 2006, p. 216).[30] If all of this is correct, then my analysis shows that the need for corporate responsibility and agency is only justified in cases that include justified false beliefs. Stated differently, justified false beliefs are a condition for corporate responsibility and agency. However, the justification for these false beliefs may need to be reconsidered in light of the prospect of responsibility gaps and the relevance of such gaps. In such a context, the demands for epistemic justification may be stronger than initially thought. Nonetheless, my analysis asserts that responsibility gaps may exist. Hence, at least in some cases, there may be a need for corporate responsibility.

References

Axelrod, R. M. (1984). *The evolution of cooperation*. New York: Basic Books.

Bacharach, M. (1999). Interactive team reasoning: A contribution to the theory of co-operation. *Research in Economics, 53*(2), 117–147.

Bacharach, M. (2006). *Beyond individual choice: teams and frames in game theory*, N. Gold & R. Sugden (Eds.). Princeton: Princeton University Press.

Baier, K. (1958). *The moral point of view: a rational basis of ethics*. Ithaca: Cornell University Press.

Braham, M., & van Hees, M. (2011). Responsibility voids. *The Philosophical Quarterly, 61*(242), 6–15.

---

[30] The following observation does not affect the argument by Pettit (2007, p. 175) that corporations can meet the three conditions for fitness to be held responsible, namely "value relevance", "value judgment", and "value sensitivity".

Bratman, M. E. (1993). Shared intention. *Ethics, 104*(1), 97–113.
Chant, S. R. (2015). Collective responsibility in a Hollywood standoff. *Thought: A Journal of Philosophy, 4*(2), 83–92.
Chapman, B. (1998). More easily done than said: Rules, reasons and rational social choice. *Oxford Journal of Legal Studies, 18*(2), 293–329.
Chisholm, R. M. (1964). The ethics of requirement. *American Philosophical Quarterly, 1*(2), 147–153.
Copp, D. (2006). On the agency of certain collective entities: An argument from "normative autonomy". *Midwest Studies In Philosophy, 30*(1), 194–221.
Dancy, J. (2004). *Ethics without principles*. Oxford University Press.
Dietrich, F., & List, C. (2017). What matters and how it matters: A choice-theoretic representation of moral theories. *The Philosophical Review, 126*(4), 421–479.
Dowding, K., & van Hees, M. (2008). In praise of manipulation. *British Journal of Political Science, 38*(1), 1–15.
Duijf, H. (2018a). Beyond team-directed reasoning: Participatory intentions contribute to a theory of collective agency. *Logique et Analyse, 61*(243), 269–298.
Duijf, H. (2018b). Responsibility voids and cooperation. *Philosophy of the Social Sciences, 48*(4), 434–460.
Gilbert, M. (2000). *Sociality and responsibility: New essays in plural subject theory*. Rowman & Littlefield.
Gold, N., & R. Sugden (2007). Collective intentions and team agency. *The Journal of Philosophy, 104*(3), 109–137.
Horty, J. F. (2012). *Reasons as defaults*. Oxford: Oxford University Press.
Kornhauser, L. A. (1992). Modeling collegial courts. II. Legal doctrine. *Journal of Law, Economics and Organization, 8*(3), 441–470.
Kutz, C. (2000). *Complicity: Ethics and law for a collective age*. Cambridge: Cambridge University Press.
Lewis, D. K. (1969). *Convention: A philosophical study*. Cambridge: Harvard University Press.
List, C., & Pettit, P. (2011). *Group agency: The possibility, design, and status of corporate agents*. Oxford: Oxford University Press.
Luce, R. D., & Raiffa, H. (1957). *Games and decisions*. New York: Wiley.
Parfit, D. (1984). *Reasons and persons*. Oxford: Oxford University Press.
Parfit, D. (2011). *On what matters*. Oxford: Oxford University Press.
Pettit, P. (2007). Responsibility incorporated. *Ethics, 117*(2), 171–201.
Portmore, D. W. (2007). Consequentializing moral theories. *Pacific Philosophical Quarterly, 88*(1), 39–73.
Raz, J. (1975). *Practical reason and norms*. London: Hutchinson.
Regan, D. (1980). *Utilitarianism and co-operation*. New York: Oxford University Press.
Ross, D. (1930). *The right and the good*. Oxford: Oxford University Press.
Scanlon, T. (1998). *What we owe to each other*. Cambridge: The Belknap Press.
Schelling, T. C. (1960). *The strategy of conflict*. Cambridge: Harvard University Press.
Schroeder, M. (2007). *Slaves of the passions*. New York: Oxford University Press.
Sugden, R. (1993). Thinking as a team: Towards an explanation of nonselfish behavior. *Social Philosophy and Policy, 10*(1), 69–89.
Sugden, R. (2000). Team preferences. *Economics & Philosophy, 16*(2), 175–204.
Tuomela, R. (2005). We-intentions revisited. *Philosophical Studies, 125*(3), 327–369.
Van Lange, P. A. M., & Balliet, D. (2015). Interdependence theory. In M. Mikulincer, P. R. Shaver, J. A. Simpson, & J. F. Dovidio (Eds.), *APA handbook of personality and social psychology: Vol. 3. interpersonal relations* (pp. 65–92). Washington: American Psychological Association.

Chapter 7
Conclusion: The Conditions for Responsibility Voids and Gaps

What is the relation between collective blameworthiness and individual blameworthiness? What are the conditions under which responsibility voids can arise? I provided a systematic study of the possibility and scope of the problem of responsibility voids and gaps. In particular, I identified conditions that circumvent such voids and gaps. In this book, I adopted a pluralistic perspective on moral responsibility by studying a range of responsibility systems, each of which specifies who is to be held responsible and for what. I often distinguished between member and individual responsibility. For example, I made a distinction between individual obligations and member obligations (Chap. 3), knowingly doing simpliciter and knowingly playing your part (Chap. 4), standard individual intentions and participatory intentions (Chap. 5), and individual reasoning and participatory reasoning (Chap. 6). I will first discuss the contributions of the chapters to answering these main research questions and will then discuss several possibilities for future enquiries.

To start, I have shown in Chap. 3 that the relation between collective blameworthiness and individual blameworthiness is not straightforward. I assumed that blameworthiness entails a failure to fulfil an obligation. It is an important observation that a group could fulfil its collective obligation even though none of its members fulfils her individual obligation. And, conversely, a group may fail to fulfil its collective obligation even though each member fulfils her individual obligation. These observations are the inspiration for studying the conditions that must be met if responsibility gaps or voids are to exist. In particular, the conditions that must be met if a given group is to be collectively blameworthy for a certain outcome even though none of its members is an appropriate target of moral criticism.

We have seen that communication and agreements can help circumvent such gaps. If agreement is unproblematic, then the group members should adopt a *good* plan to regulate their group action. That is, the group members should adopt an interchangeable and optimal group plan. Such a good group plan guarantees that if each member fulfils her member obligation then the group fulfils its collective obligation. Or, conversely, when a good plan has been adopted, a group fails to

© The Author(s), under exclusive license to Springer Nature Switzerland AG 2022
H. Duijf, *The Logic of Responsibility Voids*, Synthese Library 456,
https://doi.org/10.1007/978-3-030-92655-7_7

fulfil its collective obligation only if at least one of its members fails to fulfil her member obligation. And, moreover, in these circumstances, a group fails to fulfil its collective obligation only if at least one of its members fails to fulfil her individual obligation in the updated decision context. Hence, ceteris paribus, if agreement is unproblematic, there can be no responsibility void nor gap. So, for *objective responsibility systems* based on dominance theory we get:[1]

(C3) If agreement is unproblematic and communication unrestricted, then responsibility voids and gaps cannot arise—unless members are released from their individual and member obligation.

In Chap. 4 I have studied an epistemic condition for moral responsibility. It is important to contrast objective and subjective obligations. Subjective obligations depend on the accessible information: simply stated, an agent is subjectively obliged to φ only if she knows how to φ. Given the assumption that collective blameworthiness relies on the violation of a collective obligation, under this subjective reading, collective blameworthiness entails that the group collectively knew how to fulfil its subjective obligation yet did not do it. My theory of collective know-how illustrates that, as a consequence, a group fails to fulfil its subjective collective obligation only if at least one of its members knowingly risks that she herself causes the group to fail to fulfil its collective obligation. In other words, she knowingly risks being a co-author of the collective failure. Prima facie, this yields a reason for considering that particular member an appropriate target of moral criticism.[2] As a result, *informational responsibility systems* are vulnerable to responsibility gaps only in certain circumstances:

(C4) Responsibility gaps cannot arise—unless members who knowingly risk being a co-author of the collective failure are excused.

In Chap. 5 I explored *intentional responsibility systems*. Given the importance of acting intentionally for levels of culpability, I proposed that responsibility attributions sometimes rely on the intentions. Accordingly, collective blameworthiness relies on collective intentionality. I have argued that whenever a group of individuals strives for some joint goal, each group member should adopt a participatory intention. A participatory intention is a standard individual intention with a particular kind of content: an agent who adopts a participatory intention can be taken to be aiming at the realization of a best group action.

Following the discussion of Chap. 3, if a group adopted a good plan in order to avoid a certain outcome, then that outcome can only result if at least one of its

[1] To avoid misunderstandings, the numbering of the conditions in this chapter corresponds to the associated chapter, so, for example, C3 is associated with Chap. 3 and C6a until C6d are associated with Chap. 6.

[2] Whether these considerations yield *pro toto* reasons for member blameworthiness is up for debate. I have discussed two reasons that may trump this derivation: epistemic reasons, such as when one knows that some other group members will also not carry out their part, or motivational reasons, such as when one does not want to devalue one's individual interests for the collective good.

members did not intend to avoid the outcome. Moreover, if the group adopted a good plan to regulate its group action yet fails to fulfil its collective obligation, then at least one of its members fails to act in a way that is faithful to her participatory intention. As a consequence, in these circumstances, *intentional responsibility systems* yield a reason for considering some members an appropriate target of moral criticism:

(C5a) If agreement is unproblematic and communication unrestricted, then responsibility voids and gaps cannot arise—unless members are exempted from acting in a way that is faithful to their participatory intention.

I considered two intentional responsibility systems in more detail. First, the weakest intentional responsibility system holds that an agent can be held responsible for a given outcome if and only if they did not intend to avoid it. Accordingly, a group can be held collectively blameworthy if and only if it did not collectively intend to fulfil its collective obligation. I argued that, from this perspective, collective blameworthiness entails that at least one of its members did not intentionally participate in jointly fulfilling the group's collective obligation. Hence, those particular members may be considered appropriate targets of moral criticism for undermining the constitution of the collective intention to fulfil the group's collective obligation. In other words:

(C5b) Responsibility gaps cannot arise under the weakest intentional responsibility system—unless members who refrained from intentionally participating in jointly fulfilling the collective obligation are excused.

Second, the strongest intentional responsibility system states that an agent can be held morally responsible if (and only if) they intend to not fulfil their obligations. A group can hence be held morally responsible only if it collectively intentionally failed to fulfil its collective obligation. My theory of participatory intentions shows that the latter entails that each member intentionally participates in this collective intentional omission. Their intentional participation can form the grounds for moral criticism. For example, Kutz's *Complicity Principle* (2000, p. 122) substantiates the claim that intentional participation triggers inclusive authorship of the consequences of the collective intentional act. As a consequence, *every* member of the group is complicit in the group's harmful group act. Irrespective of the validity of the Complicity Principle, we have:

(C5c) Responsibility gaps cannot arise under the strongest intentional responsibility system—unless members who intentionally participated in harmful collective actions and omissions are excused.

In sum, these cases demonstrate that the grounds for morally criticizing group members vary. In the first case of unproblematic agreement and communication, the criticism could be based on the fact that individuals did not intentionally participate in avoiding a particular outcome, or that they did not act in a way that is faithful to their participatory group intention. In the second case, moral criticism would revolve around the absence of a participatory intention. In the last case, moral criticism focuses on the intentional participation in a collective wrongdoing and the complicity principle helps establish a connection between the collective and member blameworthiness in these circumstances. Responsibility voids or gaps can only arise if these grounds are insufficient for holding members morally responsible. So, the conditions that must be met if responsibility voids or gaps are to exist vary across these three cases.

In Chap. 6 I have explored *a reasoning-based responsibility system*, which assumes that an agent's obligations are determined by the reasons bearing on the actions available to her. I adopted practical-reasoning schemas to explicate a decision-theoretic way of conceiving such reasons. Roughly stated, to assess whether an individual is responsible for a certain outcome, I proposed to investigate the practical reasoning that has led to her decision. Moreover, inspired by the team-reasoning literature, I have distinguished between competitive and cooperative decision contexts, each with their distinct mode of reasoning or practical-reasoning schema.

The application of the reasoning-based framework to the study of responsibility gaps yielded a disparity: competitive decision contexts are free from responsibility gaps, whereas cooperative decision contexts may host them. The conditions that must be met if responsibility gaps are to exist in cooperative decision contexts depend on the type of uncertainty that the group faces: external uncertainty or coordination uncertainty. In cases of external uncertainty, the group member who has the least accurate expectations is most blameworthy. However, if her expectations were reasonable then her blameworthiness may be pre-empted and a responsibility gap may result. In cases of coordination uncertainty, theories of agreement-making and salience may help overcome the threat of responsibility gaps. But if agreements are problematic and a focal point is absent, then cases of coordination uncertainty potentially host such gaps. In sum:

(C6a) Responsibility gaps cannot arise in competitive decision contexts.
(C6b) Responsibility gaps cannot arise in cooperative decision contexts—unless members who have false beliefs regarding external factors or in-group coordination are excused.

The reasoning-based responsibility system was also used to spell out which facts must obtain if responsibility voids are to exist. In cooperative decision contexts, the conditions for the existence responsibility voids are similar to those for the existence of gaps. In competitive decision contexts, these facts are as follows: First, such voids can arise if the moral theory permits agent-relative moral preferences, where these moral preferences may give rise to a moral social dilemma. More precisely, voids can arise in cases where it is in everybody's personal interest to act in a certain way, yet each individual would be better off if they together acted differently. In these cases, nobody can be held morally responsible even though they could have together acted in a way that better satisfied each one's moral preference. Second, responsibility voids can arise if false expectations or beliefs regarding external factors or the actions of other agents are morally justified. After all, if agents are excused for their false beliefs, then it is plausible that they are morally blameless when choosing a suboptimal course of action. As a consequence, nobody would be to blame if morally undesirable outcomes result from these suboptimal courses of action. Hence:

(C6c) Responsibility voids cannot arise in competitive decision contexts—unless agent-relative moral preferences exist or agents who have false beliefs regarding external factors or the actions of other agents are excused.

(C6d) Responsibility voids cannot arise in cooperative decision contexts—unless agents who have false beliefs regarding external factors or coordination are excused.

Having summarized the contributions of the chapters to the overall theme of the book, the possibility and scope of the problem of responsibility voids and gaps, I would like to conclude with several applications and extensions for future work.

The present work has focused on the question of whether collective blameworthiness entails that some member is to some extent an appropriate target of moral criticism. It is, however, important to investigate *to what extent* members can be appropriate targets of moral criticism in certain collective action problems. Consider the following example by Matthew Braham and Martin van Hees:

> An example of overdetermination in which we may want to impute different degrees of causal impact to the agents involved is when two firms simultaneously pour toxins into a river with one firm dumping twice as much as the other, but in which the actions of both firms are in itself sufficient to cause a certain harm. (Braham & van Hees, 2009, p. 324)

Braham and van Hees (2009) provide a theory of degrees of *causation*. In light of the modes of acting that are associated with levels of culpability, it would be interesting to investigate whether a theory of degrees can be given for the modes of *knowingly* and *intentionally*—my work in Chaps. 4 and 5 could be taken as a starting point. If so, these theories of degrees of causality, knowingly, and intentionality could be imported into the analysis of individual moral responsibility in collective action contexts.

Degrees of responsibility are especially important for studying moral responsibility—both collective and individual—in *hierarchical groups*. The present work abstracts away from structural features, but it is plausible that the group's structure plays a role in the distribution of responsibility among the group's members. Consider the following case:

Commanded Killing Suppose a military commander commands his subordinate to shoot an innocent civilian. The subordinate goes ahead and shoots the civilian. Can we justify that the commander is to some degree blameworthy? Moreover, can we justify that the commander is blameworthy to a greater extent than the subordinate?[3]

It is intuitive that unstructured groups are more readily open to a uniform distribution of the extent of members' blameworthiness rather than an unequal distribution,

[3] This example is inspired by Himmelreich (2015, Chap. 4, p. 60), who argues that "the commander is an agent of the [shooting]".

which seems more plausible in hierarchical groups. After all, a subordinate acting on the orders of a superior seems less blameworthy than the superior. The central ideas of this book may shed some light on the puzzle of moral responsibility in hierarchical groups. For example, with regard to causal responsibility, it may not be clear why the commander is to blame. After all, the commander did not shoot the innocent civilian. However, if we take seriously the idea that collective intentionality may be constituted by the adoption of certain collective decision procedures (List & Pettit, 2011), then it seems that the commander's decision to order the shooting of the innocent civilian constitutes a collective intention to do so. As such, my theory of participatory intentions may signify that both the commander and the subordinate are appropriate targets of moral criticism for their involvement in the shooting. The study of moral responsibility in authority-based structured groups is therefore a viable and proximate extension for future work.

The group's structure could be non-authoritarian and less formal than the *Commanded Killing* example presupposes. Consider the following example:

Opinion Leader Suppose a committee consisting of three members, Marie, Mel, and Mo, is to decide on a particular proposal by simple majority voting. However, imagine that Mo keeps an eye on Marie and is likely to follow Marie's judgement. Suppose that Marie voted in favour of the proposal, that Mo followed Marie's judgement, and that Mel voted against the proposal. The proposal is therefore accepted by Marie and Mo voting in favour. Suppose it is a bad proposal. Can we justify that Mo is blameworthy? Can we justify that Marie is more blameworthy than Mo?[4]

In future work it will probably be fruitful to relate the study of structured groups to network theory (Newman, 2010). That is, a structured group may be represented by a network of individuals with possible relations between them. The nature of the relation between two individuals may be authoritarian, as in the *Commanded Killing*, or be purposeful influence, as in the *Opinion Leader*. Nonetheless, the application of central concepts from network theory, such as centrality, robustness, and diffusion, may help to address moral responsibility in structured groups. For instance, if a certain outcome is robust in a certain network of individuals then we may say that the individual causal responsibility for the outcome is diminished because each individual is less capable of avoiding the outcome.

Given that Chap. 3 has shown that cases in which agreement is unproblematic are free from responsibility voids and gaps, a different route for future enquiries would be to investigate, more systematically, whether such voids and gaps could arise in cases where agreement is problematic or where *disagreement* is irreconcilable. Indeed, in Chap. 6, we have seen that responsibility voids can arise in competitive decision contexts if agent-relative moral preferences exist. Is every situation of disagreement or conflict vulnerable to responsibility voids and gaps? To explicate the conditions for the existence of responsibility voids and gaps in these cases, it

[4] This example is inspired by the "opinion leader" example of Bovens and Beisbart (2011, § 3.1), who propose a measure of voting power for such cases.

seems vital to study what would constitute problematic disagreement. To illustrate the complexity of this topic, consider the following example:

> Suppose we have two individuals, Ann and Bob, and a single action of going for a walk that needs to be evaluated with respect to the two relevant (and exhaustive) possibilities, that of it being a hot day and of it being a cool day. Suppose that Ann likes to walk when it's hot, but not when it's cool, and that Bob's preferences are just the reverse. Suppose also that Ann believes that it is most likely to be a hot day and that Bob believes that it will be cool. Then they may both agree that it is a good idea for them to go walking, even though they disagree about everything that this choice depends on. (Bradley, 2005, p. 223)

This illustrates that there are cases that seem to simultaneously host both disagreement and agreement. After all, Ann and Bob agree it is a good idea for them to go walking, while they disagree about all aspects that this choice depends on. Although the example seems artificial, it should be noted that the underlying problem is relevant for financial markets. Voluntary transactions in financial markets are often based on conflicting beliefs and preferences. After all, in standard rational choice theory, the reason for trading goods is that each participant in the trade expects herself to be better off.

The final direction for future research that I would like to mention is the study of moral responsibility in *institutional contexts*. Institutions have several characteristics. Besides the structural aspects of institutions alluded to before, it is important to note that the stability of institutions is often conceptualized as an equilibrium notion. Francesco Guala and Frank Hindriks, for instance, propose a 'rules-in-equilibrium' conception of institutions; they write:

> Are institutions rules or equilibria of a game? We can now see that the answer is "both": an institution may be considered as an equilibrium or as a rule of the game, depending on the perspective that one takes. (Guala & Hindriks, 2015, p. 185)[5]

To study moral responsibility in an institutional context, it is thus important to investigate equilibria. A group is in equilibrium if its members' beliefs and incentives are stable, that is, if none of its members has an incentive to deviate from equilibrium-play given her beliefs.[6] To illustrate, consider the following problematic equilibrium:

Speeding Drivers Suppose a number of drivers are all speeding on the motorway. Each driver knows that it would be better if all of them slowed down to the legal speed limit. However, each driver also thinks that if she unilaterally slowed down, then the speed difference would probably result in a severe accident, which may yield several casualties. The group of speeding drivers may therefore be viewed as being in equilibrium.

The example illustrates that it may be risky for each driver to attempt to break out of the established equilibrium. Nevertheless, the group of speeding drivers is in

[5] See also Guala (2016).

[6] Note the similarity with the concept of a Nash equilibrium (Definition 2.5). However, this formal notion lacks the network of beliefs that are key in the notion of an equilibrium.

an equilibrium that is suboptimal, which may yield institutional blameworthiness. Can we justify that some or all of the speeding drivers are blameworthy or complicit in this institutional wrongdoing? From the perspective of my theory of collective know-how (Chap. 4), we could say that the group of speeding drivers is blameworthy for speeding while collectively knowing how to achieve the optimal outcome in which each keeps to the legal speed limit. Moreover, in this example we can see that each member knows she is a co-author of the collective failure. The nature of the problem in equilibrium-based collective wrongdoing is epistemic: each member knows that others will not carry out their part in collectively achieving the optimal outcome.

Alternatively, with regard to Chap. 6, it is important to highlight that an equilibrium is standardly viewed as a stable state for *individualistic* reasoners. That is, an equilibrium is a state from which no member has an individual incentive to deviate. However, we have seen that such competitive decision contexts are free from responsibility gaps. So either there is no collective blameworthiness or some of the individuals are blameworthy for not endorsing a *we-perspective*, which is highlighted in my reasoning-based analysis of responsibility gaps.

One could argue that this case calls for institutional *reform*. That is, the drivers are required to break out of the established equilibrium and move to the optimal solution: each should slow down. If we view an institution as an equilibrium, then institutional reform requires an update in the behaviour and the expectations of the group members. In some cases, this reform may be achieved by updating the expectations, such as when Sweden authorities announced changing from driving on the left-hand side of the road to the right on 3 September 1967. The emergence of more mundane norms and institutions may, however, rely primarily on opportunities for mutually advantageous behaviour rather than updating expectations. I offer an alternative way to achieve institutional reform: update the group members' perspective from individualistic to community-directed. This would yield a transformation from a competitive context to a cooperative one.

It is to be expected that the relation between collective and individual blameworthiness will not be a straightforward matter. Formalizations of moral responsibility can enhance our capacity to track down responsible agents. To ensure that responsibility allocations are tractable and fair, progress can be made by exploring and explicating the facts that must obtain if problematic scenarios—such as responsibility voids or gaps—are to exist. Through reverse engineering, we could design social interactions so that morally undesirable outcomes are circumvented and fair responsibility allocations are guaranteed. Understanding the logic of responsibility voids is a vital step towards ensuring that distributing responsibility is feasible and fair.

References

Bovens, L., & Beisbart, C. (2011). Measuring voting power for dependent voters through causal models. *Synthese, 179*(1), 35–56.
Bradley, R. (2005). Bayesian utilitarianism and probability homogeneity. *Social Choice and Welfare, 24*(2), 221–251.
Braham, M., & van Hees, M. (2009). Degrees of causation. *Erkenntnis, 71*(3), 323–344.
Guala, F. (2016). *Understanding institutions: The science and philosophy of living together*. Princeton: Princeton University Press.
Guala, F., & Hindriks, F. (2015). A unified social ontology. *The Philosophical Quarterly, 65*(259), 177–201.
Himmelreich, J. (2015). *Agency as difference-making: causal foundations of moral responsibility*. PhD Thesis, The London School of Economics and Political Science.
Kutz, C. (2000). *Complicity: Ethics and law for a collective age*. Cambridge: Cambridge University Press.
List, C., & Pettit, P. (2011). *Group agency: The possibility, design, and status of corporate agents*. Oxford: Oxford University Press.
Newman, M. (2010). *Networks: An introduction*. New York: Oxford University Press.

The manufacturer's authorised representative in the EU is Springer Nature Customer Service Centre GmbH, Europaplatz 3, 69115 Heidelberg, Germany. If you have any concerns regarding our products, please contact ProductSafety@springernature.com

Printed and bound by CPI Group (UK) Ltd, Croydon, CR0 4YY
30/09/2026
02225497-0002